Discovering Christ
In Galatians

Discovering Christ in Galatians

Donald S. Fortner

Go *publications*

Go Publications
The Cairn, Hill Top, Eggleston, Co. Durham, DL12 0AU, ENGLAND

© Go Publications 2008
First Published 2008

British Library Cataloguing in Publication Data available

ISBN 978-0-9548624-5-9

For information on other Go Publications titles and New Focus magazine:

www.go-publications.co.uk
www.go-newfocus.co.uk

Printed and bound in Great Britain
by Lightning Source UK Ltd

This book is dedicated to:

Pastor Scott Richardson
Fairmont, West Virginia

An Example of Faith and Faithfulness in Christ

Contents

Foreword

In a day and age when many gospels, that are no gospel, proliferate; when many subtle peddlers of another gospel 'which is not another' abound; then to have a book that presents the teaching of Paul's epistle to the Galatians unreservedly as the true and only Gospel is vital.

Galatians is unequivocal in its defence of Gospel truth: of the absolute sovereignty of God, of unconditional election, and of free grace — and so is Don Fortner. Galatians will not let us labour under the fond delusion that we can contribute one iota to our salvation — nor does Don Fortner. Righteousness is imputed in justification and sanctification: the righteousness of Christ our covenant Substitute and Surety. Paul is at pains in this Galatians epistle to insist that our life in Christ began as a life of faith not works, and must continue to the end as a life of faith. The writer is at pains in this book to insist upon precisely the same glorious truth, against any and all who would pervert, subvert, add to or take away from the Gospel of salvation by faith alone, through grace alone, in Christ alone.

This is sovereign grace polemic. It is biblical apologetic; the vindication of free salvation. We cannot modify the Gospel at any point without destroying it. There have always been, are now, and will be, legalistic influences and antinomian trends that would do just that. Don Fortner writes: 'There are two great evils to which our fallen human nature is consistently drawn, evils that must be constantly avoided. The one is the horrid evil of legalism. The other is the equally horrid evil of licentiousness. Both are evil products of the flesh.'

Therefore, a robust apologetic, the vindication of free and sovereign grace, and of a sanctified and holy life in the Spirit, is as much needed today as when the Holy Spirit through the apostle Paul first gave this bulwark epistle to the Church, for her defence and security, her liberty and purity.

One of the greatest benefits of reading *Discovering Christ in Galatians*, one that has benefited me immensely, comes from patiently taking time to look up and read the scripture references given in the text. They are not there for decoration but for our instruction, edification and spiritual refreshment.

This is a vigorous defence of the faith once delivered to the saints. But it is delivered with the empathy of a faithful pastor, the learning of a gifted theologian, and the experience of a fervent preacher.

Read it, rejoice in it, and grow in it to the eternal benefit of your soul, and to the glory of your God and Saviour, the Lord Jesus Christ.

May the Lord bless His Word.

Dr Len Allen
Wolverhampton

Introduction

'I Do Not Frustrate The Grace Of God'

If I had opportunity to address all the preachers, religious leaders, theologians, and religious people of this world at one time, who believe and teach that salvation is in any way, to any degree dependent upon or determined by the will or work of man, I would lay this solemn charge, this horrible indictment against them: You frustrate the grace of God and make the death of the Lord Jesus Christ an insignificant, meaningless, useless thing. That is precisely the charge Paul laid against those who taught such heresy in Galatia. Then, he declared, as spokesman for all who believe and preach the gospel of God's free, sovereign, saving grace in Christ, 'I do not frustrate the grace of God: for if righteousness come by the law, then Christ is dead in vain' (Galatians 2:21). That is just how serious the book of Galatians is.

When Paul sat down to write this Epistle, he was clearly provoked and angry. This book was intended (intended by Paul and by God the Holy Spirit who inspired it) to be a deliberate, forceful confrontation. There are no friendly greetings, no gentle salutations, no kind soothing reflections in this book. Everything in these six chapters is 'in your face' confrontation.

An Angry Apostle

To say the least, the apostle was a little hot under the collar. Why? What provoked Paul and stirred his anger? The Galatian churches, churches God raised up under the influence of Paul's ministry among them, were being led away from Christ and his gospel by false teachers in their midst. These men, professing to be the servants of Christ, were slandering Paul, accusing him of being a false prophet, and denying the gospel of God's free and sovereign grace in Christ. All the while they pretended to promote and defend it. They were trying to make Christianity a mere extension of Judaism, just as multitudes do today.

They did not openly deny that salvation is by the free grace of God in Christ. They did not openly state that Christ is not enough, that Christ is not sufficient, or even that works must be mixed with faith. The messengers of Satan are far too subtle for that. They were teaching salvation by grace through works; but they did not state it quite that way. The Galatian heretics taught that true faith is a faith that expresses itself in the observance of the Mosaic law and that any faith that did not express itself in law obedience was a false faith. These men and their heresy were being embraced by the Galatian churches.

Paul was shocked. How could they be confused about this? If salvation is by grace, it cannot be by works. If salvation is by works, it cannot be by grace. 'If by grace, then is it no more of works: otherwise grace is no more grace. But if it be of works, then is it no more grace: otherwise work is no more work'. (Romans 11:6). There can be no mixture of the two.

The issue at Galatia, unlike the issues at Corinth (horrible as they were), was the gospel of God, the glory of God, the finished work of Christ, and the souls of men. Therefore, Paul jumped in, as one writer put it, 'with both fists flying'. Paul had reason to be provoked. His anger was completely justified.

One Gospel

It is ever the practice of those who oppose the gospel of God's free grace to slander the men who preach it. The legalists at Galatia knew they could not refute Paul's doctrine by scripture. If they were to turn men away from Paul's message, they must turn them away from him. Therefore, they sought to discredit Paul as God's messenger.

For this reason, the opening verses of Galatians 1 identify Paul decisively as an apostle of God, not an apostle of men, or an apostle by the authority of men, but of and by the Lord Jesus Christ and God the Father. With that as his authority, Paul denounces as false every rival gospel. He tells us that every 'gospel' that teaches the sinner to look for righteousness and salvation anywhere except in Christ alone is no gospel at all, but a frustration of the grace of God; and with regard to those who preach another 'gospel' he says, 'let him be accursed' – 'Let him be damned forever'. Paul could not have used stronger language to convey his thoughts on this matter.

'I marvel that ye are so soon removed from him that called you into the grace of Christ unto another gospel: Which is not another; but there be some that trouble you, and would pervert the gospel of Christ. But though we, or an angel from heaven, preach any other gospel unto you than that which we have preached unto you, let him be accursed. As we said before, so say I now again, If any man preach any other gospel unto you than that ye have received, let him be accursed' (Galatians 1:6-9).

The gospel of God is good news about something done, not good advice about something you must do. The gospel is the good news of redemption obtained, righteousness brought in, sin put away, and salvation secured by the obedience and death of Christ as the sinner's Substitute (Daniel 9:24; John 19:30; Hebrews 1:1-3; 9:12, 26, 28; 10:10-14). Anyone who asserts that something must be done by the sinner before these things can be accomplished is a false prophet, preaching a false gospel, and those who follow him follow him to hell.

That is just how serious this matter is. And that is exactly what Paul asserts in Galatians 1:6-9. Having said that, the fat was in the fire. In verses 10-24 Paul asserts that, contrary to the accusations of his detractors at Galatia, he had no desire to please men and made no effort to do so. The gospel of God was not something he learned from men. He learned it by divine revelation. His authority as an apostle and preacher, though confirmed by the other apostles (2:1-10), was not derived from them, but from Christ himself.

Peter's Compromise

So far was Paul from being a compromising man-pleaser that when Peter compromised the gospel by his actions at Antioch Paul withstood him to the face (2:11-17). While at Antioch, Peter enjoyed a good barbeque dinner with the Gentile brethren there, until he saw some of his Jewish brethren approaching. At the sight of these men, Peter got up from the table and separated himself from the Gentiles, as if to say, 'Oh, I should not have done that. The law of Moses forbids eating good barbeque'.

When he did that, by his mere act, he led many into error, even Barnabas. By his mere action, Peter led others to believe that righteousness, justification, salvation, and acceptance with God is not totally the work of God's grace, but in some way dependent upon our own obedience to the law of God.

Frustrating Grace

Peter's actions were far more evil than most imagine. His implied doctrine was a frustration of the grace of God. He implied that justifying righteousness can be obtained by the works of men. Therefore, Paul publicly withstood him to the face before both the Jews and the Gentiles at Antioch.

'But when I saw that they walked not uprightly according to the truth of the gospel, I said unto Peter before them all, If thou, being a Jew, livest after the manner of Gentiles, and not as do the Jews, why compellest thou the Gentiles to live as do the Jews? We who are Jews by nature, and not sinners of the Gentiles, knowing that a man is not justified by the works of the law, but by the faith of Jesus Christ, even we have believed in Jesus Christ, that we might be justified by the faith of Christ, and not by the works of the law: for by the works of the law shall no flesh be justified. But if, while we seek to be justified by Christ, we ourselves also are found sinners, is therefore Christ the minister of sin? God forbid' (2:14-17).

Justification

We are justified by the faith of Christ, not by our faith in Christ, but by the faith and faithful obedience of Christ himself unto death as our Substitute (Romans 4:25). By our faith in Christ we receive and enjoy the blessedness of justification. We are not justified by something we do, but by Christ alone. To suggest, or imply in any way that our works, or even our experience, have anything at all to do with making us righteous before God for justification is to deny the gospel altogether. Paul puts it this way, 'I do not frustrate the grace of God: for if righteousness come by the law, then Christ is dead in vain' (2:21). If righteousness could be established by something men do, then Christ died for nothing! Again, Paul could not have used stronger language to denounce the heresy of mixing works with grace for justification. Salvation is by grace alone, in Christ alone, received by faith alone, without works of any kind.

Antinomianism

Paul understood exactly what he was saying, and understood exactly what his detractors would say about his doctrine. He could almost hear them screaming with clinched fists, 'Antinomianism! That is antinomianism! If our works have nothing to do with righteousness, if we can be saved without obeying God's law and doing good works ourselves, you are telling us that we can go out and live like we want to in lawlessness, licentiousness, and lasciviousness.'

I know that is what they said, both because that is what Paul says they said (2:17), and because I have heard those words countless times. The legalist never really wants to live as he pretends to live. The very language he uses to denounce free grace betrays the fact that if he could be saved without serving God, he would not serve him.

The fact is, any man who preaches salvation by grace alone, without works, will be accused of antinomianism and of promoting licentiousness; but the charge is baseless and false (2:17).

Sanctification

In chapter 3 Paul moves from justification to sanctification. He argues with the Galatians (and us) that their experience of grace forbids the idea that righteousness can be obtained by their works. 'O foolish Galatians, who hath bewitched you, that ye should not obey the truth, before whose eyes Jesus Christ hath been evidently set forth, crucified among you? This only would I learn of you, Received ye the Spirit by the works of the law, or by the hearing of faith? Are ye so foolish? having begun in the Spirit, are ye now made perfect by the flesh?' (3:1-3).

Sanctification and justification are two distinct works of God's grace; but the two cannot be separated. Those who are justified are also sanctified. And sanctification as well as justification is a work of grace alone. Once we have received righteousness in justification by faith in Christ, we do not make ourselves more holy, more righteous before God by our works in sanctification. Believers grow in grace: in faith, in love, and in consecration to God. But believers do not become more holy and righteous before God as they grow in grace. The only time the word 'holy' is used in the scriptures in connection with a man in a relative sense is in Isaiah 65:5. There the Lord God says such people who think they are holier than others 'are a smoke in my nose'.

Christ is both our justification and sanctification (1 Corinthians 1:30; Hebrews 10:10-14). His name is Jehovah-tsidkenu i.e. 'The Lord our Righteousness' (Jeremiah 23:6). We have no righteousness before God but him. To suggest that we make ourselves righteous by our works in sanctification is to mix grace and works; and that is a frustration of the grace of God, 'I do not frustrate the grace of God: for if righteousness come by the law, then Christ is dead in vain' (2:21).

No Mixture

In a word, Paul's doctrine is this: Any mixture of grace and works in the matter of righteousness is a total denial of grace, for it is a frustration of grace. Therefore, he tells us that the whole purpose of the law was fulfilled when Christ suffered, died, and rose again as our Substitute. The law was our schoolmaster unto Christ (3:19-4:31). Once Christ came and fulfilled it, the law's work was finished, 'Christ is the end of the law for righteousness to everyone that believeth' (Romans 10:4).

There is no place for legal bondage in the household of faith. Those who would bring God's saints under the yoke of legal bondage deny the whole gospel of the grace of God and every believer's experience of grace. All who attempt to make themselves righteous by the works of the law are still under the curse of the law.

'For as many as are of the works of the law are under the curse: for it is written, Cursed is every one that continueth not in all things which are written in the book of the law to do them. But that no man is justified by the law in the sight of God, it is evident: for, The just shall live by faith' (3:10-11).

Those who would bring believers under the yoke of legal bondage deny every believer's experience of grace (3:1-5). They deny the Old Testament scriptures, which assert that Abraham was justified by faith without works (3:6-9). They deny the efficacy of Christ's atonement, asserting that Christ died in vain, that he did not actually secure the blessing of grace for God's elect by his death (3:13-14). They deny the whole purpose of the law as a schoolmaster unto Christ (3:15-29). They deny the blessed liberty of the gospel and the grace of God, the very liberty Christ obtained for us by his obedience to the law and death by the law, by trying to bring us back under the yoke of bondage (4:1-11).

'But when the fulness of the time was come, God sent forth his Son, made of a woman, made under the law, To redeem them that were under the law, that we might receive the adoption of sons. And because ye are sons, God hath sent forth the Spirit of his Son into your hearts, crying, Abba, Father. Wherefore thou art no more a servant, but a son; and if a son, then an heir of God through Christ' (4:4-7).

Christ died for God's elect (his eternally adopted children), that we might receive the Spirit of adoption in regeneration, giving us faith to look upon God through the blood of our Saviour with confidence as our heavenly Father (Hebrews 10:19-22). Trusting Christ, we are no longer servants, but sons. The promoters of law righteousness would have us swap sonship for slavery! No wonder Paul was fearful for their souls! No wonder he stood in doubt of them (4:19). These Gentile believers, to whom the law was never given, were being duped by their false teachers to swap the liberty of Christ for the bondage of Moses.

'But now, after that ye have known God, or rather are known of God, how turn ye again to the weak and beggarly elements, whereunto ye desire again to be in bondage? Ye observe days, and months, and times, and years. I am afraid of you, lest I have bestowed upon you labour in vain' (4:9-11).

In the latter part of chapter 4 (vv. 21-31) Paul uses Sarah and Hagar and their sons Isaac and Ishmael as an allegory. The allegory teaches us, that as Hagar and Ishmael (the fruit of Abraham's shameful works by which he attempted to perform God's righteous promise) had to be cast out of Abraham's house, so all our own works righteousness (all attempts to make ourselves righteous before God) must be cast out as filthy rags. It is written, 'Cast out the bond woman and her son'. There is no room in the house of grace for the works of the flesh, for legal obedience.

Stand Fast
In the fifth chapter Paul urges us to stand fast in the blessed liberty of the gospel, warning us that if we do anything by which we hope to gain God's favour, improve our standing in God's favour, or keep ourselves in God's favour, we have abandoned the gospel and abandoned grace altogether. He says, 'Christ is of no value to anyone who attempts to make himself righteous before God'.

'Stand fast therefore in the liberty wherewith Christ hath made us free, and be not entangled again with the yoke of bondage. Behold, I Paul say unto you, that if ye be circumcised, Christ shall profit you nothing. For I testify again to every man that is circumcised, that he is a debtor to do the whole law. Christ is become of no effect unto you, whosoever of you are justified by the law; ye are fallen from grace' (5:1-4).

There is no antinomianism here, no licentiousness, no encouragement to sin. Far from it! The rest of the book of Galatians is a declaration that this liberty of grace is life in the Spirit. As we walk in the Spirit, looking to Christ alone for righteousness and salvation, we will not fulfil the lusts of the flesh. It is self-righteousness and legalism that causes men and women to bite and devour one another (in the name of righteousness!). Grace teaches believers to restore their fallen brethren, to bear one another's burdens, to love one another, and so to fulfil the law of Christ. Grace teaches us not to sow to the flesh and reap corruption, but to sow to the Spirit and reap life everlasting. Our only hope is the cross of Christ. Our only motivation, our only rule of life is the cross. And all who have this hope and live by this rule are blessed as 'the Israel of God'.

'But God forbid that I should glory, save in the cross of our Lord Jesus Christ, by whom the world is crucified unto me, and I unto the world. For in Christ Jesus neither circumcision availeth any thing, nor uncircumcision, but a new creature. And as many as walk according to this rule, peace be on them, and mercy, and upon the Israel of God' (6:14-16).

The Cross
The sum and essence of all true doctrine, the essence of all true Christianity, and of all motivation in the lives of God's elect in this world is the cross of our Lord Jesus Christ (6:14). When Paul writes, 'God forbid

that I should glory, save in the cross of our Lord Jesus Christ,' he is telling us that his only trust, his only hope before God is that which Christ accomplished as our all-sufficient, effectual Redeemer at Calvary.

Throughout the book of Galatians the cross of Christ is central. The cross, as Paul uses it, refers not to the wooden cross upon which Christ died, or the historic fact of the cross, but the doctrine of the cross – redemption and salvation by the death of our Lord Jesus Christ as our sin-atoning Substitute.

The cross is deliverance by blood atonement (1:3-5). The cross is life (2:19-20). The cross is righteousness (2:21). The cross is the removal of our curse (3:13). The cross is the certainty of God's blessing (3:14). The cross is the centre of our faith (3:22). The cross is the ground of our adoption (4:4-7). The cross is an offence to the unbelieving (5:11). The cross is the source of all grace (5:22-24). The cross is that by which we are crucified unto the world and the world unto us (6:14-15). And the cross is our rule, our peace, our mercy, and our life (6:16-18).

> I must needs go home by the way of the cross,
> There's no other way but this;
> I shall ne'er get sight of the gates of light,
> If the way of the cross I miss.
>
> I must needs go on in the blood sprinkled way,
> The path that the Saviour trod,
> If I ever climb to the heights sublime,
> Where the soul is at home with God.
>
> So I bid farewell to the way of the world,
> To walk in it never more;
> For the Lord says, 'Come', and I seek my home,
> Where He waits at the open door.
>
> The way of the cross leads home,
> The way of the cross leads home,
> It is sweet to know as I onward go,
> The way of the cross leads home.

Jessie B. Pounds

Paul, an apostle, (not of men, neither by man, but by Jesus Christ, and God the Father, who raised him from the dead;) And all the brethren which are with me, unto the churches of Galatia: Grace be to you and peace from God the Father, and from our Lord Jesus Christ, Who gave himself for our sins, that he might deliver us from this present evil world, according to the will of God and our Father: To whom be glory for ever and ever. Amen.

(Galatians 1:1-5)

Chapter 1

Read: Galatians 1:1-5

Paul An Apostle Of Christ

The Book of Galatians shows us the way to true freedom. Genuine liberty is neither legalism nor licentiousness. It is the blessed freedom of voluntary bondage to Christ. It is the liberty of willing captivity to the Son of God; surrendering our lives to the rule and dominion of Christ as our Lord, voluntarily giving up our lives to him; being conquered by his omnipotent, saving grace (Mark 8:34-35; Luke 14:25-33).

This true freedom is discovered when sinners are graciously forced to willingly cease from every effort to save themselves and trust Christ alone as Lord and Saviour; glorying only in his cross, and trusting him as 'the Lord our Righteousness', by whose blood and righteousness all the demands of God's holy law have been fully met and satisfied forever (Jeremiah 23:6; Romans 10:4). All who have been brought by God's sovereign, irresistible grace to trust Christ are dead to the law. You cannot be freer than that!

The law of God no longer has dominion over us. Guided by the Holy Spirit and bringing forth fruit unto God ('the fruit of the Spirit'), the saints of God, out of gratitude and love to Christ and for God's free gift of salvation in him, adorn the doctrine of God our Saviour and seek to live for his honour and glory as the children of God in this world. The terror and fear of the law no longer rule our lives, but the love of Christ. The proud hope of earning rewards from the Almighty to gratify our lusts no longer motivates us, but the grace of God. The prison door has been opened; and we have entered into the glorious liberty of the sons of God.

Not only have we found the blessing; but we have become a blessing. For it is through the children of God that God blesses the world.

The Epistle

Paul addresses this epistle to the churches of Galatia in Asia minor. These churches were established during Paul's first missionary journey and were located in Pisidian Antioch, Iconium, Lystra, Derbe, and perhaps other places. It is difficult to determine exactly when this letter was written, but it was definitely among the apostle's first epistles. We know that it was written after the council at Jerusalem, because it describes Paul's relation to the other leaders at that great meeting. It was written after the two previous visits to Galatia, which are recorded in Acts 13-16. It must not have been long after this for Paul speaks of the conversion of the people there as a recent thing (Galatians 1:6). It was probably written on his second missionary journey while he was at Corinth, before the arrival of Timothy and Titus. This would fix the date of writing about 50-53 A.D.

That which prompted Paul to write this book was the sinister, and to some extent successful, influence of Judaisers[1] who crept in among the saints. It was his purpose to counteract this dangerous error by re-emphasizing the glorious gospel of God's free-grace in Jesus Christ; and by urging the believers to adorn their faith and prove its genuine character by loving and caring for one another.

In this book Paul calls for a return to the gospel of God's free and sovereign grace in Christ, denouncing all human merit and legal effort, and warning solemnly against apostasy from the faith of the gospel. He tells us plainly that the yoke of legal bondage is a bewitching system of works religion that utterly denies the grace of God and brings people to eternal ruin (Galatians 3:1; 5:1-4). Here Paul gives a clarion call for a return to the old Gospel. It is God's power and God's means by which he saves (Galatians 1:6-9).

Divisions

The divisions of this book are very simple and clear:

> The Origin and Authority of the Gospel (chapters 1-2)
> The Vindication of the Gospel (Chapters 3-4)
> The Application of the Gospel (Chapters 5- 6)

---

[1] Judaisers are people who teach that believers are still under the law of Moses as a rule of life, though they profess to be followers of Christ.

An Apostle

The Judaisers who sought to undermine Paul's ministry and his doctrine accused him of falsely pretending to be an apostle of Christ. Their deceitful practice is common in all ages. The doctrine of the gospel cannot be refuted. Therefore, those who wish to keep others from hearing and embracing the gospel attempt to slander the men who teach it. In this first section of Galatians, Paul is forced (and inspired by God) to set forth his authority as an apostle of Christ, as a messenger of Christ to eternity bound men and women.

The apostolic office was a temporary office in the New Testament church. There are no apostles, in the official sense of the word, today. However, the word basically means 'messenger'. In that sense all true gospel preachers are apostles. But how do we know who the messengers of Christ are? How are we to determine who are true messengers of Christ to our souls? Paul gives us some guidelines in these opening verses of Galatians.

Paul could have said many things about himself that would have given him credibility in the eyes of men. He was a man of great learning and tremendous usefulness, and was highly respected by his peers. But it was not Paul's desire to have his name held in high esteem. He took no titles of distinction or superiority to himself. He was but a sinner saved by grace, just like his brothers and sisters in Christ at Galatia. He does not identify himself as the apostle, but as an apostle. He was one of many messengers of Christ.

What a tremendous weight of responsibility he carried on his heart as a messenger of Christ! He daily carried upon his heart 'the care of all the churches' (2 Corinthians 11:28). Any man to whom this responsibility is given knows something of the high honour and great responsibility the Lord has put upon him.

When the Pharisees asked John the Baptist who he was, his reply was, I am a voice, 'the voice of one crying in the wilderness, Make straight the way of the Lord'. There are multitudes of preachers listed in every telephone directory. But we have few messengers of God, few messengers of the grace of God. The pulpit, in our day, has lost its clarity. Its testimony has been spoiled because doubtful voices have arisen and been scattered among the people. Those who ought to preach the truth and nothing but the truth are telling out for doctrines the imaginations of men and the inventions of the age. Instead of revelation, we have philosophy. Instead of divine infallibility, we have human speculation. The gospel of Jesus Christ, which is the same yesterday, today, and forever, is taught as the production of progress, a thing to be amended and reformed year by year. We live in an age of liberality, of broad views, of boundless universalism, of rapidly spreading apostasy.

Another Gospel

If the world will not come to Christ, if the people of our 'enlightened' age will not accept the gospel of Christ, the wisdom of the world tells us that we must make Christ more acceptable, we must tone down his teachings, that we must take the offence out of the gospel. Such foolishness we have come to expect from self-serving, man-pleasing religious hucksters. Sadly, today there are many who claim to believe the gospel of God's free and sovereign grace in Christ who have succumbed to the philosophy of the world. They vainly imagine that the offence can be taken out of the cross and that the gospel of the grace of God can be presented in a way that will make it palatable to unregenerate men (Galatians 5:11).

Rather than proclaiming the gospel as good news, the good news of redemption accomplished (Galatians 3:13), they present it as good advice and an offer of possible redemption. Rather than proclaiming God's grace as the special, distinct operation of salvation (Galatians 1:15-16; Ephesians 2:8-9; Colossians 1:12), they present it as a thing common to all. Rather than proclaiming the efficacy of God's grace (Galatians 3:14; Romans 9:16), they present a notion of grace that makes the operation of grace dependent upon the will of man. Rather than setting forth the distinct love of God for his own elect which results in their salvation (Galatians 2:21; Jeremiah 31:3; Romans 9:13-18; 1 John 4:19), they make the love of God a universal, and therefore insignificant, helpless passion in God. Rather than declaring that faith is that which God gives to and works in chosen sinners by the revelation of Christ in them (Galatians 1:15-16; Colossians 1:12), they make faith a work done by the sinner for God. While claiming to preach the gospel of Christ, they have so perverted the gospel that the gospel they preach is another gospel; a gospel that is no gospel at all (Galatians 1:6-9).

How often I have been told that my message is out of date, that it will not suit people, and that if I would reach the people of this age I must tone down my message and modify my doctrines. Such a message is all right for the Bible College or seminary, or for private, intellectual discussion, but it ought to be modified for the pulpit. Oh, we may use the old phrases so as to please the obstinately orthodox, but we must dress them in new meanings so as to neutralize their force and make them palatable to natural men. The spirit of the age suggests that the wise preacher will abandon all that is too severely righteous and all that is too surely of God. Away with such nonsense! God has given us the message that men need, and he has supplied us with the means of communicating that message. The message is the gospel of the grace of God revealed in Jesus Christ and his death upon the cross. And God's method of communicating that message is preaching. We must not be deterred by the opinions of men. We must not be 'corrupted from the simplicity that is in Christ' (2 Corinthians 11:3). We must not be 'removed from him that called us into the grace of Christ unto another gospel' (Galatians 1:6).

He, and he alone, who preaches the gospel that Paul sets before us in this epistle is the messenger of the grace of God. Such men have many characteristics by which they are identified. They are set forth in many ways in the Book of God. But as they are revealed in these verses, they are threefold.

One Master

He who is God's messenger is a man with one Master (vv. 1-2). As Paul opens this letter his heart and mind are filled with diverse emotions. For the perverters of the gospel there is a withering denunciation springing from holy indignation. For the churches there is marked disapproval and an earnest desire to restore. For the One who has called him there is profound reverence and humble gratitude.

Paul knew that he was a man distinctly gifted, called and sent of God to preach the gospel. He was 'an apostle, not of men, neither by man, but by Jesus Christ'. He was a man with a mission. His mission was to make known the gospel of Christ. His commission came directly from God who had called him. It came, not from any group of men, or from any single man, but from the Lord Jesus Christ and God the Father (Acts 26:13-18). And he did not put himself into the ministry. He was put into the ministry by God himself (1 Timothy 1:11-12). He was called to be an apostle (messenger) to the Gentiles (Romans 1:1; Acts 9:15; Ephesians 3:3-8). His call was not inferior to the other apostles, for they were called during our Lord's earthly ministry. Paul was called by the exalted Saviour. His call was confirmed by signs and miracles, just as the other apostles (2 Corinthians 12:11-12). Like them, he had seen the risen Christ. Only he saw him by special revelation. Paul received his gospel from Christ (Galatians 1:11-12). That was his authority.

In his opening words, Paul declares two cardinal gospel doctrines: the equality of Jesus Christ with God the Father and the resurrection of Christ. These things are essential. If Christ is not himself God, then he cannot be our Saviour. If he did not rise from the dead, then he did not put away sin.

Paul was a man committed to Christ and committed to the gospel. Christ was his Master. He was his Master's devoted servant. He was altogether separated to the gospel. Paul was God's messenger. He spoke by divine authority. Those who rejected him rejected God who sent him (Romans 1:1; Galatians 1:15-16; 1 Timothy 4:13-16; 1 Thessalonians 2:13).

It is important to note that this letter and this salutation did not come from Paul alone, but from all of the brethren who were with him and who assisted him in the ministry. Those who labour for Christ are co-labourers. The letter is to all of the churches of Galatia. These were not national churches or parts of a denominational organization, but individual congregations, local churches. Each local assembly was autonomous, functioning independently without control by the others.

One Message

In verses 3 and 4 we see that Paul was a man with just one message and the message was 'grace'. 'Grace be to you and peace from God the Father, and from our Lord Jesus Christ, Who gave himself for our sins, that he might deliver us from this present evil world, according to the will of God and our Father'. He simply proclaimed the matchless, free, eternal, sovereign, saving grace of God in Christ. He had no other issue. He had no other doctrine. He preached Christ crucified. He preached all the counsel of God (1 Corinthians 2:2; Acts 20:27).

Grace is not a helpless passion in God, a helpless desire to save sinners. Grace is not something God gives men by which they are enabled to be saved. Grace is God's free, spontaneous, unmerited favour in action, his freely bestowed loving-kindness and salvation upon guilty sinners who turn to Christ for refuge. It is free, undeserved, unmerited, and effectual. It is the effectual, irresistible, omnipotent operation of God in us. God's grace is given to all sinners that go to Christ for it (John 6:36; 1 Timothy 1:15). It is God's riches at Christ's expense. It is this gracious favour and goodwill of God by which his elect have been blessed of God, made accepted in Christ and pleasing to God in him from eternity (Ephesians 1:3-7).

Grace, and grace alone brings peace. Wherever grace is given, peace is given. We have peace with God, because Christ has reconciled us to God. We have peace in our hearts, because we have the Spirit of Christ within us (John 14:27; Philippians 4:7; Romans 8:1). We have peace in our consciences, because the blood of Christ, answering the demands of God's holy law, has been sprinkled on our hearts by the Holy Spirit. We have peace with one another, because grace has united our hearts, teaching us to love one another. We even have peace with our enemies, because we are assured that they can do us no harm. These three graces come from God the Father, the source and fountain of grace and peace, through our Mediator, Christ Jesus the Lord.

Substitution

Paul's was a message of grace and peace through Christ, our Substitute. The Lord Jesus Christ, God's darling Son, voluntarily laid down his life for his people upon the cursed tree. The Good Shepherd gave his life for his sheep, in our room and stead, as our Substitute (John 10:11, 17, 18). His purpose in doing so was to rescue us from this present evil world (John 15:19; 17:14), and he keeps us for the world to come (2 Peter 3:13-14). Paul states this blessed gospel doctrine with profound simplicity and beauty in 2 Corinthians 5:21, 'For he hath made him to be sin for us, who knew no sin; that we might be made the righteousness of God in him.'

What a profound truth, what stupendous grace, what wondrous mystery those words contain! 'He', God the Father, 'hath', in holy justice and infinite mercy, 'made', by divine imputation, 'him', the Lord Jesus Christ, his infinite, well-beloved, only begotten, immaculate Son, 'to be sin', an awful mass of iniquity, 'for us', helpless, condemned, sinful rebels!

'The heart of the gospel is redemption, and the essence of redemption is the substitutionary sacrifice of Christ' said C. H. Spurgeon. Substitution is the foundation truth of Christianity, the rock upon which our hopes are built. This is the only hope of the sinner, and the joy of every true believer. 'He hath made him to be sin for us'.

This is the greatest transaction that ever took place upon the earth, the most marvellous sight that men ever saw, and the most stupendous wonder that heaven ever executed. Jesus Christ was made to be sin for us, that we might be made the righteousness of God in him. Jesus Christ, the spotless Son of God, was made to be sin!

This transaction that took place at Calvary two thousand years ago – the great substitutionary work of Christ, the mighty transfer of sin from the sinner to the sinner's Surety, the punishment of the Surety in the sinner's place, the pouring out of the vials of divine wrath, which were due to us, upon the head of our Substitute – is the only ground upon which the holy Lord God can be, as he describes himself, both 'a just God and a Saviour'.

The Lord Jesus Christ, the Son of God, was made to be sin for us. No man living upon this earth will ever really understand this truth. Yet, we ought to be gripped by the glorious reality of it. Oh, may God cause it to get hold of our hearts! The gospel of Christ must not be pushed aside as an old piece of furniture in the house of God. The glorious gospel of substitutionary redemption is the strength, the glory, and the life of God's church.

This substitutionary work of Christ, of necessity (blessed necessity!), involves the absolute sovereignty of God (Ephesians 1:3-14; Hebrews 10:5-10). Paul was never bashful about asserting God's glorious sovereignty in all things, especially in the salvation of his elect. He states it as a matter of fact, usually without defence or explanation, assuming that all who trust Christ understand and rejoice in it. That is certainly the case here. Paul simply asserts the fact that the Lord Jesus Christ gave himself for his people and that the sure result of his doing so shall be their everlasting salvation, 'according to the will of God and our Father'.

One Motive

As Paul was a man with one Master and one message, he was a man with one motive, the glory of God (v. 5). He urged God's saints to do all to the glory of God; and that was his own heart's great ambition in all things. Most distinctly, throughout his epistles, he tells us that the salvation of our souls is for the glory of our God (1 Corinthians 1:30-31; Romans 11:33-36). He has saved us in such a way, and saved such people as we are that he shall be forever glorified by saving us (Ephesians 2:7). Imagine that! The Lord God, our great God, shall forever be praised because of his great grace toward us and wrought in us! Let our hearts ever be motivated by and our lives ruled by his glory. To him be glory for ever and ever. Amen.

I marvel that ye are so soon removed from him that called you into the grace of Christ unto another gospel: Which is not another; but there be some that trouble you, and would pervert the gospel of Christ. But though we, or an angel from heaven, preach any other gospel unto you than that which we have preached unto you, let him be accursed. As we said before, so say I now again, If any man preach any other gospel unto you than that ye have received, let him be accursed. For do I now persuade men, or God? or do I seek to please men? for if I yet pleased men, I should not be the servant of Christ.

(Galatians 1:6-10)

Chapter 2

Read: Galatians 1:6-10

The Singularity Of The Gospel

It is utterly astonishing to a believer that anyone, having heard and having professed to believe the gospel of God's free, sovereign, saving grace in Christ, could be enticed to abandon it for another gospel (which is no gospel at all!) of legality, works, or a mixture of grace and works (Romans 11:5-6). But that is exactly what had happened in Galatia. Paul's purpose in writing this epistle was to expose and reprove those as heretics who attempt to mix the works of men with the work of Christ; and to establish God's elect in the gospel of God's grace and glory in Christ.

False teachers had crept into the Galatian churches perverting the gospel of Christ. While professing to be followers of Christ, they sought to mingle the works of the law with faith in Christ. They were persuading the people to abandon the gospel Paul had taught them, adding to faith in Christ the works of the law. The apostle Paul had taught them that Christ crucified is the only, all-sufficient, and effectual Saviour of men, and that faith in him is the only way we can receive his finished salvation (Romans 5:11). He had proved the truth of all his declarations by miracles. These Galatians professed to believe the gospel as it was preached and confirmed by the apostle. They had been so thankful for Paul bringing the gospel to them that they received him as an angel of God, and would have, had it been possible, plucked out their own eyes and given them to him. Yet, within a short time, these converts were induced by the eloquent discourses of false teachers to renounce Paul and the gospel of Christ, and to receive in its place a message contrary to the glorious gospel Paul had taught them. Therefore, he wrote this letter by divine inspiration, filled with indignation, sorrow, and astonishment.

One Gospel

Here Paul declares that there is only one gospel and he proceeds to show the singularity of that gospel. This message is one of dogmatism, finality, and authoritarianism, which is a rare message in our day of broadminded compromise. Our generation is taught to be liberal and sceptical; that truth is subjective and relative, not objective and absolute. One certainly is not to be dogmatic about anything. But the gospel of Christ is, in its very essence, a non-compromising, authoritarian message of absolutes. The very reason for the flourishing of Christianity in the pagan Roman world in which it was born was the non-compromising spirit of our forefathers in the faith. Rather than relinquishing or adding to one article of faith, they would die! We must return to this dogmatism about the gospel.

The church is in desperate need of a clarion message ringing once again from her pulpits. There is too much silence regarding the message that passes for the gospel in this day. There is only one gospel. It must not be altered. It must not be mixed and diluted with human conjectures. We must uphold the gospel in its purity. Men are in a helpless, hopeless, mad dash to hell; and they will not be rescued unless Christ, the crucified Redeemer, sovereignly bestows his grace upon them. The gospel is 'good news' from heaven of how that God sent his Son to save his people. It is the declaration of what God has done for sinful, helpless humanity. It is never a proposition. It is a declaration, a declaration of redemption accomplished by Christ.

The Galatian Christians had been seduced from the pure gospel of God's grace to a mixed message of God's grace plus man's merit. Such a gospel is really not good news at all, but a perverted system of self-righteousness (1 Corinthians 1:30; Colossians 1:19-22; 2:8-23). The gospel is a declaration of what God has done for sinners in the person of his Son, apart from anything done by men. Anything other than a declaration of God's work is a perversion of the gospel. Paul here calls upon them to return to, and maintain the gospel in its purity.

> One gospel and one righteousness,
> One Way, One Truth, One Life.

Amazement

It was Paul's custom to give grateful acknowledgement of divine grace bestowed upon those he addressed, whereby they had been enabled to grow in knowledge, faith, and love. It was very common for him to express his inner satisfaction with the work of God upon them, and to give forth a prayer that they may continue to persevere in the faith. That is what we might expect to find at this point in his epistle. But, in this epistle to the Galatians, we are confronted with the exact opposite. What we find here is not satisfaction, but overwhelming amazement and painful perplexity.

The first thing we see in this book is their removal from the gospel. A change had taken place among them, and this disturbed their spiritual father. As a rule Paul was a very tolerant man. He showed great tolerance in his epistles to the Corinthians, who had behaved so shamefully in so many ways. He showed great tolerance in writing to the Philippians about those preachers who, because of envy, opposed him (Philippians 1:15-18). He was usually very tactful and expressed words of encouragement before dealing with faults and failures.

But here the very essence of the gospel is at stake. God's glory and man's salvation is the issue; and here there is no place for tolerance. The Galatians were in the process of apostasy. They were forsaking liberty in Christ for the bondage of Moses. Paul was utterly amazed. He says, 'I marvel that ye are so soon removed from him that called you into the grace of Christ unto another gospel' (v. 6).

Theirs was not merely changing theological positions. They were abandoning Christ, who in his grace and mercy had called them, and turning to another gospel, which was different from his in its very essence.

'Called You'

By and large, Paul appears to have been convinced that those to whom he was writing had been truly born of God, called by the effectual, irresistible power and grace of God the Holy Spirit to life and faith in Christ. The One who had called them was Christ himself. It was Christ from whom they were in danger of turning, not just Paul.

There is a general call and an effectual call. The Lord Jesus Christ calls sinners by his Spirit in a general way, externally, whenever the gospel is proclaimed to them. This call is made effectual by the power of God. The efficacy of the gospel call is ascribed to all three Persons of the Trinity, though specifically it is a part of the mediation of Christ (John 10:2-3, 16; Romans 1:6). The Galatians were replacing the gospel of Christ with another gospel and were being removed from Christ.

The gospel of Christ is 'good news' from a far land. It is the message of grace from God in heaven for men of the earth. It is a message of what God has done and is doing for sinners in Christ (1 Corinthians 15:1-4; 2 Corinthians 5:19-21). It is a message of salvation alone in Christ. He is the Door. He is the Way. He is the Truth. He is the Life. In all that concerns the salvation of sinners, from start to finish, 'Christ is all' (1 Corinthians 1:30).

The gospel is not good advice, but good news, the good news of Christ's finished work whereby he has made all God's elect accepted with God. It is the good news of redemption, forgiveness, justification, reconciliation, and sanctification accomplished by the blood of Christ, our crucified Substitute (Romans 5:10-11; 2 Corinthians 5:17-21; Ephesians 1:6-7; Colossians 1:12-14; Hebrews 1:1-3; 9:12; 10-14).

'Another Gospel'

Neither the Galatians nor their Judaising teachers had openly denied the gospel. Heretics are almost always more subtle than that. But their perversion of the gospel (adding obedience to the Mosaic law to the finished work of Christ) was, in reality, a total denial of it (Galatians 5:1-4).

Martin Luther was right when he wrote, 'They made good works, which are the effect of justification, its cause.' But the Galatian error extended beyond the subtle evil of mixing works with grace in the matter of justification. Paul addresses that issue in chapters one and two. But, in chapter three, he deals with an even more subtle and more bewitching form of the heresy, that had been embraced by many at Galatia, and is embraced almost universally today. That is the mixing of grace with works in the accomplishment of sanctification (Galatians 3:1-3).

It is a hazardous thing to tamper with the gospel of Christ. It must neither be abridged nor enlarged. Any gospel that makes righteousness before God to be dependent upon the works or will of man is no gospel at all. 'Christ is the end of the law for righteousness to everyone that believeth' (Romans 10:4). Christ is all our righteousness. He is our righteousness in redemption, in justification, and in sanctification.

Neither our faith, nor our works make us righteous before God. By faith in Christ we receive the righteousness he accomplished for us. By our works, our obedience to our God, we manifest the righteousness he has wrought in us by his Spirit. Horatius Bonar wrote:

> Thy works, not mine, O Christ,
> Speak gladness to this heart;
> They tell me all is done;
> They bid my fear depart.

'Accursed'
As Satan transformed himself into an angel of light, his ministers transform themselves into ministers of righteousness (2 Corinthians 11:3, 13-15). These 'deceitful workers', as Paul calls them, beguile the souls of men, persuading them that they can make themselves righteous before God (or at least contribute something to the work), and thereby teaching them not to trust Christ as 'The Lord Our Righteousness' (Jeremiah 23:6; 33:16). It is for this reason that Paul uses the strong, bold language of verses eight and nine to denounce all who preach any other gospel.

'But though we, or an angel from heaven, preach any other gospel unto you than that which we have preached unto you, let him be accursed. As we said before, so say I now again, If any man preach any other gospel unto you than that ye have received, let him be accursed' (vv. 8-9).

Here the apostle tells us how those who corrupt the gospel ought to be regarded. He includes himself and all others in this stern, clear word of condemnation. If anyone comes preaching any gospel other than the gospel of full, complete, effectual redemption and eternal salvation in and by Christ alone, let him be forever consigned to hell.

The revelation of God is final, complete, and perfect. It cannot be improved upon. Christ is God's final Word to men (Hebrews 1:1-3). He is the full revelation of the Father. He came on a mission to perform the work of redemption. He has finished the work. The Book of God is final. It tells us his whole revealed will. It reveals the totality of his work. The Word of God alone has authority in his house (Isaiah 8:20; Revelation 22:18-19). The gospel is final, revealing Christ, only Christ, and Christ alone as the Saviour of our souls (Acts 4:12; 1 John 5:10-11).

Those who would pervert the gospel, those who preach another gospel, which is no gospel at all, are to be regarded as accursed men (2 John 10-11). We should be very cautious in charging any man with preaching another gospel. But when anyone comes preaching another Christ and another gospel, (anyone who preaches that salvation is to any degree or at any one point dependent upon what you do rather than upon what God does) our responsibility is crystal clear. We must not acknowledge them as God's servants. We must not receive their instruction. And we must not be partakers of their evil deeds by assisting them in any way.

Men Or God?
In verse ten Paul states plainly that as the servant of God he could not concern himself with pleasing men. 'For do I now persuade men, or God?

or do I seek to please men? for if I yet pleased men, I should not be the servant of Christ.'

He did not try to persuade (that is conciliate) men, or make the gospel appealing to men. All such efforts arise from corrupt motives and result in the destruction of men's souls, not the salvation of them. Paul never courted the favour of men. He was concerned about the favour of God. It was not his ambition to impress, please and win the favour of men. He was concerned for and motivated by the glory of God. His only principle of life was to please his one Master, Christ Jesus the Lord. The simple fact is, no one can have two masters (Matthew 6:24). Any man who, for the sake of human favour, or out of fear for human resentment, will keep back any part of sacred truth is not the servant of Christ.

Those who teach believers to live by law misuse the law (1 Timothy 1:8-9), and attempt to place upon God's people an oppressive yoke of bondage that no man can bear. Let us use the law lawfully. We must never allow ourselves to be brought back under the bondage of the law from which Christ has set us free (Galatians 5:1-4). To do so is to abandon all hope of salvation; it is to abandon Christ altogether. Let us hold forth the gospel in its purity. It is the work of Christ, which alone saves sinners. The church of God has no other purpose for existence. We have no other mission.

But I certify you, brethren, that the gospel which was preached of me is not after man. For I neither received it of man, neither was I taught it, but by the revelation of Jesus Christ. For ye have heard of my conversation in time past in the Jews' religion, how that beyond measure I persecuted the church of God, and wasted it: And profited in the Jews' religion above many my equals in mine own nation, being more exceedingly zealous of the traditions of my fathers. But when it pleased God, who separated me from my mother's womb, and called me by his grace, To reveal his Son in me, that I might preach him among the heathen; immediately I conferred not with flesh and blood: Neither went I up to Jerusalem to them which were apostles before me; but I went into Arabia, and returned again unto Damascus. Then after three years I went up to Jerusalem to see Peter, and abode with him fifteen days. But other of the apostles saw I none, save James the Lord's brother. Now the things which I write unto you, behold, before God, I lie not. Afterwards I came into the regions of Syria and Cilicia; And was unknown by face unto the churches of Judaea which were in Christ: But they had heard only, That he which persecuted us in times past now preacheth the faith which once he destroyed. And they glorified God in me.

(Galatians 1:11-24)

Chapter 3

Read: Galatians 1:11-24

Our Gospel Is Of God

There were false teachers at Galatia who imposed themselves upon the saints there by pretending that they had their commission from the apostles. In the same deceitful manner they asserted that Paul was not an apostle. They made much of the fact that he was not one of the original twelve. They declared that he had never been acknowledged by them and that he did not properly teach their doctrine. Paul replies to this groundless charge with boldness, declaring that his apostleship was directly from heaven; and that it was therefore authoritative. The other apostles had received their office from our Lord during his humiliation. Paul was called to this office by the exalted Redeemer.

Paul, however, does not content himself with the mere assertion of his apostleship. He goes on to prove what he has said by an appeal to undisputed facts from his own life. He makes this appeal with the greatest earnestness, because these facts touch the recognition of the validity of his message in all future ages. It is not unlikely that he foresaw that the fiercest attacks upon Christianity would be made upon the doctrine revealed in his epistles. Therefore, he labours to show that what he says, Christ says, since Christ is speaking through him.

'It is not strange', said Spurgeon, 'to hear certain dubious people assert "I do not agree with St. Paul". I remember the first time that I heard this expression I looked at the individual with astonishment. I was amazed that such a pigmy should say this of the great apostle. It seemed like a cheese-mite differing from a cherub, or a handful of chaff discussing the verdict of the fire.'

In the passage before us Paul is defending his apostleship by defending his message. In this defence we see certain definite characteristics of the gospel of our Lord Jesus Christ. Paul's object (the Holy Spirit's object) in this passage is to demonstrate clearly that the gospel of God's free and sovereign grace in Christ is not of man, but of God. This gospel, which, by the effectual power of the Holy Spirit, completely changes the heart and life of a man in a very brief moment, cannot be of man. Our gospel is of God! By relating his personal experiences, Paul shows that the gospel originates with God alone, is revealed by God alone, and is applied by God alone.

Brethren

'But I certify you, brethren, that the gospel which was preached of me is not after man. For I neither received it of man, neither was I taught it, but by the revelation of Jesus Christ' (v. 11-12).

Paul addresses the Galatians as 'brethren'. In spite of their deviation he still considers them members of the same spiritual family, of which he also is a member, and of which God is Father (Ephesians 3:14-15).

What a lesson there is here for us. Many are very quick to declare that others are lost, unbelieving sinners, void of God's saving grace. Such judgment is both harsh and evil. You and I do not have the ability to discern wheat from tares or sheep from goats. Our Lord's parables make that fact abundantly clear. We ought to always presume that those who profess to believe the gospel of the grace of God, who profess to believe on the Lord Jesus Christ, genuinely do so. These Galatians had fallen into grievous doctrinal error, error which caused Paul to stand in doubt of them (Galatians 4:11, 20), just as the Corinthian saints had fallen into very grievous moral and spiritual errors (1 Corinthians 1-6). Yet, Paul addresses both the Corinthians and the Galatians as 'brethren' and deals with them as 'brethren'. He does so without compromise, or pretence, bending over backwards in giving them assurance that his heart embraces them as brethren.

A Revelation

Paul continues to show, as he did in verses 6-9, that the gospel he preached is the only message worthy of the name gospel, because it is of divine origin. The form of expression used here is very strong. When he says, 'I certify you brethren'. He means, 'I assure you most certainly. I would have you certain of it. The gospel I preach is not after men.'

The gospel of Christ is not a human invention. It is of divine origin; and its character is divine. The gospel is unchanging and everlasting. It always lays man low in the dust and exalts the triune God. It exposes sin, demands righteousness, and proclaims righteousness as the gift of God's free grace through the redemptive work of Christ. The gospel is neither good advice nor a gracious proposal. It is neither an offer of mercy nor an invitation to salvation. The gospel is good news, the proclamation of mercy, grace, and salvation in Christ. It is the revealed message of eternal redemption obtained by Christ for all who trust him. The gospel is the good news of a work finished for sinners, not a proposal of something for sinners to do.

The gospel of free and sovereign grace is of God in its origin. It is not the result of human ingenuity or devising. Righteousness wrought by another and made over to us graciously is a mystery man cannot understand. Redemption accomplished by a divine Surety and Substitute, without human merit, is foolishness to me. Salvation accomplished for us, but altogether outside of us and without us, is impossible for man to grasp, except we are taught by divine revelation. Our gospel is totally contrary to human thought (1 Corinthians 2:14; Isaiah 55:8-9; John 1:5). It was devised in the eternal mind of God and brought into being by the sovereign will of God.

Many agree that the gospel is from God in its origin yet insist that it is of man in its reception. Paul declares plainly that that is not the case, 'I neither received it of man, neither was I taught it, but by the revelation of Jesus Christ.' Paul did not receive it from his parents or by his own will (John 1:12-13), it did not come from the instruction of Gamalial, or from the other apostles. Without question, he heard the gospel from the lips of a man (Romans 10:14-17). He certainly heard it from Stephen (Acts 7:58), and may have heard the message preached many times by others; but it was not a man who gave him faith and caused him to believe and understand the gospel he heard. That is the work of God the Holy Spirit alone. He alone commands the light to shine out of darkness and causes the light of the knowledge of the glory of God in the face of Jesus Christ to shine in our hearts (2 Corinthians 4:4-6).

The only way any sinner can and will receive the gospel of Christ is 'by the revelation of Jesus Christ'. That is how Paul received it; and that is how every chosen sinner receives it (Ephesians 3:3-8). Paul's conversion was not the exception, but the rule (1 Timothy 1:16). He was the pattern and example of the way God saves his people. It is only by the sovereign, irresistible, illuminating work of God the Holy Spirit that the dark abyss of any man's soul is enlightened to see and believe the gospel of Christ (Matthew 16:17; John 3:5; 1 Corinthians 12:3; Luke 10:21-22). Paul says, 'God revealed his Son in me' (v. 16).

Conversion

Saul's persecution of the early church was notorious but now the apostle relates the history of his conversion. 'For ye have heard of my conversation in time past in the Jews' religion, how that beyond measure I persecuted the church of God, and wasted it: And profited in the Jews' religion above many my equals in mine own nation, being more exceedingly zealous of the traditions of my fathers. But when it pleased God, who separated me from my mother's womb, and called me by his grace, to reveal his Son in me, that I might preach him among the heathen; immediately I conferred not with flesh and blood' (vv. 13-16).

It is not Paul's purpose here to give us a complete autobiography. He relates only those events that support the vindication of his calling and apostleship from heaven. Thus, his record here, and that recorded by Luke in the Book of Acts (which is a history of Christ's work through the early church) do not contradict one another. They simply bring to light different events in the life of this man of God.

Paul was not seeking Christ. He was seeking to destroy the very name and memory of Christ. He was a violent persecutor. He persecuted God's peculiar treasure, his church, desiring to destroy the body of Christ. This became to him, after the Lord saved him, a source of continual sorrow. He acknowledged that he was, in those persecutions, wishing himself accursed from Christ (Romans 9:1-4). He had been a Pharisee of the Pharisees (Philippians 3:4-7). But, all the while, the Lord God was seeking him. 'It is not of him that willeth, nor of him that runneth, but of God that sheweth mercy' (Romans 9:16). The Lord God had separated him as the object of his sovereign love from eternity and from his mother's womb in providence. Then at the time appointed, 'when it pleased God', he revealed Christ in him.

That is exactly how God saves all his chosen. His grace is sovereign, eternal, and irresistible (Jeremiah 1:5; Luke 1:15; Romans 9:10-24). He has a people whom he has chosen before the foundation of the world to be his own peculiar objects of love (John 15:16; Ephesians 1:3-4, 11; 2 Thessalonians 2:13-14; 1 Peter 1:2; 2 Timothy 1:9). At the appointed time of love, he calls each of his elect by his omnipotent grace (Romans 8:30). And his call is always effectual. Yes, always (John 6:37-39; 63-65). It is by this omnipotent act of mercy and grace that God reveals his Son in chosen sinners, gives them repentance and faith, and sweetly compels them to come to Christ (Zechariah 12:10; Psalms 65:4; 110:3).

Made A Preacher

It was by that same irresistible power that the Lord God made that former blasphemer a preacher of the gospel (1 Timothy 1:13; 2:7; 2 Timothy 1:11). Any man who has been called to preach the gospel is made a preacher by the call of God. He is not merely made to want to be a preacher, made an aspiring preacher, or made willing to be a preacher. He is made to be a preacher. I know that it is customary among men to speak of men being called into the ministry before they are actually engaged in the work. But you will search the scriptures in vain to find an example of any prophet, apostle, or pastor who was called to the work of the gospel ministry who was not involved in that work.

In this matter of the call to the ministry, as in other things, the customary method can be wrong and evil. When men speak of themselves or others being called to the gospel ministry, who are not actually engaged in the work, they put the cart before the horse. In the Word of God no man is ever referred to as being called to the work, until God has put him in the work. The evil of reversing that order is quickly apparent. Once a man is convinced (or convinces himself) that he is called to be a preacher, he sets out on the relentless pursuit of an office and work to which God has not called him. If he succeeds in his pursuit, the result is disastrous. If he does not succeed in making a way for himself, it is just as disastrous for he is in constant frustration.

'If a man desire the office of a bishop, he desireth a good work' (1 Timothy 3:1). But let the man quietly wait upon the Lord God to put him into that office and work. Until that actually happens, let him faithfully serve the cause of Christ where he is with joyful contentment. Until a man can serve Christ with joyful contentment as a door-keeper in the house of God, he is not fit to serve in any other capacity. Indeed, if we are God's servants, it matters not to us where or in what capacity we serve him. 'A man's gift maketh room for him' (Proverbs 18:16).

Paul tells us, that once the Lord God had conquered him by his grace and called him to the work of preaching the gospel, 'I conferred not with flesh and blood'. He did not consult with men about what he was to do. This was not a matter of arrogant independence, but of faithful obedience to Christ. If we know what the will of God is, to consult with flesh and blood concerning it is an act of disobedience. 'Whatsoever he saith unto you, do it' (John 2:5).

Paul And Other Apostles

In verses 17-24 Paul briefly describes his earliest work and his relationship with those who were apostles of our Lord before him. He did not disregard or seek independence from those faithful brethren. The Lord simply kept him from their immediate influence for three years. He tells us in verse 17 that he spent some time in Arabia, by the will of God, and afterward came back to Damascus. How long he was there, what he did there, what his work was while he was there, we are not told.

Then, after three years, he went up to Jerusalem and spent fifteen days with Peter (v. 18). But while he was there, he had no communication with any of the other apostles except James (v. 19). By asserting this fact, Paul is simply reaffirming the fact that what he believed and preached, and his authority for believing and preaching it, did not come from men, not even from the apostles, but from Christ alone (vv. 20-21). When the other apostles heard what God had done for Paul, they rejoiced, gave thanks, and glorified God for his work of grace in him (vv. 22-24).

The nature of this work of grace, described in verse 15, requires a more full examination and is the subject of our next chapter.

But it pleased the Lord, who separated me from my
mother's womb, and called me by his grace.

(Galatians 1:15)

Chapter 4

Read: Galatians 1:15

Jesus draws the chosen race
By his sweet resistless grace;
Causing them to hear his call,
And before his power to fall.

From the blissful realms above,
Swift as lightning flies his love;
Draws them to his tender breast;
There they find the gospel rest.

Then how eagerly they move
In the happy paths of love!
How they glory in the Lord,
Pleased with Jesus' sacred word!

When the Lord appears in view,
Old things cease, and all is new;
Love divine o'erflows the soul;
Love does every sin control.

R. Burnham

All Of Grace

Christianity is a religion of grace. Grace is the love of God operating toward man. We teach our children early that grace is 'God's Riches At Christ's Expense'. Our hymns are hymns of grace. We speak of God's grace in our worship services all the time. It is the incessant theme of every pulpit where Christ is worshipped. Saved sinners find the thought and experience of grace so overwhelmingly wonderful that they never get over it. Grace is the constant theme of their talk and their prayers. Men and women have written hymns about it. They have stood for it and struggled for it, accepting ridicule and loss of privilege, if need be, as the price of their dedication. As Paul fought these Judaisers at Galatia, so Augustine fought the Pelagians, and the Reformers fought scholasticism. As the descendants of Paul and Augustine the saints of God have been fighting Romanist, Pelagian, Arminian, legalistic, and humanistic doctrine ever since. With Paul they testify, 'By the grace of God I am what I am', and their rule of life is, 'I do not frustrate the grace of God'.

Yet, there appear to be very few who profess to be Christians who believe what the Word of God teaches about grace. Why do so few people believe in God's free and sovereign grace? Because they fail to see the moral ill dessert of man; they have a wrong view of God's justice; they have a weak and unscriptural view of the merits of Christ's sacrifice; they fail to recognize man's spiritual impotence; and they refuse to recognize the sovereign freedom of God.

Pattern

Before God called him by his grace, Paul had been a persecutor of Christ and his people, and went armed with letters to Damascus to arrest men and women as followers of Christ and drag them to prison. But on his road to Damascus he saw a light, exceeding in brightness the light of the sun, and a voice spoke to him out of heaven saying, 'Saul, Saul, why persecutest thou me?' By this miraculous interposition of God, this man Saul was converted. He became a saved man. He spent three days in darkness; but when Ananias came to tell him the gospel of Jesus Christ, scales fell off his eyes. He was baptized and became an instrument of great usefulness in the kingdom of God.

We generally consider Paul's conversion very remarkable in its suddenness and distinctness, and certainly it is. Yet, at the same time it is no exception to the general rule of conversions, but is rather a type, or model, or pattern of the way in which God shows forth his longsuffering and grace to his elect. The Holy Spirit tells us distinctly that Paul was a pattern of God's method of grace (1 Timothy 1:16). That simply means that the grace of God Paul experienced shows us exactly how it is that God saves sinners.

Though he was suddenly converted on the Damascus road at God's appointed time of love (Ezekiel 16:8), the Lord God had had thoughts of grace toward Saul of Tarsus long before he was born. God did not begin to work in Paul on his way to Damascus. That was not the first occasion on which the eyes of divine love and grace had been fixed on this chief of sinners. He declares that God had separated him, and set him apart, even from his mother's womb, that he might reveal his Son in him.

Salvation is all of grace. We are not saved by our works, or our wills, our obedience, or our faith; but by the grace of God we are what we are so that 'no flesh may glory in his presence' (1 Corinthians 1:29). That great work whereby sinners are made righteous and brought to heaven is entirely a work of God's free and sovereign grace, acting in love towards hell-deserving sinners.

Commonly, when we think of the word 'salvation', we tend to think only of the time when the chosen sinner, being born of God, first believes on the Lord Jesus Christ. But that is a great mistake. Salvation includes the whole work of God's free grace in Christ: everything required to bring hell-bent, hell-deserving sinners into heaven's everlasting glory in perfect conformity to the Lord Jesus Christ. From beginning to end, the whole work is wrought of God. 'Salvation is of the Lord' (Jonah 2:9). It is altogether by grace and by grace alone. It is not determined by and does not depend upon the will, work, or worth of man to any degree.

Planned

The grace of God planned our salvation (Ephesians 1:3-14). The whole work began with God's determination to save the people of his choice in eternal, electing love. He chose whom he would save. He predestined them unto the everlasting glory of the sons of God. He arranged all things from eternity, 'according to his purpose' (Romans 8:28). And looking upon his elect in the person of his Son, our Mediator and Surety, the Lamb slain from the foundation of the world, he made them 'accepted in the Beloved', and blessed them with all the blessings of grace and salvation in Christ before the world began, 'to the praise of the glory of his grace'. In divine providence our God constantly works all things according to the purpose of his all-wise decree for the eternal salvation of his elect (Romans 8:28-31).

The cost of our salvation was borne by our God alone (Ephesians 1:7-12). The price demanded by his own holy law and justice was the precious blood of Christ (1 Peter 1:18-20). He found a way, by his own 'wisdom and prudence', to redeem and save the people of his love; and that way is Christ. The Lord God graciously trusted his chosen into the hands of Christ as our Surety, the same Surety we now trust 'to the praise of his glory'.

God the Father planned our salvation (Ephesians 1:3-6). God the Son purchased our salvation (Ephesians 1:7-12). And God the Holy Spirit performs the work of grace in us by the power of his omnipotent, irresistible grace (Ephesians 1:13-14). He brings the word of truth, 'the gospel of your salvation', to every chosen sinner at the appointed time of love, creates life and faith in the chosen; seals to the believer all the promises and blessings of the everlasting covenant; and seals the believer in the grace of God, keeping him by infallible grace, until the resurrection day, 'to the praise of his glory'.

Precedes

Grace planned salvation; and grace precedes salvation. We seldom hear or read anything about it in our day; but this grace that precedes grace is what the old writers used to call 'prevenient grace'. This prevenient grace is demonstrated in Paul's life. He was moulded by the hand of God, inwardly and outwardly, for the specific purpose of doing the very thing for which the Lord God had separated him from his mother's womb: to proclaim the unsearchable riches of his grace to the Gentiles. His personality, his education, his religious training, even his persecutions of the church were things used and over-ruled by his God for his soul's good.

I mention his persecutions of the church in this matter because Paul seems never to have gotten over the fact that the Lord had so wondrously made him a member of that very body he once tried to destroy. His past acts of sinful cruelty to God's people were matters of repentance to him, ever humbling him. The remembrance of what he had been and done as a lost man seem to have inspired in him greater zeal and boldness in the cause of Christ than he otherwise could have known.

How we ought to thank God for his secret, prevenient grace. I doubt Peter would have been so bold on Pentecost had he not fallen before the maid. Luther probably would not have been so mighty a defender of grace, had he not known what it was to seek eternal salvation by his own works. Yes, when God almighty has set his heart upon a sinner from eternity, he causes 'all things' to work together for his good.

It is impossible to say when the grace of God begins to work in his elect. You can tell when quickening grace comes, but not the grace itself.

God's grace begins in our earliest years as formative grace. He sovereignly puts us in our homes. He moulds our dispositions. He forms our thoughts. In later years God's grace is upon us as preventive grace. He keeps many from a course of open sin and degradation. Then there is that marvellous restraining grace of God. He allows many to walk in sin and yet restrains their vice and keeps them from destruction, even while they live with their fists shoved in his very face. As he says to the mighty ocean, so he says to the object of his love, 'Hitherto shalt thou come, but no further' (Job 38:11). Then, at the appointed time of love, he steps into the lives of his elect by omnipotent, saving mercy, revealing his Son in them and calling them by his grace.

Preparation

The grace of God prepares the hearts of chosen sinners for his salvation (Matthew 13:3-9). He makes them willing in the day of his power (Psalms 110:3). He makes them willing to hear his Word. He gives them a tender conscience. He creates in them a dissatisfaction with their present condition. He strips them of joy and peace, creating trouble and woe in their souls (Psalms 107). And he sends his Holy Spirit to convince them of their sin, Christ's righteousness, and of redemption accomplished by Christ's atonement (John 16:8-11). God the Holy Spirit turns the eyes of the despairing prodigal heavenward. By his invincible grace, Christ effectually calls his sheep, and causes them one by one to come to him in faith (Psalms 65:4).

Preserves

The grace of God preserves our salvation, too (John 10:27-29; Philippians 1:6; 2 Timothy 1:12). This thing called 'salvation' is God's work. He will carry it through. Christ's sheep shall never perish. Here is a divine promise: 'I give unto them eternal life; and they shall never perish' (John 10:28). That is a blanket, unconditional promise of the Son of God concerning his people. It takes into consideration all times, all circumstances, all contingencies, all events, and all possibilities.

What if they are babes in Christ and their faith is weak? 'They shall never perish'. What if they are young men in Christ and their passions are strong? 'They shall never perish'. What if they are old men and their vision grows dim? 'They shall never perish'. What if they are tempted? 'They shall never perish'. What if they are tried? 'They shall never perish'. What if all hell breaks lose against them? 'They shall never perish'. What if they sin? 'They shall never perish'. What if they sin again? 'They shall never perish'. What if they fall? 'They shall never perish'. What if they fall seven times a day? 'They shall never perish'. What if they fall seventy times in a day? 'They shall never perish'!

A Message For All God's People

This promise takes in all the flock. 'They shall never perish'. Not one of Christ's sheep shall ever perish; no, not even one! This is not a distinctive privilege reserved for a favoured few. It is a common mercy to all the chosen flock. If you are a believer, if you trust the Lord Jesus Christ, if you have received eternal life, you shall never perish! Christ himself has promised it. No, you cannot even sin away the grace of God bestowed upon you in Christ. Noah's fall did not alter God's grace. Abraham's weakness did not make God's grace less strong. Lot's wickedness did not make him less righteous before God. David's crime did not cause him to perish. Peter's denial of the Lord did not cause his Lord to deny him. 'Salvation is of the Lord' Christ's sheep shall never perish!

This doctrine of the believer's security in Christ is in every way consistent with all revealed truth. It is most surely believed among the people of God. Deny this promise and with it you deny every promise of God. If one word from God cannot be believed, no word from God can be believed. Here are seven reasons why the sheep of Christ shall never perish.

1. The promise of God must be fulfilled. 'They shall never perish' (2 Timothy 2:19; 1 John 3:19).

2. The purpose of God cannot be frustrated (John 6:37-40). God's covenant cannot be disannulled. God's purpose in election cannot be overturned. The suretiship engagements of Christ cannot be defeated (Hebrews 2:13).

3. The redemptive work of Christ cannot be nullified (Isaiah 53:10-11).

4. The Book of God declares an actual, literal, accomplished, substitutionary redemption. Since Christ died for his sheep, in their room and in their place, they cannot and shall not die. He paid all our debts. We have no debt to pay. He bore all our punishment. There is no punishment left for us to bear. Christ satisfied the offended justice of God for us. There is nothing left for us to bear, and nothing for us to satisfy. Justice pleads as strongly as mercy for the eternal salvation of those people for whom Christ died at Calvary (Romans 5:10; 8:31-34). If even one of those for whom Christ died were to perish, then his purpose in dying for them would be frustrated (Ephesians 5:25-27; Galatians 1:4-5; Titus 2:14). If even one of those for whom Christ died were to perish, then he could never see of the travail of his soul and be satisfied.

5. The believer's justification in Christ is an irreversible act of grace. The trial is over. The court of heaven has pronounced an irreversible verdict upon us — 'Justified!' God will not impute sin to a believing soul (Romans 4:8). God has put away our sins forever by the sacrifice of his Son. Our acceptance before God is in Christ. Our justification is free, full, and forever!

6. The work of God's grace can never be defeated (Philippians 1:6). That which God has begun he will carry on to perfection. God is willing to complete his work in us. God is wise enough to complete his work in us. God is strong enough to complete his work in us. Without the least presumption, every true believer may gladly sing with A. M. Toplady;

> The work which God's goodness began,
> The arm of His strength will complete;
> His promise is yea and amen,
> And never was forfeited yet:
> Things future, nor things that are now,
> Not all things below nor above,
> Can make Him His purpose forego,
> Or sever my soul from His love.
>
> My name from the palms of His hands,
> Eternity will not erase:
> Impressed on His heart it remains
> In marks of indelible grace:
> Yes, I to the end shall endure,
> As sure as the Earnest is given,
> More happy, but not more secure,
> The glorified spirits in heaven.

7. The intercessory work of Christ must prevail (John 17:9-11, 15, 20; 1 John 2:1-2). 'Our cause can never, never fail, for Jesus pleads and must prevail!' The seal of the Holy Spirit cannot be broken (Ephesians 1:13-14). 'Neither shall any man pluck them out of my hand.' We are preserved in the heart of his love. And we are preserved in the hands of his power. 'All thy saints are in thy hands'. We are in the hands of Christ our God and Saviour. We are always in his hands. What a blessed place to be! This is the place of our security. These are the hands that were pierced to redeem us. These are the hands of omnipotent power. These are the hands that

hold the reins of universal dominion. These are the hands that hold us in life. These are the hands of God himself. 'My Father, which gave them me, is greater than all; and no man is able to pluck them out of my Father's hand. I and my Father are one' (John 10:29-30). God's elect are preserved in Christ forever; forever, infallibly secure in him (Zechariah 4:6-7; Jude 24-25), because this blessed work called 'salvation' is all of grace!

Then fourteen years after I went up again to Jerusalem with Barnabas, and took Titus with me also. And I went up by revelation, and communicated unto them that gospel which I preach among the Gentiles, but privately to them which were of reputation, lest by any means I should run, or had run, in vain. But neither Titus, who was with me, being a Greek, was compelled to be circumcised: And that because of false brethren unawares brought in, who came in privily to spy out our liberty which we have in Christ Jesus, that they might bring us into bondage: To whom we gave place by subjection, no, not for an hour; that the truth of the gospel might continue with you. But of these who seemed to be somewhat, (whatsoever they were, it maketh no matter to me: God accepteth no man's person:) for they who seemed to be somewhat in conference added nothing to me: But contrariwise, when they saw that the gospel of the uncircumcision was committed unto me, as the gospel of the circumcision was unto Peter; (For he that wrought effectually in Peter to the apostleship of the circumcision, the same was mighty in me toward the Gentiles:) And when James, Cephas, and John, who seemed to be pillars, perceived the grace that was given unto me, they gave to me and Barnabas the right hands of fellowship; that we should go unto the heathen, and they unto the circumcision. Only they would that we should remember the poor; the same which I also was forward to do.

(Galatians 2:1-10)

Chapter 5

Read: Galatians 2:1-10 and Acts 15:1-29

What Happened At Jerusalem?

These two portions of holy scripture are frequently passed over lightly, because they are considered only as brief instances in the marvellous history of the early church. But these two chapters record the first serious crisis that arose in the church of our Saviour, and, though there are portions within these two chapters that require careful comparative study in order to understand them, we will be greatly rewarded if we will apply ourselves in their study.

During the days of the Apostles, and early in the ministry of the Apostle Paul, the church had to undergo a very trying crisis. That church, which was on the Day of Pentecost 'all with one accord', was seriously divided. As persecutions scattered the early believers into various parts of the world, so also was scattered the precious seed of the gospel; and many converts were made among the Gentiles. Moreover, Paul had been converted, made an Apostle, and was sent to preach the gospel among the Gentiles; and many more Gentiles were converted.

Meantime, there were some men of the sect of the Pharisees who had falsely embraced Christianity. That is to say, they had joined the church, but through subtlety. They did not really embrace the gospel of God's free and sovereign grace in Christ, but mixed with the gospel the various ceremonies and works of the law. Many were so thoroughly corrupted from the simplicity that is in Christ that they embraced the damning legalism of the Pharisees. There were some who said, 'Except ye be circumcised after the manner of Moses, ye cannot be saved.'

Under the old Jewish economy, circumcision had both a moral and a ceremonial significance. For them, to do away with circumcision was to do away with the whole Mosaic law. Many of them were not quite ready for this, as Paul's letter to the Hebrews clearly shows. The Mosaic law was ordained by God in the hands of angels. It had been the true religion for 4,000 years. It was very difficult for the Jewish believers (as it is with many today) to realize that the whole Mosaic system was typical and, therefore, transitory. Thus, the issue was not merely over circumcision, but over the whole legal system. Are Christians obliged to keep Moses' law, or are they free from it? This was the question that divided the church in those early days.

Though the Apostles unanimously settled the question, it still divides the church of Christ. There are still those who insist upon bringing the free men in Christ under the bondage and servitude of Moses' law. It is regrettable and dangerous to the souls of men that many who profess to believe and preach the free and sovereign grace of God, like the work-mongers of old, try to put God's saints back under the terrifying, galling yoke of legal bondage. Let us beware lest we become entangled again with the law (Galatians 5:1; Colossians 2:8). There is no life in the law. Christ only has life. 'In him was life', and nowhere else. May our lips, our hearts, and our doctrine, never cease to declare ...

> Free from the law, O happy condition,
> Jesus hath bled, and there is remission;
> Cursed by the law, and bruised by the fall,
> Grace hath redeemed us, once for all.
>
> Now are we free, there is no condemnation,
> Jesus provides a perfect salvation,
> Come unto me, O hear His sweet call.
> Come and He saves us, once for all.
>   Philip Bliss

Paul went up to Jerusalem, not to get instruction or authority from the other Apostles, but to settle once for all this question of law versus liberty; to show to all the world that he and all the other Apostles were in agreement in this matter of free-grace, and that no place is to be given to the law as far as the Christian is concerned. Peter, James, John, and Paul all agreed upon the doctrine of the gospel. Their message was salvation by the righteousness of Christ, without anything done by man. Grace alone is the believer's motive in life. Christ alone is the Accomplisher of redemption, justification, and sanctification (1 Corinthians 1:30; Hebrews 10:10-14). Faith alone is the means by which we receive, embrace, and enjoy all the blessings of grace. In Galatians 2:1-10 the Holy Spirit gives us an inspired commentary, explaining what happened at the Jerusalem conference in Acts 15.

A Visit To Jerusalem
Paul went up to Jerusalem by the direct revelation of God. This was apparently Paul's third visit to Jerusalem and took place fourteen years after his first visit there, making it seventeen years after Paul's conversion.[1] He was now a seasoned, prudent, powerful, and confirmed Apostle.

Why was it necessary for him to go to Jerusalem? It was not because he had questions concerning the doctrines he had taught. Neither was it needful for him to have his apostleship confirmed. Paul went to Jerusalem specifically to settle the division that the Judaisers had caused in the church over this matter of the law. He went there to show that he and the other Apostles taught the same doctrine.

Barnabas, his co-labourer, was his travelling companion. His name means 'son of exhortation', or 'son of comfort'. It was given to him by the Apostles, probably as a description of the pre-eminent character of his ministry. He was a good man, full of the Holy Ghost and faith (Acts 11:24). Titus, another of Paul's co-labourers (one who had been converted under Paul's ministry), also made the trip with him. Titus was an uncircumcised, Gentile convert. Like Paul himself, both of these men were proven, faithful gospel preachers.

Paul was sent to Jerusalem by God's direct revelation (v. 2). We should always seek the direction of God's Spirit, by the Revelation he has given us in holy scripture, in all matters. This is especially true when dealing with spiritual, doctrinal, ecclesiastical matters. The Lord God directs us in

---

[1] Taking Galatians 1:15-17 as a reference to Saul's conversion experience and the 'three years' of verse 18 as the time from his conversion to his first visit to Jerusalem would seem to fit with what Luke relates in Acts 9:26-30. In Acts 11:27-30, Luke mentions another visit to Jerusalem to deliver alms (famine relief) for the saints in Judea, which Paul does not mention here, perhaps because it has no bearing upon his argument. This third visit to Jerusalem discussed in Galatians 2:1-10 seems to be the same occasion as the Jerusalem Council of Acts 15:1-22.

his will and in his way by his Spirit, through his Word, by his providence, and through his church. Paul was sent to Jerusalem by divine revelation. Yet, he was sent by the church at Antioch (Acts 15:2-3).

Doctrinal Confession

Having arrived in Jerusalem, Paul carefully, frankly, and fully explained his doctrine to the chief apostles; James, Peter, and John. First, he wisely and properly sought the Apostles and elders of the church. He privately sought those who were of reputation. What was their reputation? They were held in reputation by the brethren as faithful gospel preachers. Paul sought out these men, first because that is the proper thing to do in such matters, giving honour to those to whom honour is due. Anytime a man has a matter of controversy to lay before an assembly, he should discuss it with the pastor of that assembly.

Then, he declared to them his gospel and the success of his labours in the cause of Christ. 'And when they were come to Jerusalem, they were received of the church, and of the apostles and elders, and they declared all things that God had done with them' (Acts 15:4). He declared his message and declared that the power of God had accompanied the gospel he preached to the conversion of chosen, redeemed sinners wherever the Lord had sent him (Romans 1:16-17; 2 Corinthians 2:15-17).

After speaking privately to the other Apostles, elders, and preachers, Paul declared these things publicly to the Jerusalem church. He acted as he did in this matter so that his mission might not be in vain. If he had gone directly to the church, he might have caused greater division. Both his intention and his message may have been misunderstood.

One great evidence of the fact that Paul and those who were in Christ before him were in full agreement is the fact the other apostles did not compel, or even suggest, that Titus be circumcised. Paul allowed Timothy, who was part Jew, to be circumcised later; but he did so not to cause offence, not because of doctrinal compulsion (Acts 16:3; 1 Corinthians 10:28-31).

Still, there was a sharp confrontation between these faithful men and some false brethren who had come in under false pretence to spy out the liberty of God's saints, seeking an accusation against them (4-5). It was the presence of these men that caused Paul to make an issue of the fact that Titus was not circumcised and would not be circumcised (Acts 15:5; Jude 4). In matters of faith, for the gospel's sake, for the glory of Christ, and for the everlasting good of eternity bound sinners, faithful men must not give an inch. Henry Mahan recently wrote …

Contending for the truth against the errors of modern religion is the duty of God's servants. I hope our spirit is one of genuine love to all the chosen of God; but today's rule of charity which requires us to keep silent on certain points in order to avoid controversy, I utterly despise. It is treason to the Lord Jesus to be silent on any point where He has spoken and the honour of His Gospel is concerned. It is easy on the flesh to deal in generalities, to denounce hyper-this or hyper-that, and to claim to be a friend to all; but it is required of the loyal servant of King Jesus to maintain His crown-rights and to stand up for His Gospel of Glory and Grace.

Gospel Unity

Paul and his brethren at Jerusalem (not the false brethren) believed the same gospel. He tells us in Ephesians that as there is but one God, so there is but one faith. All who have God given faith in Christ have the same faith. They are all united in the faith of the gospel. All true believers believe the same gospel, the gospel of God's free and sovereign grace in Christ. Joseph Hart wrote,

> When is it Christians all agree
> And let distinctions fall?
> When, nothing in themselves, they see
> That Christ is all in all.
> But strife and difference will subsist
> While men will something seem;
> Let them but singly look to Christ
> And all are one in Him.
> The infant and the aged saint,
> The worker and the weak,
> They who are strong and seldom faint,
> And they who scarce can speak.
> Eternal life's the gift of God;
> It comes through Christ alone;
> 'Tis His, He bought it with His blood;
> And therefore gives His own.
> We have no life, no power, no faith,
> But what by Christ is given;
> We all deserve eternal death,
> And thus we all are even.

Paul's comment, 'But of these who seemed to be somewhat, (whatsoever they were, it maketh no matter to me: God accepteth no man's person:) for they who seemed to be somewhat in conference added nothing to me: (v. 6) must not be read as a statement of sarcasm. It is a recognition of the esteem which these men had earned in the eyes of God's church. Gospel preachers should always be held in high esteem of those among whom they labour (1 Thessalonians 5:12-13; Hebrews 13:17). Our God is no respecter of persons. He does not receive or use any man because of any natural qualities found in him. Rather, he saves sinners freely, without condition. And, commonly, those he is pleased to use in the work of the ministry are those who are least qualified for the work by nature (1 Corinthians 1:26-29). Paul was, in every way, equal with these men by virtue of his calling, and he knew it. The same is true of all to whom the Lord God has entrusted the gospel of his grace. God's servants are nothing but clay pots, in whom the Lord God has placed the great treasure of his gospel; and they all know it (2 Corinthians 4:7).

The faithful men at Jerusalem gave Paul the same honour and recognition he gave them, embracing him as God's messenger to the Gentiles. They saw that God had entrusted Paul with the gospel for the salvation of his elect among the Gentiles, just as he had entrusted Peter with it for the salvation of his elect among the Jews. Paul had a stewardship of the gospel committed to him to go to the Gentiles (1 Corinthians 9:17; 1 Thessalonians 2:4; 1 Timothy 1:11-12; Ephesians 3:8). Peter had a stewardship of the gospel committed to him to go to the Jews. The same gospel was committed to both; and both were faithful to it. Both were faithful and both were honoured by God in their labours as the instruments by which the gospel was spread both among the Jews and the Gentiles. That which is essential for any service in the kingdom of God is trustworthiness (Matthew 25:21; 2 Corinthians 4:2). It is by the mercy and grace of God that his servants are made trustworthy (1 Corinthians 7:25; 2 Corinthians 4:1), and continue so (Acts 26:22) unto the end (Acts 20:24, 2 Timothy 4:7).

Paul and Barnabas were received into the fellowship of the Apostles as co-labourers in the gospel. Fellowship is a general term expressing the common experiences, interests, goals, and hopes of God's saints. The basis of fellowship is the gospel of Christ (1 John 1:3-7). There is no fellowship where there is no gospel unity. The fact that the Apostles received Paul and Barnabas into their fellowship publicly put their stamp of approval upon them and declared to all the church that they were all co-labourers in the kingdom of God.

One Concern

Peter, James, and John were delighted to embrace Paul. They expressed concern only about one thing. They said nothing about the Mosaic commandments, ceremonies, and rituals, because they knew that God's saints are not under the law, but under grace. They only urged Paul and Barnabas to always remember and minister to the poor. That is a tremendous fact. Those servants of God had been involved in matters of great importance -- the purity of the gospel! Nothing could be more important. But the purity of the gospel would be empty and meaningless were it preached by men who were without compassion. So Peter, James, and John urged Paul and Barnabas to remember the poor in all their labours. That they were eager to do. The exercise of love, compassion, sympathy, and tenderness toward those who are most likely to be the objects of abuse is always in season and always both the duty and the delight of poor sinners who have tasted God's rich grace in Christ (Exodus 23:10-11; 30:15; Leviticus 19:10; Deuteronomy 15:7-11; Jeremiah 22:16; Daniel 4:27; Amos 2:6-7; Matthew 7:12; Luke 6:36; John 13:29; 1 Corinthians 16:1-2; 2 Corinthians 8:9; Matthew 25:31-46). In the Word of God grace, righteousness, godliness, and good works are always associated with love, kindness, and mercy. This is the law by which the people of God are ruled and motivated (1 John 3:23).

But when Peter was come to Antioch, I withstood him to the face, because he was to be blamed. For before that certain came from James, he did eat with the Gentiles: but when they were come, he withdrew and separated himself, fearing them which were of the circumcision. And the other Jews dissembled likewise with him; insomuch that Barnabas also was carried away with their dissimulation. But when I saw that they walked not uprightly according to the truth of the gospel, I said unto Peter before them all, If thou, being a Jew, livest after the manner of Gentiles, and not as do the Jews, why compellest thou the Gentiles to live as do the Jews? We who are Jews by nature, and not sinners of the Gentiles, Knowing that a man is not justified by the works of the law, but by the faith of Jesus Christ, even we have believed in Jesus Christ, that we might be justified by the faith of Christ, and not by the works of the law: for by the works of the law shall no flesh be justified. But if, while we seek to be justified by Christ, we ourselves also are found sinners, is therefore Christ the minister of sin? God forbid. For if I build again the things which I destroyed, I make myself a transgressor. For I through the law am dead to the law, that I might live unto God.

(Galatians 2:11-19)

Chapter 6

Read: Galatians 2:11-19

Free Justification

We now approach the heart of this epistle, which, concise as it is, may be regarded as the keystone of the New Testament, for it most conspicuously sets forth and defends the Biblical answer to the fundamental question, 'How shall a man be justified before God?' (Job 25:4). The entire scope of Divine Revelation focuses on the answer. This gives Paul's reproof of Peter at Antioch very high significance. No issue could be more vital, for on it was suspended the survival or the shipwreck of the early church.

Paul was the man of the hour, specifically raised up by God to meet the Galatian crisis. As in the case of Joseph, of Moses, of Samuel, of David, of Elijah, and of Daniel, the crisis depended upon the work of one; one man called, gifted, equipped, and sent of God to meet the need of his church at this crucial time. That man was Paul, the Apostle to the Gentiles. God has little use for committees and corporations. His greatest works in the history of mankind have been wrought by single men; men single eyed and strong in the Holy Spirit for the cause of truth. God 'called Abraham alone and blessed him'. So Paul was called alone. No capital was behind him; no society, or party was behind him; no religious order was behind him. Even Barnabas had deserted his cause. Like Luther, and Calvin, and Knox, he stood alone in the time of great urgency.

What was it that Paul so boldly and singularly stood for on this occasion? Justification by Christ alone. Christ and Christ only was Paul's subject. He would have nothing outside of Christ and nothing in addition to Christ for the justification of guilty sinners. Any other message is

another gospel. It was either Christ or nothing. He is all in all in the matter
of salvation. There is no such thing as Christ doing his part to save us
and us doing our part. We have no part except that of a poor beggar, who
empty-handed receives a gratuitous gift of mercy and compassion.

In the verses before us Paul continues to prove the essential
independence, both of his gospel and of his apostolic position. That
gospel which had been so enthusiastically endorsed by those 'pillars' at
Jerusalem was, when necessity demanded, asserted even in confrontation
with one of those 'men of repute'. This episode in which Paul reproved
Peter may well have occurred during the interval between the Jerusalem
conference and the beginning of the second missionary journey. We are
told in the book of Acts that it was then that Paul and Barnabas stayed for
some time in Antioch (Acts 15:22-35).

Sinners are justified before God freely, by grace alone, upon the merits
of Christ's blood, apart from anything done by them; and they receive
this free-justification by faith. This was Paul's message. This is the
message of the gospel (Romans 3:19-26). This is the doctrine of all true
believers.

Peter's Error

'But when Peter was come to Antioch, I withstood him to the face, because
he was to be blamed. For before that certain came from James, he did eat
with the Gentiles: but when they were come, he withdrew and separated
himself, fearing them which were of the circumcision. And the other Jews
dissembled likewise with him; insomuch that Barnabas also was carried
away with their dissimulation. But when I saw that they walked not
uprightly according to the truth of the gospel, I said unto Peter before
them all, If thou, being a Jew, livest after the manner of Gentiles, and not
as do the Jews, why compellest thou the Gentiles to live as do the Jews?'
(Galatians 2:11-14)

We are not told why Peter visited Antioch at this time; but that is not
important. The important fact is that Peter committed an error of conduct
so serious that Paul felt constrained to oppose him to his face. Paul did
not go about as a whisperer, backbiter, or talebearer. He withstood Peter
to his face as a brother trying to correct the error of another brother. He
handled the matter publicly, because Peter's action was public and caused
great public harm.

This event does not, in any way, suggest that those things Peter
wrote under divine inspiration are lacking in authority, infallibility, and
inerrancy. The Word of God nowhere teaches that the men who were used
of God to pen the scriptures were infallible. They were not. They were,

like all other believers, sinners saved by grace. The scriptures they penned are infallible, but not them. However, this single event does completely destroy the Roman Catholic doctrine of the infallibility and supremacy of Peter, and of the pope as Peter's imagined successor.

Peter was to be blamed. His conduct was totally inexcusable. His behaviour was to be condemned. Why? Before the Jews came to Antioch, he had been eating with his Gentile brethren. The reference here is probably to the fellowship meals, or love feasts of the early Christians. It appears that the Lord's Supper was usually held at the conclusion of these feasts. There were many abuses to which such social meals could lead, as is pointed out in 1 Corinthians 11:17-34. In Corinth there was a segregation according to wealth, the rich separating from the poor. In Antioch the segregation that occurred was of an ethnic character, the Jewish brethren separated from their Gentile brothers in Christ.

Peter knew that the distinction of meats was now laid aside, as well as the distinction of Jew and Gentile, and that nothing, meats or men, was common or unclean of itself (Acts 10:28-48; 15:8-11). The Lord had taught him plainly that we are not under the law, but under grace in this gospel age, because Christ has fulfilled the law. He knew that even Jewish believers were no longer obliged to keep the law. Certainly, then the Gentiles, who were never given the law, were not obliged to keep the law.

In spite of Peter's clear understanding of these things, when some men came from the church at Jerusalem, of which James was the pastor, Peter ceased to eat with the Gentiles, who were also believers. It may seem to some that Peter did nothing so terribly wrong. After all, all he did was this: when he saw his Jewish friends coming, Peter simply got up from the table and stepped away from the Gentile brethren, hoping that none of the Jewish brethren would smell the pork chops on his breath. But his action was horrible in its implication. Behaving as he did, Peter hypocritically implied that there is still a distinction between meat and drinks, clean and unclean, and between Jew and Gentile. He acted out of cowardice, fearing the wrath of the Jews (the wrath of Jewish believers!). When Peter got up from the table and walked away from the Gentile brethren, though he apparently said nothing orally, he spoke loudly by example and led others in his error, even Barnabas (v. 13).

Lessons To Learn
There are some obvious lessons we ought to learn from this. First, the Word of God shows us again and again that the best of men are only men at best; sinful, weak, inconsistent, and full of faults. When left to ourselves, even briefly, there is nothing we would not do and justify

ourselves in doing. A noble Noah may be found in a drunken stupor. A faithful Abraham may be found asking his wife to lie and play the harlot because of fear. A righteous Lot may be found choosing to dwell in Sodom. A devoted David may be found committing adultery and murder to cover it. Peter was no exception. Neither is the one writing or the one reading these lines. Let us ever recognize this fact. It will help to make us behave graciously toward our fallen brethren and help to keep us from being severe in our judgment concerning one another.

Second, we need to be aware of the fact that if we seek to please men, we will fail in obedience to our God (Proverbs 29:25). It is impossible to serve two masters. If we are ruled by the will and glory of God, we cannot be ruled by either the fear of men's frowns or the hope of their favour. If we are ruled by the fear of men, we cannot be ruled by the fear of God.

Third, we must constantly be aware of the great influence of our behaviour upon others. The common proverb, 'Actions speak louder than words', is as true as it is common. We are responsible for the influence we have upon others by our example. None of us, I am confident, have any idea how powerful our example is in its influence over others, especially when the example is evil. Parents, teachers, and pastors must be constantly aware of this fact. None of us live as an island. Everything we do influences those around us. The world's politicians, for the most part, have forgotten this, and have by their displays of greed and moral bankruptcy led the people under their power to lives of utter debauchery. Sadly, I fear, the same must be said of parents, teachers, and preachers around the world in this dark, dark age. Let all who fear God mark the trend of the day and, for the sake of our Lord Jesus, resolve to lead and influence others by good example, by deed as well as by word.

Paul's Rebuke

Paul saw immediately what Peter was doing. And saw that his implications were intentional. His implications were that the law is still the rule of life for believers and that God's saints are to be compelled to live by it (v. 14). This was totally contrary to the true gospel of the grace of God (Romans 6:14-15; 7:4; 10:4; Colossians 2:16-23). There is no room in the kingdom of grace for the bondmen of the law. There is no place in the household of faith for the whip of the law. Believers are motivated and ruled by the constraint of Christ's love, gratitude for his grace, faith in Christ, and the glory of God (2 Corinthians 5:14; 8:8-9; 1 John 3:23; 1 Corinthians 10:31). In the gospel there are no prohibitions about eating and drinking (1 Timothy 4:4-5). In the church of God there is no such thing as Jew and Gentile (Ephesians 2:13-22; Galatians 3:28). Peter had lived like the Gentiles;

but now he was, by his action, saying that the Gentiles should live like the Jews. This was inconsistent and obvious to all. Therefore Paul rebuked him publicly (1 Timothy 5:20).

Matthew Henry wrote, 'Paul having thus established his character and office, and sufficiently shown that he is not inferior to any of the apostles, no, not to Peter himself, from the account of the reproof he gave him he takes occasion to speak of that great fundamental doctrine of the gospel, that justification is only by faith in Christ, and not by the works of the law.'

Gospel Doctrine

'We who are Jews by nature, and not sinners of the Gentiles, Knowing that a man is not justified by the works of the law, but by the faith of Jesus Christ, even we have believed in Jesus Christ, that we might be justified by the faith of Christ, and not by the works of the law: for by the works of the law shall no flesh be justified. But if, while we seek to be justified by Christ, we ourselves also are found sinners, is therefore Christ the minister of sin? God forbid. For if I build again the things which I destroyed, I make myself a transgressor. For I through the law am dead to the law, that I might live unto God' (Galatians 2:15-19).

The verb 'justify' is in the passive voice, thus, literally, it is 'to be justified'. It occurs here for the first time in Paul's epistles, and no less than three times in one verse (v. 16). Justification is not something we do. It is something done for us and given to us freely. It is the gracious act of God, whereby, on the basis solely of Christ's accomplished mediatorial work, he declares the sinner just. The work was done by the decree of God in eternity (Romans 8:29-30). Yes, all God's elect were in the purpose of God justified from eternity, by the Lamb of God slain from the foundation of the world. Our justification was obtained by Christ when he died at Calvary as our Substitute. He was delivered unto death by the sword of divine justice because of our sins imputed to him, and raised again by the glory of God because of our justification accomplished by his sacrifice (Romans 4:25). Faith in Christ does not accomplish justification, but receives it as the free grace gift of God (Romans 5:1, 10-11; 8:1, 30, 33; Titus 3:7). Faith in Christ is not a condition upon which justification is granted, but one of the many, blessed fruits of justification accomplished. It is not our faith that justifies us, but Christ who is the Object of our faith.

Justification is a judicial act of God. It does not come as the result of man's effort (Romans 3:20, 28; Galatians 3:11; 5:4). It is not even the result of faith (Ephesians 2:8). It took place when Christ satisfied the demands of the law as a Substitute for his elect (Romans 3:24; 2 Corinthians 5:21; Ephesians 1:7). Man can never earn it. He only receives it by faith. And even the faith by which we receive it is the gift of God's grace (Ephesians 2:8). 'Man is not justified by the works of the law, but by the faith of Jesus Christ.'

Because we are justified by Christ alone, by the faithful obedience of Christ unto death as our Substitute, we have no obligation to the law. We are dead to the law. This is not a license to sin (v. 17; Romans 6:1-2, 15; 7:7). It is the blessed liberty of grace. We dare not return to the law, as Peter did by his abhorrent symbolic behaviour. To do so is to return to its curse and condemnation (v. 18).

The law of God can never give life. It only deals out death. It can never produce holiness. It only stirs up sin. The law brings the knowledge of sin, and condemns it (Romans 7:7-9). The law was our schoolmaster unto Christ. Once we have come to Christ in faith, the law has no power or authority over us (Galatians 3:24).

I have a very good friend in North Carolina, Robert Spencer. He and I became good friends just a few years ago, after I ran into him and his wife, Lib, in an elevator. He was then President of the International Lions Club, on his way to one of their meetings. I was on my way to fulfil a preaching engagement in the same town. I had known Bob many years earlier as 'Mr Spencer'. He was my sixth grade school teacher. I was a young rebel, constantly in trouble. Mr Spencer, on many occasions, with the complete authority of the State (and of my parents), inflicted pain on my posterior because it was his job to do so, to bring me to maturity. In those days I dreaded his presence and feared his wrath. Now, he is my friend. I look forward to seeing him and always enjoy his company. Even if he thought about whipping me today, he would not dare. He no longer has any authority or the power to do so. So it is with the law. Once the sinner has come to Christ, the law has no more dominion over him (Romans 6:14-15; 7:4; 10:4).

'I through the law am dead to the law, that I might live unto God' (Galatians 2:19; Romans 6:7; 7:4; 2 Corinthians 5:15). We are not dead to the law that we might live unto ourselves, but unto our God, for his glory. And if we would live unto God, we cannot live unto the law. We must never return to it in any way, to any degree, for any reason; not even to appease and win the favour of weaker brethren, as Peter did at Antioch. We trust Christ alone for salvation (Romans 10:1-4). He alone is our righteousness (1 Corinthians 1:30). To return to the works of the law is to deny him altogether (Galatians 5:1-4).

I am crucified with Christ: nevertheless I live; yet not I, but Christ liveth in me: and the life which I now live in the flesh I live by the faith of the Son of God, who loved me, and gave himself for me.

(Galatians 2:20)

Chapter 7

Read: Galatians 2:20

Christ And Me

Paul has already shown us that if he were to rebuild those things which he once destroyed, that is, if he were to return to the Pharisaic teaching of salvation by legal works, he would be a transgressor, because he would be acting contrary to his deepest convictions based on his past experience. To this he adds that such action would also destroy the meaning of Christ's death on the cross. Paul had experienced such faith in Christ crucified as to thoroughly replace any confidence he ever had in human merit. This is the connection of verses 20 and 21 to the remainder of chapter two.

Paul introduces his declaration of oneness with Christ by this statement: 'I am crucified with Christ'. What a baffling assertion! Here is the great Apostle to the Gentiles, at the love feast at Antioch, addressing an audience, which consisted of both Jewish and Gentile believers. Peter and Barnabas were in the congregation. Undoubtedly some of those false brethren who caused so much dissension over the law of Moses were still there as well (Acts 14:25-15:2). At this meeting place there was a deplorable situation. Strong cliques had developed, and segregation was being practiced. Jews were eating exclusively with Jews, leaving Gentile believers no other alternative than to eat with other Gentiles. This violation of the principle of the 'oneness' of all believers in Christ had been caused by Peter's dissimulation. He and the Judaisers were behaving as though the cross of Christ had been of no avail in taking down the middle wall of partition between them and the Gentiles (Ephesians 2:11-22).

Crucified With Christ

With this as the background, Paul declares, 'I am crucified with Christ: nevertheless I live; yet not I, but Christ liveth in me: and the life which I now live in the flesh I live by the faith of the Son of God, who loved me, and gave himself for me.' He has asserted clearly and boldly that no man was ever to be justified by his own works, however righteous they may be, but only by Christ. Now he brings his doctrine to its culmination and practical application in these ringing words, 'I am crucified with Christ'. Something marvellous had taken place, rendering Paul a justified man, which had an eternally abiding significance.

What Paul here declares of himself is true of all God's elect. All of God's elect are in such union with Christ that his righteousness, his life, his death, and his resurrection are theirs. Everything our Saviour was and is as our Mediator, everything he did and experienced as a man, is ours, and we have done in him.

In saying, 'I am crucified with Christ', Paul is describing something altogether spiritual. He was not literally, physically crucified with Christ. Christ was crucified for him in his room and stead. But he was crucified with him and in him as his Mediator, Surety, Substitute and Representative. Paul is not describing a present experience, but a finished work. This phrase would be better translated – 'I have been crucified with Christ'. He is not talking about self-crucifixion. He is not talking about self-mortification. He is not talking about something he had experienced, but about something done for him by Christ.

The Lord Jesus Christ was and is forever the Representative of all his people. All that he did and suffered was in their name and on their account. When he obeyed the law of God for us, we obeyed the law in him. When he suffered the unmitigated wrath of God for us and died under the penalty of his holy law, we suffered and died in him, representatively. When he was buried, we were buried. When he arose, we arose. When he took his seat in heaven, we were seated with him (Ephesians 2:5-6).

When our Mediator was crucified, all our sins, the whole body of them, were laid upon him. He bore them in his own body on the cursed tree, and bore them away. He destroyed and made an end of them. He put away our sins by the sacrifice of himself (Hebrews 9:26). He has blotted them out, removed them from us as far as the east is from the west, and cast them into the infinitely deep sea of divine forgetfulness, so that they shall never be remembered by our God against us again forever!

This was done when Christ died and we died in him. In regeneration (sanctification) we are delivered from the dominion of sin by the grace and power of God the Holy Spirit. By the power and efficacy of Christ's accomplishments at Calvary, the world is crucified to us and we to the world in the experience of grace. But we were crucified with Christ when Christ was crucified for us.

'Nevertheless I Live'

This is our present experience of grace. Being born again by the grace of God, having the gift of faith wrought in us by the invincible, irresistible power of his grace, we who were dead in trespasses and in sins live. Every believer is a paradox. He is dead to the law, and yet lives to God. He has been crucified with Christ, and yet lives by Christ. Indeed, the crucified Christ lives in him.

What does Paul mean by 'Yet not I'? He is telling us that he is now a new creature in Christ (2 Corinthians 5:17). He was no longer Saul the blasphemer, the persecutor, and injurious man. He was no longer Saul the Pharisee. He is not telling us that his old nature was gone, or even improved (Romans 7:14-24). Rather, he is telling us that a new man has been created in him by the grace of God; and that new man living in him is Christ. This new life was not something he had obtained by his own efforts, or by his own righteousness. It was the gift and work of God in him (1 John 3:1-9). A new, righteous nature had been created in him by grace. And that new nature implanted in him, that righteousness imparted to him was Christ himself (Colossians 1:27; 2 Peter 1:4).

And 'Christ Liveth In Me'

Christ is the Author, Giver, and Sustainer of spiritual life; but he is more than that. Christ is our life! He is formed in us. He dwells in us. He is united to us, and we to him. We are 'members of his body, of his flesh, and of his bones'. We are one with him (Ephesians 5:30-32). We who are born of God are so united to him, so thoroughly one with him that his life is our life and our spiritual life is his. It is Christ living in us! 'And the life which I now live in the flesh', here Paul is speaking of his temporary earthly existence, his physical existence in this world. 'I live by the faith of the Son of God', not the faith or faithfulness our Saviour exercised as a man while he lived in the earth, but the faith he gives to his elect by the effectual call of his Spirit. It is the faith of which he is both the Author and the Object. This is the faith by which we live in this world.

Paul did not say that he lived upon faith in Christ, but 'by' it. We do not live before God upon our faith, but upon Christ the Object of our faith; ever looking to him alone for pardon, righteousness, peace, joy, comfort, every supply of grace, and eternal salvation.

He who is our Saviour, the Object of our faith, is 'the Son of God'. He is himself God, one with and equal with his Father, the only begotten Son of God, full of grace and truth.

Distinguishing Love

How Paul must have delighted to write the words 'Who loved me'. He understood that the Lord God his Saviour loved him before the foundation of the world with an everlasting, immutable, indestructible love. Let every believing heart be assured of this great, glorious fact. God our Saviour loved us from everlasting and loves us freely (Jeremiah 31:3; Hosea 14:4). His love for us is not in any way dependent upon or determined by us. He loves us eternally. And he loves us personally and particularly with a distinguishing love.

Let others talk as they may about 'God's universal love'. Such language is both contrary to holy scripture and would utterly destroy all inspiration and motivation in us to honour him and live for him. If God's love for Jacob and his hatred of Esau are made to be the same thing, Jacob has no reason at all to praise, worship, and serve him. But that is not the case. God's love for his own elect is a particular, special love, a love by which he distinguishes his own elect from all others, a love that inspires the hearts of those who know it to live for him.

Particular Redemption

Not only has Jesus Christ loved me, he gave himself for me. He gave himself for me! Feed on that. Christ Jesus the Lord, the Son of God gave himself for me! He gave himself into the hands of justice; gave himself unto death; gave himself in my room and stead; as an offering and sacrifice to God for sin to redeem me because he loved me! He gave himself for me freely and voluntarily because of his great love for me. Redemption is passionate, personal and particular.

Our Saviour gave his life a ransom for many. He died to redeem and save all his people, his whole church, all the members of his mystical body. That is a blessed fact of divine Revelation. Yet, Paul speaks of this matter as singularly respecting himself, almost as if he was the only person Christ loved and redeemed. It was Christ's love for him, Christ's death for him that overwhelmed him. Faith does not deal with indefinite ambiguities, but with blessed, personal realities (Ephesians 1:13-14). As John Gill put it, 'Faith deals with Christ not in a general way, as the Saviour of the world, but with a special regard to a man's self: this is the life of faith; and these considerations of the person, love, and grace of Christ, animate and encourage faith in its exercises on him.'

One With Christ

'I am crucified with Christ: nevertheless I live; yet not I, but Christ liveth in me: and the life which I now live in the flesh I live by the faith of the Son of God, who loved me, and gave himself for me.' Here is man, but here is the Son of God as well, and the two personalities are singularly interwoven. Christ and the believer are one! As we are naturally one with Adam, as he is our representative in the Covenant of Works, so we are one with Christ as he is our Representative in the Covenant of Grace. How can this be? (Romans 5:18-19).

Paul says, 'I am crucified with Christ'. He means by this that we are one with Christ. Thomas Goodwin puts it beautifully, 'As in the womb, head and members are not conceived apart, but together, as having relation to each other; so were we and Christ (as making up one mystical body to God) formed together in the eternal womb of election.'

> Lord Jesus, are we one with Thee?
> O height, O depth of love!
> Thou one with us on Calvary,
> We are with Thee above.
>
> Such was Thy grace, that for our sake
> Thou didst from heaven come down,
> With us of flesh and blood partake,
> In all our misery, one.
>
> Our sins, our guilt, in love divine,
> Confessed and borne by Thee;
> The gall, the curse, the wrath, were Thine,
> To set Thy members free.
>
> Ascended now in glory bright,
> Still one with us Thou art;
> Nor life, nor death, nor depth, nor height
> Thy saints and Thee can part.

O teach us, Lord, to know and own
This wondrous mystery,
That Thou with us art truly one,
And we are one with Thee.

Soon, soon, shall come that glorious day,
When seated on Thy throne,
Thou shalt to wondering world's display
That Thou art with us one.

We have such a union with Christ that when he died, we actually died in him, thus God's wrath was satisfied (Isaiah 53:4-6, 8, 12; Matthew 20:28; Galatians 1:4; 3:13). Our union to Christ is such that when he was quickened from the dead, we were made alive in him (Ephesians 2:3-6; Colossians 2:12-14; 3:1; Romans 8:1, 33-39). Because we are one with him, living in him, we shall never die (John 10:28; 11:25-26).

I do not frustrate the grace of God: for if righteousness come by the law, then Christ is dead in vain.

(Galatians 2:21)

Chapter 8

Read: Galatians 2:21

'I Do Not Frustrate The Grace Of God'

Why was Paul so dogmatic and bold in publicly withstanding Peter when Peter led the division of the church at Antioch, when he caused the Jewish believers, and even Barnabas, to separate themselves from their Gentile brethren? The answer to that question is found here in Galatians 2:21. Peter's actions were a frustration of the grace of God. That is to say, Peter (by his actions) led these believers back to the law as the basis of acceptance with God.

Therefore Paul writes, 'I do not frustrate the grace of God'. The word translated 'frustrate' means to 'cast away, deny, despise, reject, and make void'. He here asserts that any and every assertion that salvation is the result of something men do is to cast away, deny, despise, reject, and make void the grace of God. It is a frustration of the grace of God the Son revealed in the sacrifice of himself for our sins. The teaching that salvation is in any way, or to any degree, the result of human effort is a denial of the whole gospel (Galatians 5:1-4). It is a frustration of the gospel of the grace of God, because such doctrine declares that righteousness comes by the law rather than by Christ alone (Galatians 5:5-6). Those who make righteousness (justifying righteousness and/or sanctifying righteousness) dependent upon the works of men have denied, despised, rejected, and rendered null and void the gospel of the grace of God. They have departed from it altogether. Why?

'For if righteousness come by the law, then Christ is dead in vain.' There was no need for the Son of God to die, if righteousness can be obtained some other way. Nothing can be more contemptuous of our God and Saviour than to assert there was no reason for his death. Such doctrine is monstrous. It asserts that God slaughtered his Son for no reason. Of course, nothing could be further from the truth. The Holy Spirit tells us plainly that the reason it was necessary for Christ to die was precisely because righteousness could not come to poor sinners like us, except by the substitutionary sacrifice of God's dear Son (Romans 3:24-28). Only in this way can God be both just and the Justifier of his people. He could not be both a just God and a Saviour in any other way (Isaiah 45:21-25). It is beyond monstrous to imagine that the infinitely wise, good, and just God would sacrifice his darling Son were there no necessity for it.

Criminal Doctrine

That makes the doctrine of salvation by works a criminal doctrine. It was for this reason that Paul was determined to give it no place. He opposed fervently everything that bore any resemblance to salvation by human merit. Therefore, when Peter sided with the Judaisers at Antioch, and seemed to teach that the Gentile believers must live by the law, he publicly withstood him to the face.

The gospel of Christ is a declaration of salvation by grace, the good news of salvation accomplished by the obedience of God's Son unto death as the sinner's Substitute. Paul vehemently opposed every idea that the keeping of the law could merit God's favour. He asserted dogmatically, clearly, and constantly that men are not saved by works in any degree, but entirely by the grace of God. 'By grace are ye saved through faith; and that not of yourselves, it is the gift of God.' God has 'saved us and called us with an holy calling, not according to our works, but according to his own purpose and grace, which was given us in Christ Jesus before the world began'. Grace means grace, and grace alone (2 Timothy 1:9). Any mixture of works with grace is a complete denial of grace (Romans 11:6). To teach, as multitudes do, that salvation can be obtained by anything apart from the sacrifice of Christ, or by anything placed in connection with the sacrifice of Christ, done by man; is to frustrate the grace of God and say that Christ died in vain

There is no evil in the world so vile, so blasphemous, so destructive to the souls of men as the doctrine of salvation by human effort. Martin Luther declared, 'This is blasphemy more horrible than can be expressed'. Nothing robs God of his glory as God like Arminian, free-will, works religion. Yet, there is no evil more common among men.

Inevitable Consequences

Paul asserts that there are certain, inevitable consequences to the doctrine of salvation by works. He specifically names two. First, if righteousness comes by the law, then the grace of God is cast away. Secondly, if righteousness comes by the law, then Christ died in vain.

All who hope to be saved by their own efforts reject the grace and free favour of God. They regard God's grace as useless and frustrate it, cast it behind their backs, and trample it beneath their feet. If righteousness comes by the law then there is no need for grace. If keeping the law will win God's favour, we do not need his grace.

Paul has specifically spoken of the legal ceremony of circumcision; but that ceremony is used only as an expression of legal obedience. This becomes obvious when we read what he says in chapter three. 'As many as are of the works of the law are under the curse: for it is written, Cursed is everyone that continueth not in all things which are written in the book of the law to do them' (Galatians 3:10).

Many would have us believe that Paul's assertions concerning the law and the believer's freedom from it only apply to the ceremonial law, and only apply to the attempts of men to be justified by their obedience to the law. They insist that, though justifying righteousness cannot be gained by our obedience to the law, sanctifying righteousness is. But Paul moves from justifying righteousness to sanctifying righteousness in chapter three. 'O foolish Galatians, who hath bewitched you, that ye should not obey the truth, before whose eyes Jesus Christ hath been evidently set forth, crucified among you? This only would I learn of you, Received ye the Spirit by the works of the law, or by the hearing of faith? Are ye so foolish? having begun in the Spirit, are ye now made perfect by the flesh?' (Galatians 3:1-3). It is in this context that he asserts that all who attempt to live before God upon the basis of their obedience to the law are damned (v. 10).

The fact is, Christ is made of God unto his elect 'wisdom, righteousness, sanctification, and redemption' (1 Corinthians 1:30). We have no other righteousness but Christ. He is both our justification and our sanctification (Hebrews 10:10-14). He is the whole of our acceptance with the Father (Ephesians 1:6).

To make our obedience to the law the basis of our righteousness, either for justification or for sanctification, is not only a frustration of the grace of God, it is also a frustration of the law of God. Those who teach that we make ourselves righteous, or make ourselves more righteous, by our obedience to the law bend the demands of the law to accommodate our weakness and sin, asserting that though the law is holy it can be satisfied by our unholy attempts to keep it.

If righteousness cannot be gained by our obedience to God's law, it is certain that righteousness cannot be gained by the religious deeds and ceremonies men perform. Doing penance, no matter how sincerely, can never give a sinner acceptance with God. Righteousness cannot be gained by the waters of baptism, by taking the Lord's Supper, or by any other religious ritual or deed.

When Paul speaks of legal righteousness, he is talking about works righteousness of any kind. All teaching of works righteousness casts aside and frustrates the grace of God. Any mixture of works with grace is the total denial of grace (Romans 11:6). You cannot trust Christ and yourself. Those who would mix works and grace would seldom say, 'I am saved by my own works'. Yet, in reality, that is exactly what they believe. Ask them about the grounds of their assurance. They will always bring up their works. Ask them about the basis of their comfort. They will always bring up their works. Ask them about their eternal reward in heaven. They will always bring up their works. Why? They trust in themselves that they are righteous. 'For they, being ignorant of God's righteousness, have not submitted themselves unto the righteousness of God.' They just do not understand that 'Christ is the end of the law for righteousness to everyone that believeth' (Romans 10:3-4; Luke 18:9-14).

Dead In Vain

The second inevitable consequence of works religion is the horrible, blasphemous assertion that Christ died in vain, that the Son of God died for nothing, that his blood is useless. There are many ways in which this blasphemy is asserted by worksmongers.

Some assert that man is not totally depraved. If man is not totally depraved, he does not need a Saviour. Others assert that Christ's death as the sinner's Substitute was neither sufficient nor effectual. Let it be stated in whatever pretty phrases men may invent, the doctrine that the Son of God did not actually put away the sins of his people by the sacrifice of himself (Hebrews 9:26); did not actually obtain eternal redemption for God's elect when he died (Hebrews 9:12); did not actually redeem and justify his people; did not actually bring in everlasting righteousness and make an end of sin; but only made these things possible, frustrate the grace of God, trample under foot the blood of Christ, and do despite to the Spirit of God (Hebrews 10:29). They do so by making the blood of Christ 'an unholy' (that is a common) thing.

Such blasphemy makes the efficacy of Christ's sacrifice to depend entirely upon the will of the sinner. That is what the Holy Spirit calls the basest form of idolatry, 'will-worship' (Colossians 2:23). It is the worship of one's own will, trusting one's own will, rather than trusting and worshipping the Son of God. Did not our Saviour cry, 'It is finished'? Did he not seal the covenant with his blood? Did not the Father accept his sacrifice?

The doctrine of justification by works is sin and blasphemy against all three Persons of the Sacred Trinity. It blasphemes God the Father, asserting that he sacrificed his Son in vain for no cause. It blasphemes God the Son. It is the very denial of his deity and of him being Jehovah's righteous Servant, asserting that he failed in his mission (Isaiah 42:4), that he shall never see the travail of his soul with satisfaction (Isaiah 53:11), and that he really finished nothing when he died at Calvary (John 19:30). And it blasphemes God the Holy Spirit, asserting that he bears false witness of Christ, when he convinces sinners of their sin, Christ's finished work of righteousness, and judgment finished (justice satisfied) by his death (John 16:8-11).

Cherished Heresy

The doctrine of salvation by works gives no hope to sinners and would silence the praises of the saints in heaven. Yet, it is a very popular doctrine, accepted and promoted by all false religion. It is a cherished heresy. The reason is obvious – it sets aside the glory of God and makes room for the sinner to boast.

'Every religion except one', Augustus Toplady wrote, 'puts you upon doing something in order to recommend yourself to God ... It is the business of all false religion to patch up a righteousness in which the sinner is to stand before God. But it is the business of the glorious gospel to bring near to us, by the hand of the Holy Spirit, a righteousness ready wrought, a robe of perfection ready made, wherein God's people, to all the purposes of justification and happiness, stand perfect and without fault before the throne.'

The sinner's only hope before God is God's free, sovereign, effectual, irresistible grace in Christ, grace flowing freely to us through the effectual, accepted, sin-atoning blood of Christ. Philip Doddridge wrote:

> Grace, 'tis a charming sound,
> Harmonious to mine ear.
> Heaven with the echo shall resound,
> And all the earth shall hear.

Grace first contrived the way,
To save rebellious man;
And all the steps that grace display,
Which drew the wondrous plan.

Grace first inscribed my name,
In God's eternal book;
'Twas grace that gave me to the Lamb,
Who all my sorrows took.

Grace led my roving feet,
To tread the heavenly road;
And new supplies each hour I meet,
While pressing on to God.

Grace all the work shall crown,
Through everlasting days;
It lays in heaven the topmost stone,
And well deserves the praise.

In this wonderful, glorious thing called 'salvation', 'Christ is all!' He opened the gates of heaven and shut the gates of hell for all his people, when he entered once into the holy place with his own blood and obtained eternal redemption for us. He is all our Wisdom, all our Righteousness, all our Sanctification, and all our Redemption. The grace of God can never be frustrated, made void, or nullified (Job 23:13; Psalms 33:11; Proverbs 19:21; Isaiah 46:10; Hebrews 6:17). The Lord Jesus Christ did not die in vain (Isaiah 53:11). All for whom he shed his blood at Calvary shall be seated with him in glory.

O foolish Galatians, who hath bewitched you, that ye should not obey the truth, before whose eyes Jesus Christ hath been evidently set forth, crucified among you? This only would I learn of you, Received ye the Spirit by the works of the law, or by the hearing of faith? Are ye so foolish? having begun in the Spirit, are ye now made perfect by the flesh? Have ye suffered so many things in vain? if it be yet in vain. He therefore that ministereth to you the Spirit, and worketh miracles among you, doeth he it by the works of the law, or by the hearing of faith? Even as Abraham believed God, and it was accounted to him for righteousness. Know ye therefore that they which are of faith, the same are the children of Abraham. And the scripture, foreseeing that God would justify the heathen through faith, preached before the gospel unto Abraham, saying, In thee shall all nations be blessed. So then they which be of faith are blessed with faithful Abraham. For as many as are of the works of the law are under the curse: for it is written, Cursed is every one that continueth not in all things which are written in the book of the law to do them. But that no man is justified by the law in the sight of God, it is evident: for, The just shall live by faith. And the law is not of faith: but, The man that doeth them shall live in them. Christ hath redeemed us from the curse of the law, being made a curse for us: for it is written, Cursed is every one that hangeth on a tree: That the blessing of Abraham might come on the Gentiles through Jesus Christ; that we might receive the promise of the Spirit through faith. Brethren, I speak after the manner of men; Though it be but a man's covenant, yet if it be confirmed, no man disannulleth, or addeth thereto. Now to Abraham and his seed were the promises made. He saith not, And to seeds, as of many; but as of one, And to thy seed, which is Christ. And this I say, that the covenant, that was confirmed before of God in Christ, the law, which was four hundred and thirty years after, cannot disannul, that it should make the promise of none effect. For if the inheritance be of the law, it is no more of promise: but God gave it to Abraham by promise.

(Galatians 3:1-18)

Chapter 9

Read: Galatians 3:1-18

'Who Hath Bewitched You?'

Paul is astonished that those very same men and women who had received him and the gospel of God's free and sovereign grace in Christ, were now so easily turned away from the gospel and counted him as their enemy (4:13-16). 'I marvel', he wrote in chapter 1, 'that ye are so soon removed from him that called you into the grace of Christ unto another gospel', which is not even similar to the Gospel of Christ. Here he again writes in utter astonishment, 'O foolish Galatians, who hath bewitched you'?

The Galatian church was being turned away from the Gospel. They were being persuaded to exchange Calvary for Sinai; Christ for Moses; sonship for slavery; liberty for bondage; and faith for works. They had been charmed into evil, hoodooed by false prophets who flattered them with the notion that they must seek righteousness by their own works; and that they could attain it. Oh, how foolish, how senseless they were! Yet, there are multitudes today, who, in the face of this horrible example, follow after the Galatians, clinging to Moses, legal principles, religious ceremonies, the commandments of men, and their own filthy rags of self-righteousness; refusing to submit themselves to the righteousness of God, refusing to trust Christ alone for all righteousness with God (Romans 9:31-10:4).

Justification By Faith

Paul had proved that the gospel he proclaimed – justification received by faith in Christ apart from any human effort – is the gospel of God. He now proceeds to show in chapters 3 and 4 that both the universal testimony of holy scripture and the experience of every saved sinner verify the doctrine of the gospel. Sinners receive the justification that Christ accomplished at Calvary (Romans 4:25) by faith alone, apart from anything done or experienced by them.

When the scriptures speak of justification by faith, they are speaking of faith's reception of the finished work of Christ, not of faith's contribution to it and completion of it. It is this reception of Christ and his finished work as our all-sufficient, effectual Substitute and Saviour by which our hearts and minds are reconciled to God. Sinners are not judicially pardoned by their faith, but by the blood of Christ. We simply receive the knowledge of that pardon and the peace that knowledge brings by faith in Christ (Romans 3:24; Hebrews 9:11-12; Ephesians 1:7; Romans 4:25-5:5, 10).

Bewitching Doctrine

In verse one of this chapter Paul does the same thing with the Galatian church that he did with Peter at Antioch (2:11-17). He confronts them head-on because of their departure from the gospel. He writes, as he does, not in a harsh spirit to reproach them, or provoke them to anger. His language was not a violation of our Lord's admonition (Matthew 5:22). Rather, he wrote with the tenderness of a pastor's heart (2 Timothy 3:15), as one like the Saviour (Luke 24:25), concerned for the souls of men.

The Galatians had been bewitched. They had been turned away from the simplicity of the gospel. The word 'bewitched' implies deceitful charm, a seduction. They had been charmed away from the gospel by teachings that flattered the flesh. There is witchery in the very air of works religion. It is a deceitful flattery of the flesh. As the deceitful harlot allures a foolish man to her bed by appealing to his pride, so Babylon's religion seduces foolish men and women and destroys them forever (Proverbs 7:1-27). Satan's ministers transform themselves into ministers of righteousness, teaching sinners to live good, morally righteous lives, even to live by the law. Thereby the fiend of hell beguiles the souls of fools from the simplicity (the singleness of faith) that is in Christ (2 Corinthians 11:3, 13-15).

The Galatians had verbally denied Christ. They had begun to mix works with grace, their own righteousness with Christ's righteousness, their performances with Christ's blood. They had been tricked into thinking that Christ's work must be supplemented by their own works. Paul's object in this epistle (and in all his epistles) is to demonstrate the fact that Christ supplemented is Christ supplanted (Galatians 5:2). In the matter of faith, Christ is all or he is nothing.

'Before whose eyes Jesus Christ hath been evidently set forth'. These men and women were in great danger of total apostasy. Paul was very concerned for their souls (Galatians 4:11, 20). The doctrine they had embraced from false teachers was horrible and deadly. Yet, Paul is hopeful that they will recover. He addresses them as brethren, people who know and trust Christ, and reasons with them upon the basis of their professed faith in Christ.

Paul himself had preached Christ to them. He had clearly set forth the Lord Jesus Christ, the Son of God as the crucified, accepted Substitute for sinners. With this phrase, Paul gives us a clear description of what preaching is. It is the setting forth of Jesus Christ and him crucified (1 Corinthians 2:2).

Many preach a vague, indistinct Christ, who did something or other, but no one knows what or why; not Paul. He distinctly painted a picture of Christ before the eyes of his hearers (2 Corinthians 1:18-20; 4:3-6; Romans 10:4; 1 Corinthians 1:23-24; Galatians 6:14). To do the souls of men good we must set Christ crucified before them. There is no righteousness for sinners except the righteousness of God in Christ; the righteousness brought in by his perfect obedience to the law in his life and his infinitely meritorious, effectual satisfaction of its justice by his blood.

Life's Beginning

Paul in verses 2-5 moves from a denunciation of justification by works to the denunciation of sanctification by works. Justification is righteousness imputed. It is a work done outside our experience. Sanctification is righteousness imparted in the new birth. Both are totally the works of God's free grace, works of grace to which we contribute nothing. W. A. Clarke wrote:

> God's jewels of election-love
> Were sanctified in Christ above;
> In oneness with his nature pure,
> Joint-heirs with him for evermore

The Spirit of God comes into our lives in regeneration sovereignly (John 3:8). He comes in and works his work by the 'hearing of faith' through the preaching of the gospel (1 Peter 1:23-25). The gifts of the Spirit come through the preaching of faith, not of law works (Romans 10:16-17; Acts 11:14; 2:38; 5:31-32; Ephesians 1:12-13; John 7:38-39).

Sanctification comes not by the law, but by Spirit wrought faith in Christ (1 Corinthians 1:30). I am fully aware that this is not commonly accepted. But I am just as fully convinced that it is the teaching of holy scripture. To those who try to teach salvation by grace alone and still make sanctification to be the result of our works, I ask only that they show their doctrine from the Word of God. That cannot be done.

The words 'sanctify', 'sanctified', 'sanctifieth', and 'sanctification' are used more than thirty times in the New Testament. We are said to be sanctified by the purpose of God, by the blood of Christ, by the Spirit of God, by faith in Christ, and by the Word of God. But never, not even once, are we said to sanctify ourselves. Sanctification is the work of God alone. We are not made perfect, complete, by the works of the flesh. Our life in Christ began as a life of faith, and must continue to the end as a life of faith (Colossians 2:6).

Abraham's Justification

The first mention of a man having righteousness accounted (imputed) to him is found in Genesis 15:6. That man was Abraham, (vv. 6-9). He was not justified by being circumcised. Circumcision had not yet been commanded. Abraham was justified by faith alone (Genesis 15:6; Romans 4:2, 9-10, 13, 20-25). If Abraham was justified by faith without works, then all those and only those who are justified by faith without works are the children of Abraham. That is to say, the people of God, the heirs of God's covenant and God's promises, those who are saved, the Israel of God are all those, and only those, who trust Christ alone for all their acceptance with God (John 8:39; Philippians 3:3). Isaac Watts wrote:

> In vain we ask God's righteous law,
> To justify us now,
> Since to convince and to condemn,
> Is all the law can do.
>
> Jesus how glorious is thy grace!
> When in thy name we trust,
> Our faith receives a righteousness
> That makes the sinner just.

Cursed

Justification must be by faith and cannot come by the works of the law, because all who live (profess to live) under the law are under the curse of the law (v. 10). No man can obey God's holy law. No man can perform the righteousness required by the law. No man can satisfy the debt owed to the law. Only Christ, the God-man, could do that. Sincere obedience is not sufficient. Obedience must be perfect. The law can do nothing but condemn and kill (Romans 3:19). It can never justify and give life. If we would be justified, we must be justified freely by the grace of God through the redemption that is in Christ.

It is very important for us to take note of the fact that Galatians 3:10 is a quotation of Deuteronomy 27:26. It is important for this reason, those who endeavour to make the law of God the believer's rule of life insist that when the New Testament teaches our total freedom from the law in Christ (Romans 6:14-15; 7:4; 10:4), it is only talking about freedom from the ceremonial, Levitical law. But the passage cited here has nothing to do with the ceremonies of the law. Deuteronomy 27:14-26 speaks only of what is called 'the moral law'. Galatians 3:10 specifically states that all who attempt to live before God by the ten commandments are yet under the curse of the law.

Evident Fact

Justification must be by faith, because the life of faith is above the law (vv. 11-12). The life of faith has a superior principle. Faith works by love (2 Corinthians 5:14; Galatians 5:6; Hebrews 8:10; 1 John 3:23). The life of faith has a superior power. Christ lives in us (1 John 3:9). The life of faith has a superior promise. Moses, in the law, promised only temporal blessedness to moral obedience. Christ in the gospel promises eternal life to the obedience of faith (v. 12, John 17:2).

Many Old Testament saints knew God, walked with God and were justified long before the law was given at Sinai (Abel, Noah, Job, Abraham); and many were justified during the legal dispensation; but none were justified by obedience to the law. The law was given to identify, expose, and condemn sin and to lead us to Christ. It has no other function. The scriptures declare, 'The just shall live by faith' (Habakkuk 2:4; Romans 1:17; Hebrews 10:38). The law is not of faith. The law does not demand faith. It demands obedience, perfect obedience, external obedience, internal obedience, constant obedience, utter obedience, obedience in thought, in motive, and in attitude. Therefore, it is written, 'The just shall live by faith'.

Redeemed

Justification must be by faith, because Christ has redeemed us from the curse of the law (vv. 13-14), thereby fulfilling the law and bringing the law to its end. Christ is the end of the law (Romans 10:4). He is the conclusion of the law. He is the purpose for which the law was given, the One to whom it pointed. And he is the termination of the law (Hebrews 10:1-14). He endured its curse for us and redeemed us from it (2 Corinthians 5:21; Isaiah 53:5-6).

'Christ' – the appointed, anointed, accepted Redeemer and Saviour, God's own dear Son – 'hath' – once and for all, with finality, by his one great sacrifice for sin – 'redeemed' – effactually ransomed and delivered by a just and legal payment – 'us' – God's elect, every sinner who trusts him – 'from the curse of the law' – from all possibility of judgment, condemnation, penalty, and death by the law – 'being made a curse for us' – being made to be the object of God's just wrath, the object of the law's just curse, by being made to be sin for us! – 'For it is written, Cursed is everyone that hangeth on a tree' (Deuteronomy 21:22-23).

Christ died in our room and stead, satisfying all the demands of God's holy law as our Substitute for this purpose, that the same blessings that God gave Abraham: justification, imputed righteousness, and eternal life, might come upon us through him (Romans 4:7-10). Abraham was not justified by works, or by circumcision, or by anything within himself. He was justified by Christ (Romans 4:20-25).

When Paul says, 'that we might receive the promise of the Spirit through faith', he is not saying that we receive the gift of the Holy Spirit in regeneration by faith. It is this gift and operation of the Holy Spirit that creates faith in us (Galatians 5:22; Ephesians 1:19; 2:8-9; Colossians 2:12). The promise of the Spirit is the gift of faith which was symbolized in circumcision, by which all the blessings of God are sealed and assured to us; the Spirit of adoption that enables us to confidently call God himself our Father, through faith in Christ (Romans 8:15; Galatians 4:4-7; 1 John 3:1-3).

Promises

Justification must be by faith, because all the promises of God are made to faith (vv. 15-18). Justification before God cannot be by the law, because all these promises were made by God in a covenant 430 years before the law was given. A covenant or testament made by a man cannot be overturned or nullified once it is confirmed. Certainly, if a man's covenant cannot be nullified, God's covenant cannot be.

These promises of acceptance with God, justification and eternal life, were not made to Abraham's physical seed, but to Christ as the federal head and representative of God's elect; his church, his body, Abraham's spiritual seed. They were made to him for us before the world began (Ephesians 1:3-6; 2 Timothy 1:9; Titus 1:2). The Levitical law, which was given 430 years after the covenant God made with Abraham concerning Christ and the blessings of grace in him (Genesis 12:1-3), does not and cannot nullify God's covenant grace or make his promises of mercy, grace, salvation, and eternal life in Christ of no effect.

What Paul says in verse 18 is very much the same thing he says in Romans 4:16 and 11:6. 'Therefore it is of faith, that it might be by grace; to the end the promise might be sure to all the seed; not to that only which is of the law, but to that also which is of the faith of Abraham; who is the father of us all ... And if by grace, then is it no more of works: otherwise grace is no more grace. But if it be of works, then is it no more grace: otherwise work is no more work.' If justification can be obtained by something we do, it cannot be received by faith in Christ. Faith and works cannot stand together. If we bring in works, we push out faith, push out grace, and push out Christ completely. But God gave the inheritance of grace to Abraham by promise. Isaac Watts wrote:

> How long beneath the law I lay,
> In bondage and distress!
> I toiled the precept to obey.
> But toiled without success.
> Then all my servile works were done,
> A righteousness to raise;
> Now, freely chosen in the Son,
> I freely chose his ways.
> To see the law, by Christ fulfilled,
> And hear his pardoning voice,
> Will change a slave into a child,
> And duty into choice.

In the matter of salvation Christ is all (1 Corinthians 1:30-31). Let us trust him, love him, serve him, and seek his honour always and in all things, who loved us and gave himself for us (1 Corinthians 10:31). John Kent's lovely hymn reminds us that our salvation, from beginning to end honours Christ and is 'All for the lifting of Jesus on high'.

1. Jehovah, in council resolved to fulfill
The scheme from eternity, laid in His will.
A scheme too profound for a seraph to pry,
And all for the lifting of Jesus on high.

2. 'Twas not from the creature salvation took place,
The whole was of God, to the praise of His grace;
And all to His glory shall tend by and by
To accomplish the lifting of Jesus on high.

3. His wisdom contrived the adorable plan,
Grace, mercy, and peace, and good-will towards man;
The Great Three-in-One did the same ratify,
And all for the lifting of Jesus on high.

4. Here all the perfections of Deity shine,
Love, wisdom, and power, and goodness divine:
His justice and grace received honour thereby;
'Twas all for the lifting of Jesus on high.

5. When first the great project to angels was known,
They hailed Him in songs as the Lamb on His throne:
The concave of heaven resounds with their cry,
God-man, Mediator, they lift Him on high.

6. Creation proclaims the great work of thy hand,
All beings and things in the order they stand;
Productions of chance, they are led to deny,
'Twas made for the lifting of Jesus on high.

7. All things for His sake did Jehovah prepare,
For of Him, and to Him, and through Him, they are;
All systems and worlds that revolve in the sky,
Were made for the lifting of Jesus on high.

8. Set up as the head of His mystical frame,
He honoured the records of fate with His name;
And nothing was wanting, which God could supply,
To aid the uplifting of Jesus on high.

9. When man was created, what wisdom we see,
The whole he possessed was the image of Thee;
But, O! in his fall, we are led to espy,
'Twas all for the lifting of Jesus on high.

10. When Adam to eat of the fruit was inclined,
It answered the end which Jehovah designed;
No purpose or wisdom was altered thereby,
'Twas all for the lifting of Jesus on high.

11. Here Satan was nonplussed in what he had done,
The fall wrought the channel where mercy should run;
In streams of salvation, which never run dry,
And all for the lifting of Jesus on high.

12. From hence it appears, He made nothing in vain,
For Adam, thus formed, was a link in the chain;
In him 'twas decreed, that his members should die,
And all for the lifting of Jesus on high.

13. The man that betrayed Him, prediction foretold,
The pieces of silver for which He was sold:
To prove His salvation, the world we defy,
He fell for the lifting of Jesus on high.

14. The law that was given on Sinai of old,
Was still the great mercy and love to unfold,
Which did in the womb of eternity lie,
And all for the lifting of Jesus on high.

15. In fulness of time, He came under the law,
Its jots and its tittles, He answered we know;
And, stretching His arms, did on Calvary die,
To accomplish His lifting to glory on high.

16. He slept in the tomb, till the morning arose,
That signed His release, and confounded His foes;
Then, bursting its bars, He ascended the sky,
To reign in His glory, Eternal, on high.

O foolish Galatians, who hath bewitched you, that ye should not obey the truth, before whose eyes Jesus Christ hath been evidently set forth, crucified among you?

(Galatians 3:1)

Chapter 10

Read: Galatians 3:1

The Preservative

The Galatians received the gospel Paul preached unto them with great enthusiasm. The Galatians were apparently a very warm-hearted, but fickle people. Paul found, to his great grief, that while he had been away from them, certain false teachers came in among them and turned them aside from the simplicity of the gospel of Christ. He was thus constrained to speak very plainly in this matter. In this verse he uses strong terms. 'O foolish Galatians, who hath bewitched you, that ye should not obey the truth?' I hope that no such witchery has befallen any who read these lines. Yet, being men, we are all subject to the dangerous doctrines of devils that would move us away from the blessed 'simplicity that is in Christ' (2 Corinthians 11:3). There are bewitching doctrines in the air these days. Many are found among men and women who profess faith in Christ, and among those who are responsible to preach the gospel of Christ, to whom these words might be properly addressed.

Evidently Set Forth

Here Paul reminds us of our conversion by the grace of God. He addresses us as those 'before whose eyes Jesus Christ hath been evidently set forth, crucified among you'. The word here translated 'evidently set forth' is a word that refers to the placards that were openly displayed in a public place for all to see. Having no newspapers, public announcements were made in this way in ancient times. They were placed in areas where the public mingled so that everyone could read them.

When Paul preached the gospel to the Galatians, they could see the Lord Jesus crucified among themselves. They, in their minds and by faith, followed the procession of the Roman soldiers through the streets of Jerusalem. They heard the ringing of the hammers as the Saviour was nailed to the cursed tree. They saw his tears and heard his cries of agony and pain. They felt his suffering as his blood flowed from his head, his hands, his feet, and his wounded side. Seeing him thus crucified, they were convicted in their hearts. They forsook their paganism and idolatry, being born into the kingdom of God. They became new creatures. The old life, the old world, the old ways, the old pleasures were passed away, and all things had become new. They were born again by the sovereign power of the Spirit of God, through the hearing of the Word of faith. They forsook their old gods and embraced the true and living God, even Jesus Christ our Lord.

Paul's Message
Here we have a marvellous testimony to the message Paul preached. What was the theme of his sermons? It was this – that Christ died for our sins, was buried, and rose again the third day, 'according to the scriptures' (1 Corinthians 15:3-4). When Paul preached, he preached the gospel (1 Corinthians 9:16). Christ, 'the Son of God', and him crucified was this man's message (Acts 9:20; 1 Corinthians 2:2). That is the faith. That is the substance and the essence of Christianity. The beginning, the middle, and the end of the Christian faith is 'Jesus Christ and him crucified'. When Paul preached the gospel, he preached Christ. When John wrote about the revelation of the Father and eternal life, he was writing about Christ. When James spoke of the great Lawgiver and Judge, he was talking about Christ. When Paul wrote to the Hebrew believers about the Great High Priest in heaven and the Mediator between God and man, he wrote about our Saviour. The Christian faith is Christ. Take that away, take the Lord Jesus Christ out of it, and it is nothing.

This is the gospel that Paul preached and the power and effect of it upon the Galatians was effectual to the salvation of their souls. It placed the light of heaven in their hearts. They cried, 'Abba Father', and Christ was formed in them. In Christ they had liberty and life. Paul rejoiced in their spiritual transformation and thanked God for his operations of grace on their behalf.

But now Paul's astonishment is aroused by something else. It appeared that the Galatians were being taken away from their hope in Christ by false teachers who entangled them again in the yoke of the law. They had taken their minds off of Christ and focused them on something else. This is a danger of which we need a word of caution in our day. The only way that we can escape this evil, which Paul so severely condemns, is the use of proper precautionary means. Only as the Holy Spirit keeps us will we be preserved from the fascination of heresy and kept true to the gospel of Christ. We will be kept from error concerning our Christian faith only if we keep our hearts and minds fixed by faith upon Christ as the all and all of the faith.

The Danger

Believers were not free from the subtle dangers of heresy in apostolic times any more then we are today. No sooner was the gospel preached and embraced in any place, than Satan sent false apostles who attempted to destroy its influence by corrupting its message, 'bewitching' those who were converted by satanic perversions of the gospel. These were not out and out denials of the gospel, but more dangerous, subtle denials of it, but denials of the gospel nonetheless. Judaism subverted the gospel in the Galatian church, attempting to mix grace and works. Gnosticism arose early in the Colossian church, denying the supernatural and spiritual, making conversion to be a matter of knowledge and learning. Asceticism crept in quickly among Corinthian believers, teaching that the way to spirituality is avoiding those things that are natural, depriving the flesh of pleasure. Annihilationism also plagued the church at Corinth, teaching that there is no future resurrection.

Very shortly after the days of the Apostles, Arianism crept in, subverting the souls of many by a denial of the absolute, eternal deity and sonship of Christ. Augustine, in his day, had to resist the influence of Pelagianism, which denied the moral guilt of man, and rendered the work of Christ unnecessary. During those long, dark years of Roman Catholic supremacy, the superstitions of the papacy prevailed almost universally. Shortly after the protestant reformation, the Church of England began to return to the doctrines of the Roman Catholic church. During the days of John Gill and John Brine in England and Jonathan Edwards in America, Unitarianism and Socinianism crept into a great many Baptist and Congregationalist assemblies.

In our day Satan continues to pervert the gospel of God's free and sovereign grace in Christ in many ways. Russellites (Jehovah's Witnesses) and Mormons, though embraced by many as Christian societies, have at the core of their creeds the denial of Christ's divinity. Many religious groups, commonly acknowledged as Christian denominations, teach that men and women (even infants!) are saved (regenerated) by baptism, by receiving the bread and wine of the Lord's Supper, and by performing good works. None would say that we are saved by what they call 'sacraments', or by good works alone, without the grace of God and the blood of Christ. But they universally declare that salvation is not by grace alone and not by Christ alone.

But more subtle and, therefore, more dangerous heresies abound throughout what is considered evangelical Christianity. Things are no different today than when Augustus Toplady wrote ...

> Every religion except one puts you upon doing something in order to recommend yourself to God ... It is the business of all false religion to patch up a righteousness in which the sinner is to stand before God. But it is the business of the glorious gospel to bring near to us, by the hand of the Holy Spirit, a righteousness ready wrought, a robe of perfection ready made, wherein God's people, to all the purposes of justification and happiness, stand perfect and without fault before the throne.

Arminian, free-will, works religion is the religion of the day. Rare are the churches in which there are no altars of man's making, with ascending degrees (steps) of righteousness and holiness upon which men expose their shame in will-worship (Exodus 20:22-26; Colossians 2:23). Few there are in conservative churches (those commonly considered evangelical, let alone others) who know who God is and how he saves sinners by his almighty free grace upon the basis of Christ's finished work, with no contribution of any kind from the sinner.

Multitudes are deceived into thinking that salvation, eternal life, and acceptance with God is theirs because they made a decision for Jesus. They actually believe that salvation is gained by responding to an altar call, deciding for Jesus, repeating the words of a prayer, or simply saying, 'I want to be saved'. Few have any understanding of the teaching of holy scripture that faith is the gift and operation of God the Holy Spirit (Ephesians 1:19; 2:8-9; Colossians 2:12), wrought in the hearts of chosen redeemed sinners by the revelation of Christ in them (2 Corinthians 4:4-6; Galatians 1:15-16), by the preaching of the gospel (1 Peter 1:23, 25).

Many try to show some respect for Christ, acknowledging him as a great man, a good prophet, and a good example to follow, while denying that he is God. Such a pretence of respect is as blasphemous as it is dishonest. If Jesus Christ is not God the eternal Son, he was a liar, an impostor, and can be of help to no one. His life and death are as meaningless as the life and death of Mohammed. In fact, to declare that Jesus of Nazareth was only a man is to declare that he was an absolute lunatic. Only a lunatic would publicly declare himself to be eternal, self-existent God, if he was, in fact, nothing but a man.

Multitudes, who vigorously defend the eternal Godhead of our Saviour in theory, utterly deny it in reality. Perhaps, you think, 'How can that be true?' When they speak of the work of Christ, they speak of him as a failure. They openly avow that Christ died in vain for the multitudes who perish under the wrath of God, that he tries to save multitudes he is unable to save, and that he wills what he shall never see accomplished.

You may ask, 'How is this related to Galatians 3:1 and that by which the Galatians were bewitched?' The fact is, the very essence of all forms of legalism is the work of man. The supposition that man must make some contribution to the grace of God – that man must add something to the work of Christ, that man must do something to complete the work of the Holy Spirit, that something must be done by the sinner to complete the work of God – in making sinners stand perfect and without blame before him. That is precisely what Paul is dealing with in this passage.

The scriptures are crystal clear. Any mixture of works with grace is a total denial of grace (Romans 11:6). The Lord Jesus has, by his obedience unto death as our Substitute, 'perfected forever them that are sanctified' (Hebrews 10:10-14). He is all our righteousness (Jeremiah 23:6; Romans 10:4); and we are altogether 'complete in him' (Colossians 2:10). Christ is all our Righteousness and Sanctification, as well as all our Wisdom and Redemption before God (1 Corinthians 1:30). In all the work of salvation, 'Christ is all' (Colossians 3:11).

The Preservative

I am fully aware that these heresies, by which many make shipwreck of their souls, are under the control of our heavenly Father, and that they come to pass according to his purpose (1 Corinthians 11:19). Yet, they are a danger to be avoided, and avoided with determined care. How can we be kept from falling into these terrible heresies? If we would be kept sound in the faith, we must get the proper object fixed in the centre of our hearts – Christ and him crucified. The singular preservative for our souls is Christ. The instrumental method by which God preserves his people in grace and faith, and keeps his elect from the damning heresies by which others are ruined, is the preaching of the gospel of Christ; the preaching of Christ and him crucified.

Wherever Paul went he set forth the Person and work of Jesus Christ. Religion without Christ is useless religion; and any pretence of preaching, without the preaching of the gospel of Christ, is useless pretence. Christ is the Alpha and the Omega of holy scripture. Christ must be the Alpha and the Omega of our faith. He is the Foundation. He is the Cornerstone. He is the Capstone. Christ is all our hope. Christ is all our assurance. Christ is all our peace.

Paul did not simply preach about Christ, when he preached he set forth Christ, set him forth conspicuously and clearly. He took pains to make Christ and him crucified clearly beheld by his hearers. Christ crucified was his doctrine (Acts 9:16, 20; 1 Corinthians 2:2). This is the doctrine by which men and women are preserved from the bewitching doctrines of free-will, works religion. Any doctrine divorced from Christ crucified is false doctrine. Any ordinance or religious ceremony divorced from the crucified Christ is meaningless ritualism. Any works, acts of religious devotion, or sacrifices motivated by anything other than love for, faith in, and gratitude to Christ are exercises in self-righteousness.

Christ crucified is the essence of all truth, for he is the Truth. Let him be set forth clearly among men that he may be embraced by them. He is our God, our Creator, and our Judge. And he is our Substitute, the One by whose blood we are redeemed, by whose righteousness we are righteous, by whose grace we are saved. Shun every doctrine that detracts from his glory. Judge every ministry, every doctrine, every religious thought by this one standard – does it exalt and magnify Christ our God and Saviour?

Simplicity
Christ is the gospel. To preach the gospel is to preach Christ. Christ is the Truth. To preach truth is to preach Christ. The gospel of God is not a complex mystery, but the revelation of God, and the revelation is given in simple, clear, unmistakable words: one body, one Spirit, one hope, one Lord, one faith, one baptism, one God, one Mediator, one thing needful (Ephesians 4:4-6; 1 Timothy 2:5; Luke 10:38-42). There is only one Way, one Truth, one Life, just as there is only one Lord Jesus (John 14:6). It is this very simplicity that men and women stumble over. It is an offence to them (Galatians 5:11).

We prefer things more complicated. We want signs, wonders, and a display of wisdom. We want a challenge, something to do, something to discover, something to decipher, something, anything that will allow us to have some part in the great work of grace. This was the thing that destroyed both the Jews and the Gentiles in Paul's day; and this is the thing that destroys men today. It is ever the nature of man to live under the vain delusion that he is good and that he can make himself righteous before God. And it is ever the trademark of false religion to put men to work producing righteousness for themselves (Romans 9:33-10:4).

For this reason, Christ must be constantly and evidently set forth, crucified before men. This is the message of God, which is the power of God unto salvation to every believing sinner (Romans 1:15-17). It is this message that transforms sinners. It is this message that comforts God's saints. It is this message that honours God. And it is this message that is honoured by God. If we would be of any service to the souls of men in this world, let us seize every opportunity and use every means at our disposal to set before them Jesus Christ and him crucified, as he is set forth throughout the Book of God.

This only would I learn of you, Received ye the Spirit by the works of the law, or by the hearing of faith?

(Galatians 3:2)

Chapter 11

Read: Galatians 3:2

The Holy Spirit And The Hearing Of Faith

'This only would I learn of you'. Here Paul strikes at the heart of the Galatians' great error. He demonstrates that the gift of the Holy Spirit, that is to say grace, salvation, eternal life, and all the blessings of the covenant of grace of which the gift of the Spirit is the seal and assurance, come to chosen, redeemed sinners only by the hearing of faith, not by the works of the law (Galatians 3:13-14; Ephesians 1:13-14).

'Received ye the Spirit by the works of the law, or by the hearing of faith?' John Gill says, 'This question supposes they had received the Spirit; that is, the Spirit of God, as a spirit of wisdom and knowledge in the revelation of Christ; as a spirit of regeneration and sanctification; as a spirit of faith and adoption; and as the earnest, seal, and pledge of their future glory.'

True Believers

Paul addresses the Galatians as brethren, as genuine believers. His hope was that their apostasy was not a total departure from the faith. He hoped they had not yet made shipwreck of their souls. It is very important to observe this fact. Writing by divine inspiration, Paul shows us that men and women may embrace much error regarding gospel doctrine, who do truly trust Christ. The Galatians were involved in grave error, just as the apostle Peter had been at Antioch (2:11-16). They appeared to be in danger of total apostasy (5:1-4). Indeed, some may have totally abandoned the faith they had once professed to believe. But Paul's language in this verse clearly indicates that there were some in the Galatian church who were truly born of God, who had true faith in Christ, who were possessors of the Holy Spirit, yet had embraced in measure the horrible heresy of legalism.

I stress this as a matter of importance, because there is a terrible, proud, self-righteous tendency among God's people in this world, and among preachers of the gospel, to set themselves up as judges of others, to quickly condemn as reprobate everyone who falls into doctrinal error regarding the gospel. What sad divisions there are in the visible church (among true believers) because of this tendency. In matters of judgment concerning others, if we err, let it be on the side of leniency, not severity.

Still, Paul uses the language of stern reproof. His purpose is to settle the issue in our hearts and minds. When he says, 'This only would I learn of you,' he is saying, answer this question and the matter is settled: 'Received ye the Spirit by the works of the law, or by the hearing of faith?' If salvation's initial experience (regeneration and conversion) is altogether the work of the Holy Spirit in us, a work of grace alone received by faith alone then the whole of salvation must be the same. The Holy Spirit, who had been given to them in their initial experience of grace (Acts 10:44; 11:16), was to them, as he is to God's saints now, the proof of God's favour and their acceptance with God in Christ. If we receive justification without works, we also receive sanctification, perseverance, and glorification without works. Albert Barnes says,

> They had been converted. They had received the Holy Spirit. They had had abundant evidence of their acceptance with God; and the simple matter of inquiry now was, whether this had, occurred as the regular effect of the gospel, or whether it had been by obeying the law of Moses?

This gift of the Holy Spirit is in no way connected with obedience to the law of Moses, or of any other law. It was not a matter of works. This, Paul implies, is a matter of such absolute clarity to any believer that none who know God can call it into question. The indescribably rich gift of God's salvation has nothing to do with something we do.

The Hearing Of Faith

When Paul asks, 'Received ye the Spirit by the works of the law, or by the hearing of faith?', he is asserting that it is ludicrous to imagine that we merited and procured the Spirit of God by our obedience to the law; or that the Spirit of God came into our hearts by the preaching of the law. Though the law gives a knowledge of sin, it can do nothing else. The law is a killing letter. It brings a sense of wrath, condemnation, and death, but not the Spirit of life in Christ Jesus.

The Holy Spirit comes by 'the hearing of faith', that is by the hearing of the gospel. The preaching of the gospel is the declaration of righteousness and justification, redemption and forgiveness accomplished by Christ (Romans 4:25; Galatians 3:13; Hebrews 9:12). 'In this way', as John Gill stated, 'the Spirit of God is received. While the Gospel is being preached he falls on them that hear it, conveys himself into their hearts, and begets them again by the word of truth.' In other words, if we are God's children, it is because we have heard the voice of God in the gospel and responded to it by faith. Thus Horatius Bonar could write:

I heard the voice of Jesus say, 'Come unto me and rest;
Lay down, thou weary one, lay down thy head upon my breast.'
I came to Jesus as I was, weary, and worn, and sad.
I found in Him a resting place, and He has made me glad.

I heard the voice of Jesus say, 'Behold, I freely give
The living water – thirsting one, stoop down, and drink, and live.'
I came to Jesus, and I drank of that life giving stream;
My thirst was quenched, my soul revived, and now I live in Him.

I heard the voice of Jesus say, 'I am this dark world's light;
Look unto Me, thy morn shall rise, and all thy day be bright.'
I looked to Jesus and I found in Him my star, my sun;
And in that light of life I'll walk till travelling days be done.

The scriptures teach that all of God's children have heard in their hearts the voice of Christ, and have responded to that voice by faith (Romans 10:17). The believer's life is from beginning to end a life of faith. We are not saved by the law, sanctified by the law, nor kept by the law, but by faith in Jesus Christ (Habakkuk 24; Romans 1:17; Galatians 3:11; Hebrews 10:38).

The Holy Spirit is the gift of God, with and by whom all the gifts of grace, salvation, and eternal life are received into the soul. It is by the Spirit that the works of the Saviour are known and received. The Holy Spirit is himself the seal of God's favour, the seal of his covenant, and the token of our peace with God. When he enters our hearts we are saved, resurrected from death to life, and brought into a conscious awareness of adoption (Galatians 4:6-7; 2 Timothy 1:9-10). He is the source of light, life, faith, love, and liberty in our souls. He even sanctifies our bodies, making our very bodies the temples of God (1 Corinthians 6:19-20).

The experience of God's people, as it is recorded in the Acts of the Apostles, is a clear demonstration of the fact that the Spirit of God comes to sinners by the hearing of faith. He had been promised to the disciples, and he was given as they in faith waited for him (Acts 1:4-5, 8; 2:1-4). The same thing happened at Samaria (Acts 8:12-17). Thus the Holy Spirit came upon Cornelius and his household through the hearing of faith (Acts 10:44-45). When Paul preached the gospel among the Gentiles, the Holy Spirit fell sovereignly on those who heard (Acts 15:7-12).

The Holy Spirit And Salvation

When Paul speaks of the reception of the Holy Spirit by the hearing of faith, he is not talking about a second work of grace, but about the initial experience of grace in salvation. Ephesians 1:13, as it is translated in the King James, has been horribly misinterpreted by many to imply that after sinners are saved, if they are really good, praying, spiritual Christians, then they may receive a higher form of spiritual life by receiving the Holy Spirit. That text in the King James Version reads, 'In whom ye also trusted, after that ye heard the word of truth, the gospel of your salvation: in whom also, after that ye believed, ye were sealed with that Holy Spirit of promise.' That translation might appear to teach that there is an interval between faith in Christ and the seal of the Spirit. But that is incorrect. Ephesians 1:13 would be far more accurately translated, 'In whom you also trusted, having heard the word of truth, the gospel of your salvation: in whom also, having believed, you were sealed with that Holy Spirit of promise.'

In other words, every chosen, redeemed sinner is, by the effectual call and irresistible grace of God the Holy Spirit, granted faith in Christ when he is made to hear the word of truth, 'the word of faith', the gospel of his own salvation accomplished by Christ. And, trusting Christ, he is sealed with the Holy Spirit of promise. He has sealed to him, that is he is given the conscious assurance of all the blessings of God's everlasting mercy, love, and grace in Christ (Ephesians 1:3-7); and he is sealed in grace, sealed up in infallible, indestructible security in the grace of God (John 10:27-30).

There can be no question regarding this interpretation of Paul's teaching about God's people receiving the Holy Spirit, because it is the universal testimony of holy scripture that no sinner is saved who has not received the Holy Spirit. All the graces of faith, hope, and love that are wrought in us are the fruit of the Spirit (Galatians 5:22-24). It is the Holy Spirit who reveals Christ in us, grants us faith in him by the mighty operations of his grace, and assures us of our acceptance with God in Christ (Galatians 1:15-16; Ephesians 2:8; Philippians 2:13; Colossians 1:12).

Salvation is the knowledge of the one true and living God as he is revealed in his Son, the Lord Jesus Christ (John 17:3). But there is no possibility of anyone knowing God, knowing Christ, except God the Holy Spirit take the things of Christ and reveal them unto him (John 16:8-14). If we belong to Christ, we have received the Holy Spirit (1 Corinthians 12:13). We have been enlightened by the Holy Spirit. He showed us our guilt, convincing us of sin. He convinced us of righteousness, of righteousness accomplished and brought in by Christ our Substitute. He convinced us of judgment, judgment finished, justice satisfied, condemnation forever removed by the death of Christ in our room and stead at Calvary. It is God the Spirit who has revealed the glory of God in the face of Jesus Christ to us (Romans 3:24-26; 2 Corinthians 4:3-6).

This great gift of grace is altogether without our works. We received faith by the Holy Spirit (Ephesians 2:8-9). Our works could never bring it. We received peace by the Holy Spirit (Romans 5:1-5). Our works could never give it. We have been sanctified by the Holy Spirit. It is God the Spirit who formed Christ in us in the new birth, making us partakers of the divine nature (2 Peter 1:4). Our works could no more sanctify us than they could justify us. We have communion with God the Father by the Holy Spirit. Our works could never give us access to him. The Holy Spirit teaches us to pray and helps us in prayer (Romans 8:26). The law could never do so. The Holy Spirit, as we have seen already, is our seal and pledge and assurance of heaven (Ephesians 1:13). The law never secured that for anyone. The Lord Jesus Christ brings his people into rest by the operation of the Holy Spirit; something Moses and Joshua could not do (Hebrews 4:9-10). The Holy Spirit is a fountain of living water springing up in the soul (John 7:36-39). The works of the law are a broken cistern.

The Connection
Clearly, the doctrine of holy scripture is that salvation is wrought in us by the power and grace of God the Holy Spirit, without our works. But what

is the connection between the hearing of faith and receiving the Holy Spirit, between the hearing of faith and the experience of salvation? It is just this, 'Faith cometh by hearing, and hearing by the Word of God.'

Not only has the Lord God ordained who shall be saved, as well as the very time and place when he will work his grace in them, he has also ordained the means by which grace, salvation, and faith shall come to them; and that means is the preaching of the gospel. This is exactly what he says in his Book, God's elect are 'born again, not of corruptible seed, but of incorruptible, by the Word of God, which liveth and abideth forever.' And he does not leave us to guess what he means by that. He says, 'And this is the Word which by the gospel is preached unto you' (1 Peter 1:23-25).

When the time of love has come (Ezekiel 16:8), when the Lord God will call out a sinner, he raises up a man to preach the gospel to that sinner and causes their paths to cross by one means or another. He causes the chosen sinner to hear the gospel preached; but the sinner has no ability to understand it. He cannot receive the things of God. They are foolishness to him (1 Corinthians 2:14). But when the Spirit of God conveys the gospel to the heart, he comes with it, enlightens the mind, gives understanding, and sweetly, irresistibly, effectually inclines the heart to believe and the will to receive and embrace Christ, as he is set forth in the gospel (John 1:12-13; 6:63; 1 Corinthians 2:9-13; Hebrews 4:12). Then, believing on the Son of God, having received God's salvation by the hearing of faith, the saved sinner sings with David, 'Blessed is the man whom thou choosest, and causest to approach unto thee' (Psalms 65:4).

Are ye so foolish? having begun in the Spirit, are ye now made perfect by the flesh? Have ye suffered so many things in vain? if *it be* yet in vain. He therefore that ministereth to you the Spirit, and worketh miracles among you, *doeth he it* by the works of the law, or by the hearing of faith?

(Galatians 3:3-5)

Chapter 12

Read: Galatians 3:3-5

'Are Ye So Foolish?'

The Galatians were acting foolishly, in utter stupidity. They had received the message of the gospel under the powerful demonstration of the Holy Spirit. They had trusted Christ as he was revealed to them by the Holy Spirit. They had received the great blessings of the gospel under the sovereign influence of the Holy Spirit. But now they were being bewitched.

The servants of Satan came among them preaching another gospel. The old serpent began to deceive many and turn them away from the simple faith of the gospel. These false teachers were saying that something must be added to faith; and that, though we are justified by faith in Christ, yet we are not perfected, or sanctified by faith. They taught that if men would be true Christians, if they would be sanctified, then works of the flesh must be added to the righteousness of Christ to achieve this. They did not openly deny the gospel. They did not come out and say, 'You must be saved by grace and by works.' Satan is too slick for that. What these Judaisers said is that though we are saved by grace, we must finish the work ourselves. Paul says, 'Are you so foolish? Having begun in the Spirit, having been justified by the work of Christ and having received it by the Spirit, do you now think that you can perfect yourselves?'

Flesh And Spirit

Our Saviour declares, 'It is the Spirit that quickeneth; the flesh profiteth nothing' (John 6:63). The Spirit is life. The flesh is death. The indwelling of God the Holy Spirit is the indwelling of Christ, the indwelling of Life. It is by the Holy Spirit that we are born again. We have faith by the gift and operation of the Spirit. It is the Holy Spirit who gives us assurance of the forgiveness of sin, and of sonship. It is the work of the Holy Spirit to illuminate our minds, assure our hearts, and keep us sealed in grace as the purchased property of Christ. It is the Holy Spirit who bears witness with us, and who enables us to bear witness to others. The flesh can do none of these things.

The flesh speaks of the absence of Christ. As it is used here, the word flesh indicates anything apart from Christ, or in addition to Christ, which we depend upon as meritorious before God. The Galatians were beginning to renounce Christ as the all-sufficient Saviour. Having begun in the Spirit, they were now placing their confidence in fleshly things; such as legal works, as the observance of ceremonies, the practice of circumcision, sabbath keeping, and even the things they ate and drank, or did not eat and drink! They hoped to make themselves perfect, complete, and holy by the works of the flesh. What stupendous, disastrous stupidity!

Paul seems to say, 'Your beginning was so hopeful, but your continuation is so sorrowful. And just think of it, those false guides whom you are following have a name for this process of going down hill. They call it 'becoming perfect'. How foolish! What Paul here says of the Galatians applies equally to those who trust in anything except Christ for salvation in our day. If a man bases his hope for life, or anything in heaven upon anything apart from, or in addition to Christ, he is depending on the flesh. Christianity is 'Christ in you', and Christ in you is the work of God the Holy Spirit.

Trinitarians

Christians are Trinitarians. We believe, according to the plain statement of holy scripture, that there is one living and true God, and that there are three persons in the Godhead: The Father, the Son, and the Holy Spirit. Each is equal to the other in all things. This is what the Book of God declares: 'There are three that bear record in heaven, the Father, the Word, and the Holy Ghost and these three are One' (1 John 5:7). Yet, for the purpose of our redemption, in the covenant of grace each of the Sacred Three voluntarily assumed to himself one aspect of the great work of saving the elect.

Ephesians 1 teaches this with complete clarity. In the covenant of grace God the Father is the great Architect of salvation. He purposed the great work (vv. 3-6). God the Son is the great Accomplisher of salvation. He purchased salvation (redemption and forgiveness) for his people (vv. 7-11). God the Holy Spirit is the great Applier of salvation. He produces the work of grace in the heart and effectually applies it to chosen, redeemed sinners (vv. 12-14). Let us never think lightly of God the Holy Spirit. He is not a mere influence upon us. He is our great God, and it is his office in the Covenant of Grace to apply the finished work of Christ to the hearts of the elect, and to bring them safely to heaven. Salvation, in the experience of it, is altogether the work of God the Holy Spirit.

The Beginning

At the very beginning of our experience of grace, in the new birth, in the gift of faith, and in effectual calling, salvation is the work of the Spirit. Our Lord Jesus tells us plainly that our being born of God and our believing on him is not the result of something we do (John 1:12-13). He told Nicodemus that no man could either see or enter into the kingdom of God until he is born again; and that that new birth is the sovereign, irresistible work of the Spirit (John 3:1-8).

Yes, God's elect were saved from eternity in the purpose of God. Let men argue with that as they may, God states it plainly (Romans 8:28-30; 2 Timothy 1:9). Yes, every chosen sinner was saved by Christ when he redeemed them from the curse of the law ((Romans 5:10; Galatians 3:13). In preaching the gospel we declare to eternity bound sinners, utterly helpless before God, dead in trespasses and in sins, redemption accomplished, and salvation finished by the crucified Son of God. In that sense salvation is altogether outside our experience.

Yet, salvation is something every chosen, redeemed sinner experiences in time. The chosen must be born of God. The redeemed must be called. The called must believe. The believing must follow Christ. The follower must persevere unto the end. The whole of salvation, as it is experienced in time, is the work of God the Holy Spirit. Those who are spiritually dead can no more raise themselves up to spiritual life than the physically dead can raise themselves. Resurrection to life is the work of God the Spirit (Ephesians 2:1-5). Unbelievers can no more make themselves believers than blind men can make themselves see. Faith is the fruit of the Spirit (Galatians 5:22), the gift of his grace (Ephesians 2:8), and the operation of his omnipotent, irresistible mercy (Ephesians 1:19; Colossians 2:12).

It is God the Holy Spirit who, at the appointed time of love, causes chosen sinners to hear the gospel, not in word only, but in power and in much assurance, creating life and faith within (1 Thessalonians 1:5; Romans 10:17; 1 Peter 1:23-25). He makes the gospel effectual, making it to each of the redeemed, the gospel of his own salvation accomplished by Christ (Ephesians 1:12-14).

He works faith in us by revealing Christ to us and in us by the gospel (2 Corinthians 4:4-6; Galatians 1:15-16). When Christ is revealed, the Holy Spirit convinces the sinner of his sin, of righteousness accomplished, and of justice satisfied by the crucified Son of God (John 16:8-11). And it is God the Holy Spirit who preserves us, by whom we are sealed until the day of our resurrection (Ephesians 1:14; 4:30). We persevere in faith because we are kept by his grace.

In all this great work there is nothing to be attributed to the flesh. The whole work is the work of grace, free, sovereign, irresistible, indestructible, everlasting grace, 'It is the Spirit that quickeneth; the flesh profiteth nothing'.

Indwelt

The Holy Spirit indwells every believer. The church universal is the temple of the Holy Spirit (1 Corinthians 6:19-20; 2 Corinthians 6:16). Every true local church is the temple of the Holy Spirit (1 Corinthians 3:16-17), an habitation of God by the Spirit (Ephesians 2:22). He is the antitype of the Shekinah in the Old Testament (Numbers 9:15-23; 2 Chronicles 7:1-3). And every believer is indwelt by God the Holy Spirit. He is our ever abiding, indwelling Comforter, Teacher, and Keeper. That is the doctrine of Christ in John 13-16. The Holy Spirit keeps every believer in absolute security (John 10:28; 1 Peter 1:5). He is our Sanctifier, the One whose presence with us, giving us a new nature, has sanctified us in the experience of grace. He is the Anointing and Unction of God, by whom we are taught all things (John 14:26; 1 John 2:27; 1 Corinthians 2:14).

He comforts our hearts by taking the things of Christ and showing them to us (John 14:16-18; 16:13-14). He gives us the peace of pardon by revealing Christ to us, by sprinkling (applying to our hearts and consciences) the blood of Christ, the Lamb of God crucified for us (Hebrews 9:12-14). We know that we have the forgiveness of sins, because the Holy Spirit speaks pardon to our hearts, declaring that Christ's blood has satisfied divine justice. We have assurance of salvation and eternal, immutable acceptance with God by the Holy Spirit who gives us faith in our immutably accepted Substitute (Romans 8:16; 2 Corinthians 1:22; Ephesians 1:14; Hebrews 11:1-2). It is this gift of faith that assures us that we are indeed the children of God (Galatians 5:6).

Finish

Yes, the Holy Spirit began the work of grace in us, and he will finish it. That is what the word 'perfect' means in Galatians 3:3. The legalists who were seducing the Galatians away from Christ taught that, though saved by grace, we must now finish the work God began in us by contributing the works of our flesh (self-righteous, law obedience) to the work of the Spirit to make God's work of grace complete. What horrid blasphemy! Yet, it is the commonly accepted religion of the world.

How often I have heard people say to me, after hearing the gospel of God's free, sovereign, saving grace in Christ, 'According to what you preach there is nothing for me to do. God does everything.' My response is always, 'I'm glad you heard what I said.' Did you get that? In this business of salvation, there is nothing for you to do. God does everything. He who called you will keep you. He said so. He who began his good work in you will finish it (without your help). He said so (Philippians 1:6; John 6:39). He who brought you out of the grave and raised you in the first resurrection spiritually will bring you out of the grave and raise you up to glory in the second resurrection. He said so (Romans 8:11, 23).

Faith

To walk in the Spirit is to live by faith in Christ, trusting Christ alone for the whole of our salvation. To live after the flesh is to seek in some way, to some decree, by some means to establish some sort of righteousness for ourselves. Therefore, the Apostle Paul writes, 'As ye have therefore received Christ Jesus the Lord, so walk ye in him' (Colossians 2:6). 'Walk in the Spirit, and you shall not fulfil the lusts of the flesh' (Galatians 5:16).

How did you receive Christ? We did not receive Christ by the works of the flesh, or by the hearing of the law, but by faith (Galatians 3:1-3). That is how we must live, if we would honour God. We honour God, fulfil the law, and magnify our Saviour, only by faith in him (Romans 3:31). There is no other way to do so.

How did you receive Christ? If you have received him, you received him by faith. You came to him as a sinner, trusting him as your Saviour (1 Corinthians 1:30-31). You bowed to him as a servant, receiving him as your Lord. You came to him as a Bride, like Gomer, conquered by his love, embracing him as your husband. As you received Christ Jesus the Lord, so walk in him, trusting him alone for all things.

The flesh and the Spirit can never come together. God's work of grace Paul refers to here as 'Spirit'. The law he calls 'flesh'. I know that appears strange to many, and offensive to others. The reason is clear: multitudes seek to make themselves perfect by the flesh.

The works of the law he calls flesh, because the ordinances of the law were 'carnal ordinances' (Hebrews 9:10). Imposed upon the Jews during the Old Testament. The commandments of the law are called the 'rudiments of the world' (Colossians 2:8, 20) and 'beggarly elements of the law' (Galatians 4:9). In the Old Testament, for the Jews of that Mosaic age the ordinances of the law were spiritual; the ordinances of God. But all the law was temporary by design, pointing to Christ who fulfilled the law and is the end of the law. The law was a schoolmaster to lead to Christ. Now that Christ has come, having died, and risen again from the dead, the carnal ordinances of the law became useless. Besides that, God never intended them to be anything other than temporary rudiments and first elements. We are no longer under the law. We worship and live after the Spirit (Philippians 3:3).

To return to the law is to become apostate. It is to depart from Christ and deny the grace of God. That is how serious the matter is (Galatians 5:1-4). It is for that reason that Paul spoke so strongly about the believer's freedom from the law in Christ. And it is for that reason that we must reject and flee from every attempt by men to bring us back under the yoke of legal bondage today, no matter what their pretence is for doing so, 'As ye have therefore received Christ Jesus the Lord, so walk ye in him' (Colossians 2:6).

Even as Abraham believed God, and it was accounted
to him for righteousness. Know ye therefore that they
which are of faith, the same are the children of Abraham.
And the scripture, foreseeing that God would justify the
heathen through faith, preached before the gospel unto
Abraham, saying, In thee shall all nations be blessed. So
then they which be of faith are blessed with faithful
Abraham. For as many as are of the works of the law are
under the curse: for it is written, Cursed is every one that
continueth not in all things which are written in the book
of the law to do them.

(Galatians 3:6-10)

Chapter 13

Read: Galatians 3:6-10

'Children Of Abraham'

Paul's purpose in this section is to demonstrate that the believer's standing before God is completely upon the merits of Christ, and not upon anything done by himself. Salvation in all its fulness is obtained by faith, and not by legal works. The judicial act of justification took place when Christ was delivered up to death upon the cursed tree because of our offences imputed to him and raised again because of our justification accomplished by him (Romans 4:25). Our justification is the result of justice being satisfied by the sacrifice of Christ. It is a work of grace accomplished totally outside our experience.

Yet, the scriptures speak of God's elect being justified by faith (Romans 3:28; Galatians 3:24). How can this be? The answer is very simple. We receive justification by faith. We were justified in the court of heaven upon the merits of Christ, so that God looks upon us with the same complacency as if we had never sinned. It is only because this is true that God can deal with sinners in mercy. If his justice were not already fully satisfied, he could not allow any sinner to live. We were reconciled to God by the death of his Son long before we believed. When he gave us faith in Christ, we received that reconciliation and justification by faith (2 Corinthians 5:19; Romans 5:9-11). We come to experience justification in the court of conscience by faith. That is when the Holy Spirit speaks peace to our hearts, and declares us to be free from condemnation by applying the blood of Christ to our hearts. Thus our carnal mind, which is naturally at enmity with God, is reconciled to God. It is in this sense, and only in this sense, that we are justified by faith.

Paul has shown that this doctrine of justification by grace alone is exactly what all our Lord's apostles taught. This is the doctrine of Christ. He has declared that if righteousness could be had in any other way, or by any other means, then Christ died in vain. In the opening verses of this chapter Paul shows that every saved sinner's experience verifies this truth of the gospel.

Now, he appeals to biblical history to prove that believers are not justified by the law; and that we do not live by the law, but by faith in Christ. He points us to Abraham, the friend of God. It is likely that Paul selected this reference to Abraham in order to show that at the very beginning of Israel's history it was clearly evident that God had chosen this nation in order that it might be a blessing to all nations through its 'Seed', the Lord Jesus Christ, and to show that from the beginning this blessing of grace had been received by faith alone and not by works.

In the passage before us Paul identifies who the children of Abraham are. He shows that all of God's elect in every age are truly the children of Abraham. They are the true Israelites. Abraham is the father of the faithful. He is called 'the father of all them that believe' (Romans 4:11), because he is the first person of whom the Book of God declares he 'believed God, and it was counted to him for righteousness' (Genesis 15:6; Romans 4:3; Galatians 3:6).

Abraham's Children

The true Israel of God are not the natural descendants of Abraham, but the spiritual descendants of Abraham. He was the father of the nation from whom Christ sprang, who is the Author of our faith; and all of God's children are children of faith. As the Holy Spirit puts it in Philippians 3:3, 'we are the circumcision, which worship God in the spirit, and rejoice in Christ Jesus, and have no confidence in the flesh.'

The Word of God shows this to us with unmistakable clarity. The natural, physical seed of Abraham, Jews, or Israelites, after the flesh, are not the people of God by right of their physical birth. It is true that God made definite promises to the physical seed of Abraham, but these were all fulfilled (Joshua 21:43-45; 23:14-16), and they were given upon condition of obedience. Israel, after the flesh, has denied Christ and was judged by

God for having done so (Matthew 22:1-14; 23:37-38). Paul clearly asserts that Israel after the flesh is not the true Israel (Romans 2:28-29; 9:4-7). God has cut off the natural seed in order to bring in the greater spiritual seed (Romans 11:22, 25-36). 'The Israel of God' is that holy nation and royal priesthood of saved sinners who live by the rule of the gospel (Galatians 6:14-16), 'who walk not after the flesh, but after the spirit'. Paul holds Abraham before us as 'the father of all them that believe', because we see in Abraham certain marks, certain characteristics by which all God's elect are identified in this world.

God's Declaration

Those who opposed Paul's preaching of free-grace and insisted so strenuously that the works of the law must be added to faith in Christ vehemently claimed that they were Abraham's true descendants, that they were God's true children (Acts 15:5; Galatians 2:3; 5:2-3; 6:12, 13, 15; Matthew 3:9; Luke 3:8; John 8:33, 39, 40, 53). Therefore, Paul turns to the declaration of Abraham's righteousness and makes two statements concerning it, which destroy all carnal hope, both for the Jews and for Gentiles who hope for righteousness upon the basis of their works.

First, Paul asserts that Abraham was justified by faith, apart from any works of his own, ' Abraham believed God, and it was accounted to him for righteousness' (v. 6). Abraham's justification preceded his circumcision by many years (Genesis 15:6; 17:24; Romans 4:9-12). He believed God. The Object of his faith was God, especially the Son of God, who is the Word of God (Genesis 15:1, 6). He was Abraham's Shield (Ephesians 6:16) and his Reward (1 Corinthians 1:30, cf. Romans 4:22-25; John 8:56). Abraham trusted Christ. It was Christ, the Object of Abraham's faith that was imputed unto him for righteousness, not his act of faith. His faith was the channel through which he received the blessing of justification, the righteousness of Christ.

Then, the Apostle declares, 'Know ye therefore that they which are of faith, the same are the children of Abraham' (v. 7). All who, like Abraham, believe God are justified by faith; and they are the children of Abraham. Physical lineage from Abraham guaranteed no spiritual blessing to Jews (Matthew 3:9). And being the physical descendants of godly (believing) parents secures no spiritual blessing to any today (John 1:11-13). All spiritual blessings (all the blessings of grace, salvation, and eternal life) are in Christ and come to sinners by grace alone. All who are of faith (all who trust Christ) have a right to all the promises which God made to Abraham.

The Gospel Preached To Abraham

The Holy Spirit tells us plainly that the gospel was preached to Abraham. 'And the scripture, foreseeing that God would justify the heathen through faith, preached before the gospel unto Abraham, saying, In thee shall all nations be blessed. So then they which be of faith are blessed with faithful Abraham' (vv. 8-9). For some strange reason, many are terribly uncomfortable with that fact. They are uncomfortable with it because they do not know the gospel. They vainly imagine that God saved people in a different way and by a different gospel in the Old Testament than he does today. But that is not the case.

It was never God's purpose to limit his church and kingdom to the physical nation of Israel, but to use them as a means of saving his elect among the Gentiles (Matthew 8:11-12). This he determined before the world began, and, therefore, before Abraham was called to life and faith in Christ, by the revelation of Christ in the gospel. Yes, Abraham saw Christ, knew Christ, and trusted Christ, in precisely the same way as believers do today.

I do not mean to suggest that Abraham had the full revelation of Christ that is given with the completion of holy scripture. But I do mean to assert that Abraham believed on the Son of God as he is revealed in the gospel. Our Saviour himself declared, 'Your father Abraham rejoiced to see my day: and he saw it, and was glad' (John 8:56). God promised Abraham that the Seed would be from his loins, who would be the Messiah, in and by whom all the nations of the earth would be blessed. Abraham believed in Christ, his Messiah-Redeemer. God promised him that the Messianic blessings were to be worldwide (Matthew 28:19-20; 1 John 2:2), that all the nations of the earth would be blessed in and by him.

In verse 9 Paul was inspired of God to draw a very logical and necessary conclusion. All who believe God, upon the hearing of the Gospel, are the sons of Abraham; hence, they are blessed with him. What Paul is here teaching is the important truth that the church of both the Old Testament dispensation and the New is one. All believers are one in Christ. All of God's people were chosen in Christ (Ephesians 1:4). All enjoy being clothed in the righteousness of Christ. All are redeemed by Christ (Isaiah 53; Matthew 1:21; John 3:16). All are his sheep, have one Shepherd, and belong to one fold (Ezekiel 37:22; John 10:16; Ephesians 2:14-15). The names of all the elect are recorded in one Book of Life (Revelation 3:5). All the elect are predestined to the same glory (Romans 8:29-30). All partake of the glories of the heavenly Jerusalem (Revelation 21:10-14; Matthew 8:11-12). And all will be perfected together (Hebrews 11:40).

Living By Faith

We read in verses 10-12, 'For as many as are of the works of the law are under the curse: for it is written, Cursed is every one that continueth not in all things which are written in the book of the law to do them. But that no man is justified by the law in the sight of God, it is evident: for, The just shall live by faith. And the law is not of faith: but, The man that doeth them shall live in them.'

We understand the impossibility of law righteousness. Every believer does. We know that the law demands perfection we cannot perform, righteousness we cannot produce, and satisfaction we cannot give. Knowing that fact, all who are just before God, all who have been justified by his grace and have received that justification by faith in Christ, live by faith, just like Abraham did (Hebrews 11:1-2, 17-19). They obey God because they believe him. Read the life of Abraham, and learn what it is to live by faith.

By faith Abraham left his own country to seek another (Genesis 11:27-32).
By faith Abraham left his family (Genesis 12:1; Hebrews 11:8).
By faith Abraham separated himself from Lot (Genesis 13:1-13).
By faith Abraham received a son (Genesis 17).
By faith Abraham sacrificed his son and received his son back from the dead (Genesis 22).
By faith Abraham sojourned through this earth seeking the city of God, not receiving one parcel of land for himself (Genesis 13:14-18; Hebrews 11:10).
By faith Abraham died (Hebrews 11:13).

If we seek to live by the law, Paul declares that we do not live by faith (v. 12). To embrace the law as a principle of life is to abandon faith, abandon grace, and abandon Christ (Galatians 5:1-4).

Redemption

Redeemed sinners are free from the curse and condemnation of the law. We cannot and shall not be cursed by the law, for 'Christ hath redeemed us from the curse of the law, being made a curse for us: for it is written, Cursed is every one that hangeth on a tree: that the blessing of Abraham might come on the Gentiles through Jesus Christ; that we might receive the promise of the Spirit through faith' (Galatians 3:13-14). Christ's object in redeeming us, as it is here declared, was that we might receive the blessing of Abraham, the Spirit of God, and all the gifts of grace and salvation in him by faith in Christ. What a blessed, clear statement this is of particular, effectual redemption!

> Their sins upon him all were laid,
> And he the dreadful debt has paid,
> (A debt no more to pay);
> Their surety in their law place stood
> Appeased stern justice with his blood,
> And bore their sins away.

But that no man is justified by the law in the sight of God, it is evident: for, The just shall live by faith.

(Galatians 3:11)

Chapter 14

Read: Galatians 3:11

'The Just Shall Live By Faith'

'The just shall live by faith.' God's people in this world live by faith, trusting him, believing his Word. That has always been the case and shall continue to be the case until time shall be no more. Trusting Christ as our Saviour, we trust him as our Lord, living by faith in him.

Benjamin Beddome captured the meaning of these words in one of his hymns.

'Tis faith supports my feeble soul, in times of deep distress,
When storms arise and billows roll, great God, I trust Thy grace.

Thy powerful arm still bears me up, whatever griefs befall;
Thou art my life, my joy, my hope, and Thou my all in all.

Bereft of friends, beset with foes, with dangers all around,
To Thee I all my fears disclose, in Thee my help is found.

In every want, in every strait, to Thee alone I fly;
When other comforters depart, Thou art forever nigh.

Justification

Clearly, Paul's doctrine in this text is an undeniable declaration that justification can be obtained from God only by faith in Christ, without the deeds of the law. God's elect were justified before the law was given just as we are today, by grace through faith, trusting Christ. Abel, Noah and Job, Abraham, Isaac and Jacob, and Joseph, Moses and Aaron trusted Christ just as we do today, believing God's revelation concerning his Son, and obtained justification by faith in him. Since the law had not yet been given, it is not possible that obedience to the law had anything to do with their justification.

Many were justified during the legal dispensation, but no one was justified by his obedience to the law, even in that day. The law was not given to justify, but to expose and condemn sin. The law never made anyone holy, except in a ceremonial (typical) way. The law's only purpose was to lead us to Christ, shutting us up to faith in him alone for redemption, righteousness, and grace. All the types and commandments of the law were given to reveal both our need of Christ as our Substitute and the blessed efficacy of his work as our sin-atoning sacrifice. Therefore, it is written, 'The just shall live by faith. And the law is not of faith'.

Sanctification

The apostle Paul here quotes, by divine inspiration, the prophet Habakkuk (Habakkuk 2:4). In fact, this statement, 'The just shall live by faith', must have been one of Paul's favourite passages. He quotes Habakkuk's words three times in his epistles (Romans 1:17; Galatians 3:11; Hebrews 10:38). The fact that the Holy Spirit inspired the writing of these words four times in holy scripture certainly implies that there is much in them that we need to learn and remember.

If we carefully read the context from which this quotation is taken and the context in which Paul was inspired of God to use it, it will become obvious that the Holy Spirit's intent is to teach us that as we experience justification by faith in Christ, so too we experience sanctification by faith in him. Clearly, this is what Paul is teaching in Galatians 3.

That faith by which we live is the gift and operation of God's grace in us. It is not native to man, but the gift of God, the fruit of his Holy Spirit (Galatians 5:22; Ephesians 2:8-9; Colossians 1:12). The operation of faith in the heart produces love; and love produces obedience. These gifts of grace are not the cause of life before God, but the fruit of it. These things do not produce righteousness, but flow from it. In the spring we feast our eyes on the beautiful roses and flowers blooming around our homes, with their fragrances filling the air; but no one imagines that the flowers cause the plants to live. We know that it is the living plant that brings forth the flower and its fragrance. So it is with the believer. It is the grace of God that gives us life; and the life we live in faith, righteousness, and sanctification is the fruit of his grace. Love for and obedience to Christ are the fruit of grace, not the cause. They neither give us life, nor maintain it. They are the result of life given.

Habakkuk's Questions

The Spirit of God here (and throughout the scriptures) teaches us that faith is the distinctive principle of the believer's life. By faith we embrace the Saviour and live upon him. In Habakkuk 1 (vv. 2-3) the prophet cried beneath the heavy weight of his burden, 'O Lord, how long shall I cry, and thou wilt not hear! ... Why dost thou show me iniquity and cause me to behold grievance?' Then, at the end of the chapter (vv. 13-17), he asked the Lord to explain himself to him, to explain to him why he would choose to use the Chaldeans to punish Judah? His question is, 'How is it you, O Lord God, who is of purer eyes than to behold iniquity, will execute your wrath upon Judah by a people even worse than they?'

These were not the questions of a rebel, or a reprobate unbeliever, but the questions of a faithful man perplexed by God's providential works. We might not be honest enough to put them into verbal expressions; but they are questions that frequently disturb us too. Habakkuk's questions remind us of David's great struggle in Psalm 73.

God's Answer

We must admit that we have struggled with the same questions. The earth is filled with glaring inequity. The wicked do seem to prosper while the righteous suffer. After raising these questions, Habakkuk resolves to wait for God's answer. We would be wise to do the same, and to lay the answer to heart.

In chapter 2 Habakkuk stands upon his watchtower to await God's answer, and the Lord gives it to him in a vision. He does not tell us what he saw; but it must be assumed that the remainder of his prophecy is the result of the vision God gave him. I say this because God commanded him to write out the vision and make it plain (vv. 2-3); and the declaration of God's vision was first and foremost a word of instruction, then a reproof, and finally an assurance to Habakkuk and to us (v. 4). Let us hear the instruction, bear the reproof, and rejoice in the assurance. 'The just shall live by his faith.'

The first thing we learn is that God is running things in this world right on schedule. Our time and God's time are not measured by the same clock. Israel offered sacrifices for centuries in anticipation of Christ, the coming Sacrifice, by whom sin would be put away. The Jews, in unbelief, fell into idolatry and were cast off by God, because, they refused to live by faith. They stumbled over the Stumbling-Stone (Romans 9:33-10:4). Going about to establish their own righteousness, they refused to submit to the righteousness of God, never realizing that, 'Christ is the end of the law for righteousness to everyone that believeth.' 'The just shall live by his faith.' But they refused to believe and perished.

Yet, 'when the fulness of the time was come, God sent forth his Son, made of a woman, made under the law, to redeem them that were under the law' (Galatians 4:4-5). You can count on it, not one thing willed, purposed, predestined, and promised by God will fail to be accomplished, and accomplished in exactly the way and at the precise time God has ordained. A thousand years are as a day in God's sight. He never gets in a hurry, and he is never late.

This is God's answer to all Habakkuk's questions and his answer to our own questions as well: 'The just shall live by his faith' (Habakkuk 2:4). As I mentioned at the beginning of this study, this great statement made by God to Habakkuk is repeated three times in the New Testament, all by the apostle Paul. Each place describes a specific aspect of Christ's all-sufficient and infallibly effectual work on behalf of his people as our Surety and Substitute.

Romans 1:17

The first New Testament quotation is found in Romans 1:17. It follows Paul's declaration, 'For I am not ashamed of the gospel of Christ: for it is the power of God unto salvation to everyone that believeth' (Romans 1:16). Then he says, 'For therein is the righteousness of God revealed from faith to faith; as it is written, The just shall live by faith' (Romans 1:17).

In Romans 1 Paul is standing, as it were, upon the threshold of his great Epistle on Justification, in which he shows us how sinners are made righteous and just before God, not by works, but by grace. In the Book of God we are given an inspired record of God's wondrous work of redemption in Christ. A witness of redemption accomplished by the righteousness and blood of his darling Son. Faith believes God's witness and says 'Amen', to the testimony concerning God's Son; and in so doing freely receives the righteousness of God in him: unconditional, irrevocable and eternal justification. I repeat: faith does not make us righteous. Christ did that at Calvary (Romans 4:25). Faith receives the atonement and the righteousness brought in by it (Romans 5:11). Like our brother Abel, believing God, offering God the blood of his own Son, we obtain witness that we are righteous (Hebrews 11:4).

Galatians 3:11

The second quote is here, in Galatians 3:11, 'But that no man is justified by the law in the sight of God, it is evident; for, The just shall live by faith.' Here, Paul is saying much the same thing as he wrote in Colossians 2:6, 'As ye have received Christ Jesus the Lord, so walk ye in him.' The Galatians were being tempted by false preachers, Judaising legalists, to forsake Christ and the grace of God altogether (Galatians 5:1-4). These false teachers tried to persuade them that, having been saved by grace (justified by grace), they must now keep themselves saved and make themselves perfect, that they must sanctify themselves by their own works.

Paul is not confusing justification and sanctification, but clarifying them. In the context (Galatians 3:1-10) he is clearly addressing the matter of sanctification. He is telling us that both are found in Christ, that both are received by trusting Christ, that both are works of grace received by faith. He is saying, 'If you could make yourself perfect by works, you could justify yourself by your works. But that is evidently impossible, for, "the just shall live by faith!"'

In Galatians 3:11 Paul is talking about the believer's walk of life in this world. Just as we are saved by faith, we continue to live by faith. Our life's walk is a walk of faith

Hebrews 10:38

We see Habakkuk's words again in Hebrews 10:38. Here the Holy Spirit is talking about perseverance and the assurance of it (Hebrews 10:39). When the night is darkest, faith pierces the darkness and, seeing the light of God's promise and grace in Christ, refuses to quit. Faith embraces and clings to Christ.

Back in the book of Habakkuk, the prophet of God tells us that judgment is coming. Every proud rebel shall be destroyed. But, even in the midst of the providential calamities of divine judgment in time, and when the great and final day of wrath shall come, those who live by faith have their eyes on One who is the Anchor of their souls, knowing that he is in his holy temple. 'For the earth shall be filled with the knowledge of the glory of the LORD, as the waters cover the sea' (Habakkuk 2:14, 20).

Certainly, this is talking about that last day, when judgment is over and God makes all things new. It is equally certain that this is talking about this gospel age, in which the gospel of God's free, sovereign, saving, grace and glory in Christ is spread over all the earth, even as God destroys the nations by the great whore of false religion, Babylon.

Still, there is more. If you have a marginal translation, you will see that the words of Habakkuk 2:14 might be translated, 'the earth shall be filled by knowing the glory of the Lord'. That is to say, 'We who believe God, who live by faith, knowing the glory of God in Christ, see the fulness of God's purpose in all things through all the earth' (Romans 8:28-39). This is exactly what our Lord declares to be the case in John 11:40. As it was upon Mount Sinai that the whole earth was full of the glory of God (Habakkuk 3:3-4), so it is now. If only we had eyes to see it, the whole earth is full of God's praise. One day soon, all things shall show forth his praise.

Even when God marches through the earth in wrath, with his glittering sword drawn, he is riding upon his 'chariots of salvation' (Habakkuk 3:8), and goes forth for the salvation of his people by Christ, his anointed (Habakkuk 3:12-13).

We are justified by faith; we walk by faith; we will be delivered by faith. This is the vision God gave the prophet of old. Habakkuk declares, 'God is working out his eternal purpose of grace for the salvation of his people. In wrath, he does remember mercy. He is making himself known. He is preserving his church and kingdom. Blessed be his holy name!' In consideration of all these things, the Holy Spirit tells us four times, 'The just shall live by faith.'

Habakkuk's Faith

Knowing this, the troubled, heavy-hearted prophet closes his song and his prophecy with a marvellous declaration of determined faith, bowing to the wisdom, goodness and grace of God's adorable providence, even when it appears dark and difficult. 'Although the fig tree shall not blossom, neither shall fruit be in the vines; the labour of the olive shall fail, and the fields shall yield no meat; the flock shall be cut off from the fold, and there shall be no herd in the stalls: Yet I will rejoice in the LORD, I will joy in the God of my salvation. The LORD God is my strength, and he will make my feet like hinds' feet, and he will make me to walk upon mine high places. To the chief singer on my stringed instruments' (Habakkuk 3:17-19).

That is exactly what is meant by these words, 'The just shall live by faith.' May God the Holy Spirit, whose words these are, teach and give us grace, constantly, to live by faith.

And the law is not of faith: but, The man that doeth them shall live in them. Christ hath redeemed us from the curse of the law, being made a curse for us: for it is written, Cursed *is* every one that hangeth on a tree: That the blessing of Abraham might come on the Gentiles through Jesus Christ; that we might receive the promise of the Spirit through faith.

(Galatians 3:12-14)

Chapter 15

Read: Galatians 3:12-14

Christ Our Redeemer

In Galatians 3 Paul is showing us that salvation is entirely the gracious and sovereign work of God, upon the merits of the shed blood of Christ, apart from any human effort. He makes what must be to all legalists a very astonishing and grating statement in verse 10. 'As many as are of the works of the law are under the curse'. When a man tries to save himself by doing good, by keeping laws and commandments, he is cursed in his very effort. Such a statement is in direct opposition to the natural opinion of man, and all other forms of religion. Men, by nature, assume that Christianity should address itself to men and say, 'You ought to do good. Do this and that and thou shalt live. Obey these commandments and you will have eternal life.' But the revelation of God says just the opposite. 'As many as are of the works of the law are under the curse: for it is written, cursed is everyone that continueth not in all things which are written in the book of the law to do them.'

The Law

The giving of the law was an awesome and terrifying event. Mount Sinai burned with fire. It was covered with thunder and lightning and thick darkness. The giving of the law was accompanied by the blast of a trumpet. It sounded like the day of doom, of damnation, of destruction. So awesome and terrible was that sight that Moses said, 'I do exceedingly fear and quake'. It was such a fearful time that if so much as a beast were to touch the mountain it was to be stoned, or thrust through with a dart.

The awesomeness of that drama was concluded by the law of God being given to man upon two huge tables of stone. The law is hard, unbending, and impersonal. It was written on rock, heavy rock that crushes us to powder. 'Cursed is everyone that continueth not in all things which are written in the book of the law to do them.' Paul shows us that no man can stand before God and claim salvation upon the footing of his own works, because his very works are a curse to him.

In verse 13 he tells us how sinners are saved. They cannot be saved upon their own merit, but they can be saved upon the merits of Another. Jesus Christ, the Representative Man, is the only one whose righteousness God will accept. And he graciously accepts as righteous all who are in Christ.

Sin is an accursed thing. The holy Lord God must curse it. His righteousness demands that he punish all sin and punish men for sin. But the Lord Jesus Christ, the all-glorious Son of the Everlasting Father, became a man and suffered in his manhood the curse, which was due his people. In the sacrifice of his own Son as our Substitute, God has satisfied his justice in the punishment of sin, and bestows his boundless mercy, love, and grace upon all who trust his Son, receiving salvation at his hand.

Our Ruin

All men are guilty of sin and under the curse of the law (v. 10). You and I have broken God's holy law (Exodus 20:1-17). The mere reading of the law should be enough to convince us of our guilt. We have all broken the law continually, from our youth up. No sinful human being is capable of keeping even one of the commandments. You may think, 'But the Lord knows, I have done the best I could.' But that very thought is itself a lie; and you know it. No man has ever done the best he could do. It is ever our nature to choose evil. Yet, even if it were true, the best that we can do is but sin. God's law demands perfect obedience, inwardly and outwardly, without a break.

Some try to find comfort in the supposition that, though they have sinned, they are no worse than others. But that will be no solace when God sweeps nations into hell. In that terrible day the wrath of God will be felt by every sinner as though he alone were damned. Unless you have kept the whole law of God perfectly, from the dawn of your life to the end of it, you are guilty before God.

Though it is impossible for us to keep God's law because of the corruption of our hearts, were it possible to do so, we are still guilty. We all sinned and fell in Adam (Romans 5:12). We were all born in sin (Psalms 51:5; 58:3). We do not become sinners by what we do. We do the evil that is in us because we are sinners. We were born that way. Our very nature is evil (Mark 7:20-23, Luke 11:13). Therefore we all live by nature after the lusts of our flesh, fulfilling the desires of the flesh (Ephesians 2:1-3).

Our Curse

Because we have broken God's holy law, we are under the curse of his law (Deuteronomy 27:14-26). What is the curse of the law, but the curse of God? It is a completely just and righteous curse, a curse we have earned (Genesis 2:17, Ezekiel 18:4; Romans 6:23). And the curse of God is indescribably great (Nahum 1:2-6; Malachi 4:1). He who destroyed the world once in water will soon purge it with fire. He who rained fire and brimstone upon Sodom and Gomorrah, will pour out the unquenchable fire of his holy wrath and the everlasting brimstone of torment, upon every sinner who is found by his avenging justice outside Christ, the only City of Refuge.

But let no one imagine that the wrath of God is something that may fall upon them sometime in the future. The wrath of God is presently upon the unbelieving (Deuteronomy 28:15-19; John 3:36). Eternal hell is the place where that wrath shall be forever executed, without abatement, upon the ungodly.

Redemption

But there are some people in this world who are no longer under the curse of the law, who are no longer condemned, and can never be condemned. Let every believing sinner rejoice and sing. Christ our Mediator has redeemed us from the curse of the law, being made a curse for us (1 Corinthians 12:3; Deuteronomy 21:22-23; Joshua 10:24-27).

The Word of God declares that there is only one way of redemption and that is substitution. The only way God can or will forgive sin is by the sin-atoning death and justice satisfying sacrifice of a Substitute of infinite worth and merit. The Lord Jesus Christ is that Substitute. 'For he hath made him to be sin for us, who knew no sin; that we might be made the righteousness of God in him' (2 Corinthians 5:21). The Lord Jesus Christ, the Son of God, was made to be sin for us. When he was made sin, the Lord God poured out all his infinite, holy wrath upon him. With one tremendous stroke of his terrible sword, justice was satisfied. The sword of justice that would have tormented us forever was swallowed in our holy Substitute, the Lord Jesus Christ. This is his one great sacrifice for sin.

> With one tremendous draught of love,
> He drank damnation dry!

The Redeemer

'Christ hath redeemed us from the curse of the law'. Our Redeemer is Jesus Christ, the Son of God, who was appointed and called to this work by his Father. He agreed to be our Redeemer and became our Redeemer in eternity, in the everlasting covenant. He is the Lamb slain from the foundation of the world. He was spoken of in Old Testament prophecy as our Redeemer, and was typified as our Kinsman Redeemer both by the law and by Boaz. In the fulness of time he came, not to become our Redeemer, but as our Redeemer. And he has, by the sacrifice of himself, obtained eternal redemption for us. Our Lord Jesus is abundantly qualified to be our Redeemer. As man, he is our near kinsman, to whom the right of redemption belonged by the law. As God, he was able to accomplish the great work.

The Redeemed

Those who have been redeemed by Christ are 'us', God's elect are the objects of his eternal love (Jeremiah 31:3; Romans 8:28-30, Revelation 5:9). They are a people scattered through all the world, a peculiar people, the peculiar and distinct objects of grace. They are the people of Christ, 'his people', whom he came into the world to save (Matthew 1:21), those the Father gave to him before the world began (John 6:39). Those who were redeemed by Christ are his sheep (John 10:11-16), those for whom he made and makes intercession (John 17:9, 20). Surely, no reasonable person can imagine that the Lord Jesus would lay down his life for those for whom he refuses to pray! Those Christ redeemed are those who are, in fact, redeemed. Is it not ludicrous beyond comprehension to imagine that the Lord Jesus Christ redeemed some who are not redeemed? All those redeemed by Christ are 'us' who in time are brought by grace to believe on Christ. Our faith in him in time is the result of the redemption he accomplished at Calvary.

By his death upon the cursed tree, by the infinite merit and efficacy of his blood, the Lord Jesus Christ effectually redeemed God's elect (all for whom he died); and the blessing he obtained for them is eternal redemption

(Hebrews 9:12). When Paul says, 'Christ hath redeemed us from the curse of the law', his meaning is this: 'At one time in the past, by a finished, once for all act, Christ bought us out of the curse of the law and delivered us from it to himself, by a price'. And the price of our redemption was his own life's blood (1 Peter 1:18-20). We were his by the Father's gift before he died. Now, we are his by lawful ransom. He purchased us with the price of his own blood and delivered us 'from the curse of the law', its sentence of condemnation and death, and from the execution of it in eternal wrath. That simply means that all who were redeemed by Christ have been so thoroughly and effectually delivered from the curse of the law, 'so that', as John Gill puts it, 'they shall never be hurt by it, he having delivered them from wrath to come, and redeemed from the second death, the lake which burns with fire and brimstone.'

Made A Curse

How did our Saviour accomplish this great work? The Holy Spirit tells us that Christ redeemed us from the curse of the law 'by being made a curse for us'. That does not mean that he was simply made to be like one who is cursed by the law. It does not merely mean that he was looked upon by the men of his day as an abominable, wicked man, or that God merely looked upon him as though he were such.

There is much more here than a supposed curse. When our all-glorious Substitute was made to be sin for us, he was made to be 'a curse for us'. As our Surety the Lord Jesus was made under the law. He stood before God in our place legally as our Representative. Having all the sins of all his people imputed to him, and having assumed total responsibility for us as our Surety, he stood before God as one answerable for them; the only one answerable for them. The law, finding our sin on him, charged him with them and cursed him for them.

When the Son of God was made to be sin for us, justice executed upon him the full measure of God's infinite wrath and fury, until it was fully satisfied with the payment received from him. God the Father himself, who spared not his own Son, but delivered him up for us, awoke the sword of his angry justice against him, and commanded his death, even the horrid, ignominious, accursed death of the cross. Thus, he was made a curse: 'made a curse', by the will, counsel, and determination of the eternal God. And as our great Saviour and the Father's righteous Servant, the Lord Jesus freely consented to the work. He freely laid down his life for us. He voluntarily gave himself for us. He made his own soul an offering for sin in full agreement with the Father, because of his great love for us.

'Christ hath redeemed us from the curse of the law, being made a curse for us: for it is written cursed is everyone that hangeth on a tree.' That phrase in Deuteronomy 21:23 is translated in the margin, 'He that is hanged on a tree is the curse of God'. Stronger words could not be used to describe our Redeemer's agony, the magnitude of his sacrifice, and the efficacy of his work upon the cursed tree.

When he hung on the cross the Lord of Glory was made a curse, not for himself, or for any sins of his own, for he had none. He was made a curse, the curse of God for us, in our room and stead, because of our sins that were made to be his. He was made the curse of God to make atonement for us. The curse of God fell upon his darling Son as our Surety. His own Father, who made him to be sin for us, made him the curse of God for us, that he might redeem us from the curse of the law.

God's holy law requires a penalty against sin. The penalty is death. That is its curse. The only way anyone can ever be delivered from the curse of the law is by enduring its curse, death, to the full satisfaction of justice. But no man can ever do that. Indeed, whatever hell is, it is eternal, precisely because all the damned suffering the wrath of God in hell can never satisfy its infinite curse.

Here is the great beauty, wonder, and glory of the gospel. When the Lord Jesus Christ was made the curse of God for us and all for whom he died, we endured the curse of God in him to the full satisfaction of justice; for when he died, we died in him. Now, upon the grounds of justice satisfied, both the law of God and the grace of God demand the eternal salvation of all for whom Christ died. Because 'Christ hath redeemed us from the curse of the law, being made a curse for us', God is both just and the Justifier of all who trust his Son (Romans 3:24-26). There is no other way in which he can be, as he declares himself to be, 'A just God and a Saviour' (Isaiah 45:21-22).

Brethren, I speak after the manner of men; Though it be but a man's covenant, yet if it be confirmed, no man disannulleth, or addeth thereto. Now to Abraham and his seed were the promises made. He saith not, And to seeds, as of many; but as of one, And to thy seed, which is Christ. And this I say, that the covenant, that was confirmed before of God in Christ, the law, which was four hundred and thirty years after, cannot disannul, that it should make the promise of none effect. For if the inheritance be of the law, it is no more of promise: but God gave it to Abraham by promise.

(Galatians 3:15-18)

Chapter 16

Read: Galatians 3:15-18

Salvation: The Promised Inheritance Of Free Grace

Paul's purpose in Galatians 3 is to show us that salvation, in its entirety, is the inheritance of free grace, the result of God's absolute and unconditional promise through the blood of Christ. He is showing us that no part of the inheritance can be obtained by the works of the flesh, by obedience to the law. Paul, writing by divine inspiration, uses argument after argument to demonstrate the fact that this is not some new doctrine, but that it is the doctrine of holy scripture, constantly taught throughout the Old Testament. In this passage he shows us that the blessing of Abraham, the blessing of salvation by the blood of Christ and the operation of God's omnipotent grace is an eternal, covenant blessing.

An Illustration

Paul has already shown us that the promise God made to Abraham was the promise of the gospel. That promise is an eternal, covenant promise. Here the apostle shows us the steadfastness of that covenant and the certainty of the promises of grace and salvation in the covenant, using earthly things as illustrations of heavenly things. 'Brethren, I speak after the manner of men; Though it be but a man's covenant, yet if it be confirmed, no man disannulleth, or addeth thereto' (v. 15). Because the promise was given to Abraham 430 years before the law was given on Mount Sinai, it should be obvious that the law can never nullify the promise.

It is a matter of common knowledge that once a covenant has been ratified, it cannot be changed. Its terms cannot be altered. Paul's point is this: Because the promises of grace and salvation were made before the law was given, the law cannot alter or in any way nullify those promises. Therefore, justification, salvation, sanctification, and eternal life cannot come by the law. All the blessings of the gospel come by God's free, unalterable promise, through the merits and efficacy of Christ's redemptive accomplishments to all who, like Abraham, believe the gospel.

Paul's Argument

If a man's covenant cannot be overturned by something that happens after the covenant is ratified, you can be sure God's covenant cannot be. 'Now to Abraham and his seed were the promises made. He saith not, And to seeds, as of many; but as of one, And to thy seed, which is Christ' (v. 16). The promises of the gospel were given long before the law and cannot be annulled or modified by the law that came later. The word translated 'covenant' in verse 15 refers to what we would call 'last will and testament'. There is no doubt that Paul uses the word in that sense here to illustrate his point. Yet, he is using it to refer to something far greater than a man's last will and testament. He is using it to refer to God's everlasting, immutable, unalterable covenant of grace, and the promises of it made with his Son as our Surety before the world began.

Paul stresses the fact that the promise God made to Abraham was totally wrapped up in one person, Abraham's 'Seed', the Lord Jesus Christ. The promise was, from the beginning, based upon the work that Christ accomplished from eternity as the Lamb slain from the foundation of the world, and would accomplish in time as our Surety, Redeemer, and Covenant Head. Therefore, as it has been from the beginning of time, so it is now: grace, salvation, forgiveness, and eternal life flow to believing sinners freely through the sacrifice of Christ.

That which God confirmed to Abraham in Christ by the gospel that was preached to him cannot be nullified by the law given at Mount Sinai. And that which God gave us in Christ from eternity, before the world began, which has been confirmed to us by the gospel (2 Timothy 1:9-10; Ephesians 1:3-7, 13-14), cannot be nullified by anything that appears in time. 'And this I say, that the covenant, that was confirmed before of God in Christ, the law, which was four hundred and thirty years after, cannot disannul, that it should make the promise of none effect' (v. 17).

'For if the inheritance be of the law, it is no more of promise: but God gave it to Abraham by promise (v. 18). The inheritance Paul speaks of is an eternal inheritance, everlasting life and happiness in heaven. This is the gift of God in, by, and through Christ. It is not gained by obedience to the law, but by the gift of grace. This inheritance of grace includes all the blessings of grace and glory (Ephesians 1:3; 1 Corinthians 1:30-31). Paul is distinctly asserting that this inheritance includes justification and sanctification in Christ, the distinct blessings of grace promised in the covenant to Abraham and his spiritual Seed, that is to all God's elect, both Jews and Gentiles, in Christ, Abraham's Seed.

These bounties of grace do not belong to those who seek them by the deeds of the law. They are not the heirs of the promise (Romans 4:14). These promises are obtained by faith alone, without works (Romans 4:16). And there can never be a mixture of faith and works, of grace and law, of mercy and merit. If salvation comes by promise, it cannot come by law. If it comes by law, it cannot come by promise. Salvation is the free gift of God by grace in Christ, without the works of the law. As John Gill states it, 'God gave it, freely, without any consideration of the works of the law, to Abraham by promise; wherefore justification is not by works, but by the free grace of God, through faith in the righteousness of Christ; and in this way men become heirs according to the hope of eternal life.'

430 Years
The fact that Paul speaks of the space between God's promise to Abraham as being 430 years sometimes causes confusion. There were considerably more than 430 years between the time God's covenant promises were given to Abraham (Genesis 12) and the giving of the law on Sinai (Exodus 20). Actually more than 600 years elapsed between the two events.

Did Paul make a mistake? Is there an error found in the Bible? Of course not! I am certain that Paul understated the space of time on purpose, taking the 430 years from Exodus 12:40-41, which refers to the time of Israel's sojourn in Egypt. He was simply using the event as an illustration. Without question, Paul chose this figure by the direction of God the Holy Spirit. Using this figure, he dates the covenant promise, not back to Abraham alone, but to the last of the patriarchs to whom the Lord successively renewed the promise (Jacob — Genesis 28), lumping them all together as one. By writing this way, he both gives the goats a can to chew on and the sheep something else to rejoice their hearts. Just as Abraham, Isaac, and Jacob were one before God and all blessed with the same covenant blessings, freely and fully by grace alone, so all God's elect are one in Christ and are all blessed with all the blessings of grace in the covenant, because we are one with Christ, our Covenant Head.

God's Covenant

That which Paul obviously has in mind, when he speaks of God's covenant with Abraham and the blessings of it, is the everlasting covenant of grace, so often spoken of in the Book of God (Jeremiah 31; Psalms 89; Hebrews 8; Hebrews 12; Ephesians 1; 2 Timothy 1). John Gill tells us that, 'The covenant of grace is a compact, or agreement made from all eternity among the divine Persons, concerning the salvation of the elect.' It was a contract, a promise, willingly undertaken by the Triune Persons of the Godhead.

This covenant of grace is an eternal covenant. Before there was a star in the sky, before the sun was fixed in its place, before there was an angel in heaven to sing the praises of the triune God, before there was a man on earth made in the image and likeness of God, the everlasting Father determined to have a people for himself, like his only-begotten Son. As he loved his Son, so he loved his people before the world was (John 17:22-24). It was a covenant of pure grace and free mercy, made for God's elect in Christ our Surety (Hebrews 7:22).

These are the words of that covenant as they are given in Scripture: 'Mercy shall be built up forever: thy faithfulness shalt thou establish in the heavens. I have made a covenant with my chosen, I have sworn unto my servant. Thy seed will I establish forever, and build thy throne to all generations. My mercy will I keep for him forevermore, and my covenant shall stand fast with him' (Psalms 89:2-4, 28). The Psalmist declared, 'The mercy of the Lord is from everlasting to everlasting' (103:17).

This covenant of grace, and redemption, and life, was made between the sacred Persons of the blessed Trinity before the world began. Man had nothing to do with it. The foundation of the covenant is the love of God and his sovereign pleasure. The covenant was entirely free. The grace of God is its only cause. This everlasting covenant is the basis of all of God's decrees and works. It is 'his own purpose' according to which he brings all things to pass (Romans 8:28-30). He made the angels to be the servants of those whom he had appointed heirs of salvation. He made the earth as the abode of his elect. He created a race of men to call his people from among them. He ordained the fall of that race in order to show the fulness of his love in redeeming his people from the ruins of the fall (Proverbs 16:4). He gave the law to show us the terror we deserved. He gave his Son into the hands of the law to magnify the law and make it honourable; to satisfy its holy justice, and to display his great love for us in redeeming us. He ordained every step of our lives so that each of his elect might show forth most brilliantly the riches of his grace and glory forever. He sent his Spirit to fetch us to himself.

What does all this mean to believing sinners, to poor, weak, worthless sinners who look to Christ alone for salvation and eternal life? It means, 'All things are yours', for, 'ye are Christ's, and Christ is God's' (1 Corinthians 3:21-23). It means, 'all things work together for good' to you. It means that 'no evil shall happen' to you. It means that you 'shall never perish'. God's covenant encompasses all things for us. I remind you, too, that this is an immutable covenant. It is 'ordered in all things and sure'. God will never break his covenant. Of our God it is written, he is a God 'who keepest covenant' (Nehemiah 9:32).

His faithfulness, which he will never allow to fail, is engaged in the covenant. 'My kindness shall not depart from thee, neither shall the covenant of my peace be removed, saith the Lord that hath mercy on thee' (Isaiah 54:10). 'My covenant will I not break, nor alter the thing that is gone out of my lips' (Psalms 89:34). This covenant is never to give way to another. It was hidden in ages past, under the law, in types and shadows; but it stands forever. God hath 'sent redemption unto his people: He hath commanded his covenant forever: holy and reverend is his name' (Psalms 111:9).

It is just this point for which Paul is arguing in Galatians 3:15-20. In Hebrews 13:20 he calls it 'the everlasting covenant'. The law, as a covenant of works, has waxed old and vanished away. It has been replaced by the full revelation of the covenant of grace, which will continue until the end of the world when Christ shall give up his mediatorial kingdom unto the Father, and God shall be all in all (1 Corinthians 15:24-28).

Wherefore then serveth the law? It was added because of transgressions, till the seed should come to whom the promise was made; and it was ordained by angels in the hand of a mediator. Now a mediator is not a mediator of one, but God is one.

(Galatians 3:19-21)

Chapter 17

Read: Galatians 3:19-21

False teachers crept into the Church at Galatia and convinced many that they must seek to live by the law, that the believer's justification and sanctification were not accomplished by grace alone. They taught we must be saved by grace, by faith in Christ; but we must also keep the law, if we would be saved. Paul boldly and dogmatically asserted that there can be no mixture of law and grace.

Paul could not have stated himself more clearly than he did in Romans 11:6 and Galatians 5:1-4. In those two places, he shows that if you add your works to the grace of God, for justification, for sanctification, or for righteousness of any kind before God, then you deny the grace of God altogether and are lost; are totally ignorant of the grace of God, are without Christ, and are without hope before the Holy Lord God. In Galatians 2:21, having dashed in pieces the notion of mixing law and grace, he makes this bold, dogmatic assertion. 'I do not frustrate the grace of God: for if righteousness come by the law (justifying righteousness or sanctifying righteousness), then Christ is dead in vain'.

He simply could not have used stronger language to state his case. He declares that those who teach that righteousness may be obtained before God by our personal obedience to the law both frustrate the grace of God and assert that Christ died for nothing. That is the background to this passage.

'Wherefore Then Serveth The Law?'

As we have seen, the law was added because of transgressions. These verses of Inspiration tell us the purpose of God's law. Paul, being inspired by the Holy Spirit, anticipated the carping of the legalists who would denounce his doctrine. He knew they would come along and say, 'If the law has nothing to do with the believer, if it has nothing to do with our justification and nothing to do with our sanctification, if it is not to be used as a rule of life, why was it given? What is its use?' That is the question he answers in these verses.

'Added Because Of Transgressions'

The law of God, (the ten commandments and the legal precepts of worship, civil government, and daily life given in the Old Testament), was never intended to be a means of righteousness, a means of grace, or a means of salvation. It was 'added because of transgressions' (v. 19), that is, it was given to reveal and specify man's transgressions, to show what sin is and measure man's shortcomings against it. It was not given as a code of moral ethics. It was not given as the believer's rule of life. It was not given as a motive for Christian service. It was not given as a measure of sanctification. It was not given to be the grounds of our assurance. It was not given as a basis for reward in heaven. It was never the intent, purpose, and use of the law to make sinners holy, righteous, and just before God. The Book of God is crystal clear in its language in this regard. Believers are not under the law, but under grace (Romans 6:14-15). It is impossible to be under both. We are dead to the law (Romans 7:4). 'Christ is the end of the law' (Romans 10:4).

The purpose of God's holy law is to identify and expose man's sin, shutting him up to Christ alone for acceptance with God. It is written, 'Now we know that what things soever the law saith, it saith to them who are under the law: that every mouth may be stopped, and all the world may become guilty before God' (Romans 3:19). 'Moreover the law entered, that the offence might abound. But where sin abounded, grace did much more abound' (Romans 5:20).

Before anyone is converted, he must be convinced of his sin and guilt. We preach the holy law of God to convince men of their sin. Before anyone is given the newness of life in Jesus Christ, he must be slain by the law. The law is God's deep cutting plow, by which he breaks up the fallow ground of a man's heart and conscience, and prepares the soil for the gospel. This plowing of a sinner's heart is a painful and difficult work, but must be done.

'The Seed'

Look at the next line in verse 19. The law was given until 'the Seed should come to whom the promise was made'. The Seed spoken of here is Christ. The promise spoken of is the promise God the Father made to God the Son before the world began. That promise was the promised gift of grace, salvation, and eternal life by the Holy Spirit to his elect. It was a promise made on condition of Christ's obedience and death, upon condition of righteousness established by him for us as our Substitute.

I am not guessing about this. The context declares it. The Mosaic law given at Mount Sinai was given to Israel in the hands of a mediator who was but a man. But the promise was given to Christ our Mediator from God our Father; and these two are one God. Look at the scriptures. That is the meaning of Paul's words here in verse 20, 'Now a mediator is not a mediator of one, but God is one.' God the Father promised eternal life to his elect before the world began. But he made the promise to Christ as our Covenant Surety (Titus 1:1-3). We who believe have obtained this promise of eternal life in Christ because the Lord Jesus Christ purchased it and effectually obtained it for the seed of Abraham; Abraham's true, spiritual seed (Galatians 3:13-14; Hebrews 9:12; 2:16).

'To Whom The Promise Was Made'

The law was not given to makes us righteous, but to shut us up to Christ. The law of God, set forth in holy scripture, concludes all under sin. We are all by birth, by nature, by choice, and by practice under sin (Romans 3:19-23). We are under sin's dominion, corruption, penalty, and curse. The reason for this is, 'That the promise (the same promise he has been discussing throughout the chapter, the promise of grace, salvation, and eternal life) by faith of Jesus Christ might be given to them that believe.'

Read that last sentence carefully and understand the gospel: grace, salvation, and eternal life come to chosen sinners upon the ground of and because of the faith, faithfulness, or faithful obedience of Jesus Christ as our Substitute.

It was Christ alone who brought in everlasting righteousness for us. It was Christ alone who redeemed us. It was Christ alone who put away our sins. It was Christ alone who made atonement for us by satisfying the justice of God with his own blood. It was Christ alone who, with his own blood, obtained eternal redemption for us. Our faith in him has no part in the accomplishment of these things!

What does faith do? Nothing! Faith receives. Believing God, every sinner who believes has been given grace, salvation, and eternal life by

God the Holy Spirit because God the Father promised it and God the Son purchased it! 'Salvation is of The Lord' (Jonah 2:9).

Before faith came, that is before we came to trust Christ, before God gave us faith in his Son, 'we were kept under the law'. As we read in Ephesians 2:3 we 'were by nature children of wrath', just like everyone else. Though we were justified from eternity by God's decree and justified at Calvary by Christ's blood atonement, we knew nothing about it. We lived as wrathful children, hating God, under a sense of guilt, as cursed, condemned sinners, without hope. Our first convictions, our first thoughts toward God, filled us with terror. The law condemned us, condemned us justly. When the law came, sin revived and I died! That is what Paul said (Romans 7:9).

The Law's Purpose

The law was given, not as a system by which sinners should seek to be saved, not as a rule of conduct by which believer's are to measure their spiritual might and superiority over others; but it was added as a temporary thing to restrain wickedness by the threat of punishment, until Christ came and brought in the fulness of God's covenant promise.

The law was given long after the promise of eternal life was made (Titus 1:2). It was given to reveal and expose the sin and guilt of men, to constantly remind and make men conscious of their sin. The law was given at Sinai to show sinners their need of a Substitute and to reveal Christ, the Messiah, the Redeemer, in types and pictures until he came (Hebrews 10:1-9). Even as God gave his law on Mount Sinai, he graciously showed Christ as the Mediator between God and men, typically, in Moses' mediation. Moses stood as the mediator between sinful Israel and the holy Lord God (Exodus 20:18-19). The angels of God were messengers and instruments God used in the giving of the law.

Christ Our Mediator

As Moses was mediator between God and Israel on Sinai, the Lord Jesus Christ, our God-man Saviour, is the Mediator between God and men (1 Timothy 2:5; Hebrews 8:6; 9:15; 12:24; Acts 4:12). A mediator has to do with more than one party. There can be no mediator if only one person is involved. Yet, God is one; he is the one offended, standing off at a distance, giving the law in the hands of a mediator, revealing their alienation. Therefore, justification cannot be expected through the law. Someone must step in, take up our cause, and satisfy the law for us, or we must perish. That Someone is the Lord Jesus Christ, the Son of God, our

Mediator and Surety. He took up our cause from eternity, assumed total responsibility for our souls before the world began, and has sworn to his Father that he will bring his own elect safe to glory in the perfection of his righteousness and holiness (John 10:16; Hebrews 2:13), according to the terms of the covenant (Ephesians 1:3-6); presenting us before the presence of his glory holy and without blame (Jude 24-25).

No Law Righteousness
'Is the law then against the promises of God? God forbid: for if there had been a law given which could have given life, verily righteousness should have been by the law' (v. 21). What a plain statement this is! It is utterly irrefutable. The law, which was given by Moses, cannot be contrary to the promise of eternal life to God's elect before the world began. It is absurd, monstrously absurd, to imagine that God would have sacrificed his darling Son for nothing. If righteousness could be obtained by us doing something God would never have sacrificed his Son at Calvary to bring in righteousness for us!

But the scripture hath concluded all under sin, that the promise by faith of Jesus Christ might be given to them that believe. But before faith came, we were kept under the law, shut up unto the faith which should afterwards be revealed. Wherefore the law was our schoolmaster to bring us unto Christ, that we might be justified by faith. But after that faith is come, we are no longer under a schoolmaster.

(Galatians 3:22-25)

Chapter 18

Read: Galatians 3:22-25

What Scripture Has Concluded

The whole volume of holy scripture and particularly the killing letter of the law of God, declare that all men, all that is in us by nature, and all that is done by us are under the power, dominion, and guilt of sin. All the sons and daughters of fallen Adam are defiled, sinful, and guilty.

Paul's language is inclusive of all things relating to all men: all the members of our bodies; all the faculties of our souls; all the thoughts of our minds; all the emotions of our hearts; all the intentions of our wills; all our choices; all our works; all our services to God and men; even all our best works of righteousness are but 'filthy rags'. Everything about us is sinful and polluted. The Word of God declares that we are guilty and shuts us up as prisoners under the sentence of death, without hope in ourselves.

It is necessary that such a conclusion be made, recorded, understood and accepted by sinners in order, 'that the promise by faith of Jesus Christ might be given to them that believe'. The promise of faith is the promise of eternal life and salvation, of everlasting righteousness and the never ending smile of divine approval. All that is included in the promise belongs to all who believe.

It is not our believing that fulfilled God's covenant promise and brought
in that blessed righteousness by which we now stand before him in life.
The promise is given to all who believe. But the promise was fulfilled and
comes to us 'by faith of Jesus Christ'. It was Christ to whom the promise
was made as our Surety in the everlasting covenant, upon condition of
his obedience unto death as our Substitute. It is Christ who obtained the
promise by his faithful fulfilment of his covenant engagements as our
Surety (Hebrews 10:5-14).

Whose Faith Has Come?

What faith is Paul talking about in verse 23? Whose faith is this? Is it
yours? Is it mine? The faith that came by which we were delivered from
the curse of God's holy law, by which we were justified, is the 'faith of
Jesus Christ' spoken of in verse 22. It is this, 'faith of Jesus Christ', that is
revealed to us by the gospel. Our faith in Christ is not revealed to us, it is
given to us and worked in us by the mighty operations of God the Holy
Spirit (Ephesians 1:19-20; 2:8-9; Colossians 1:12-14).

When God the Holy Spirit comes to chosen, redeemed sinners in the
saving power of his omnipotent grace, he convinces them of all that
Christ accomplished by his faithful obedience as our Substitute. When
he reveals Christ in a person, he convinces him that his sin has been put
away by Christ's atonement, that righteousness has been brought in by
Christ's obedience, and that justice has been satisfied by Christ's blood
(John 16:8-11). And the sinner, being convinced of these things, trusts
Christ.

Shut Up To Faith

Why? The Spirit of God tells us. We were thus (by the terror of the law in
our consciences damning us) shut up to Christ. Look at it in verses 23-24.
The law's purpose, function, and use is to bring sinners to Christ. Once it
has served that purpose it has no other function. That is not my opinion,
interpretation, or theological view; it is exactly what God the Holy Spirit
tells us in verse 25, 'But after that faith is come, we are no longer under a
schoolmaster.'

What does that mean? It means exactly what you think it means. It
means spiritually what Martin Luther King proclaimed with the passage
of the Civil Rights Bill. 'Free at last! Free at last! Thank God Almighty, I'm
free at last!' It is just the same with the law. Once the sinner has come to
Christ, he is free from the law. The law has no more dominion over him
(Romans 6:14-15; 7:4; 10:4).

'Our Schoolmaster'

Be sure to note that our translators put the words 'to bring us' in italicized letters in verse 24, to call our attention to the fact that these words were added by them to make the sentence read more smoothly and that there are no corresponding words in the original language of the text. The verse would be more accurately translated; 'Wherefore the law was our schoolmaster unto (or until) Christ, that we might be justified by faith.'

Everyone in Galatia would have understood exactly what Paul meant by comparing the law to a schoolmaster. A schoolmaster was a servant to whom a man would commit the care and education of his children until they reached maturity. It was his responsibility to teach and protect the children and see to it that they got their education. It was the law's purpose, like a schoolmaster, to direct God's elect to Christ and make sure they get to Christ. It was our schoolmaster until Christ came and fulfilled it by his faithful obedience to it and satisfaction of it. Once that was done the schoolmaster's service ended (Romans 10:4).

Now that the righteousness of the law has been fulfilled by Christ's obedience in life as our Representative, and the justice of the law has been fulfilled by Christ's satisfaction of it in his death (Romans 4:25), we can be and are 'justified by faith'. Because justification has been accomplished by Christ in the court of heaven, we can now be justified in the court of our own consciences by faith in Christ.

Faith looks away from self to Christ. Looking to Christ we see our justification fully accomplished in him, and we are justified by him. Trusting Christ, we receive complete, final, full justification in him and have peace with God in him 'by whom we have now received the atonement' (Romans 4:25-5:12, 18).

Since faith has come (v. 25), that is to say, since Christ has come, we are no longer under the law. It was the law's purpose, like a schoolmaster, to direct God's elect in the Mosaic age to Christ and make sure they got to Christ. The law was the children's schoolmaster until Christ came and fulfilled it by his faithful obedience to it and satisfaction of it. Once that was done the schoolmaster's service ended, the schoolmaster's useful service came to an end (Romans 10:4).

The Faith Of Christ

The scriptures speak of both 'the faith of Christ' and our 'faith in Christ'. In Galatians 3:19 Paul tells us that the law of God given at Mount Sinai was given for a specific, designated period of time; 'It was added because of transgressions till the Seed (Christ) should come to whom the promise (the promise of God's blessing, grace, and salvation) was made'. In verse

21 the apostle assures us that the law of God given at Sinai is not in any way against, or contrary to God's covenant promise of salvation by Christ, and that it was never intended to produce righteousness. The law is, as Paul puts it in 2 Corinthians 3:7, 'the ministration of death'. It has nothing to do with life. It cannot produce righteousness; 'I do not frustrate the grace of God: for if righteousness come by the law, then Christ is dead in vain' (Galatians 2:21).

The scriptures declare that we are justified 'by the faith of Jesus Christ'. That means that our justification was totally accomplished by Christ, that it was accomplished outside our experience, altogether without us, by the faith (faithful obedience) of the Lord Jesus Christ as our Substitute. Paul uses this phrase, 'the faith of Christ', seven times in his writings (Romans 3:22; Galatians 2:16, 20; 3:22; Ephesians 3:12; Philippians 3:9).

Every time he speaks of justification accomplished for us, he uses this phrase or its equivalent 'the faith of Jesus Christ'. We have been conditioned to think of faith only in connection with ourselves. We believe in Christ. We trust the Son of God. 'He that believeth on the Son hath everlasting life' (John 3:36). When we read in the Book of God about 'the faith of Christ' we automatically think, 'That must just be an odd way of saying "faith in Christ".'

Correct Translation

That is exactly what the vast majority of the commentaries do with this phrase. They tell us the words, 'faith of Christ', really means, 'faith in Christ'. These words, 'the faith of Christ', are commonly treated as though they were a mistranslation of the Greek text; but they are not a mistranslation.[1] I have checked every one of them carefully. Our translation is correct. Yet, almost every modern English translation (those so called 'great improvements' upon the old, archaic King James Version) mistranslates this phrase and make it read, 'faith in Christ'. I do not think that the mistranslations were made accidentally!

---

[1] Galatians 3:22, 'by faith of Jesus Christ'. This phrase, as elsewhere (Romans 3:22; Galatians 2:15-16; Philippians 3:9), is genitive in the Greek. It is Christ's own faith (faithfulness) that is meant: the faith belonging to and emanating from Christ, but ours by trusting in him, the faithful One. This is the faith that is the gift of God (Ephesians 2:8). We are saved by his life which includes his faith, as well as by his death (Romans 5:10). For his life was a life of faith lived for us, just as his death was the death of death endured for us. We died in him as we live in him: as our Substitute, Surety and Mediator in all things pertaining to righteousness and salvation. Christ's faith must prevail if my faith is not to ail.

We are told by the commentators and led by the modern translations to believe that the phrase is really just an unusual way of saying 'faith in Christ' and that it really refers to our faith in Christ. Such recklessness in handling the Word of God, be it deliberate or otherwise, completely alters the meaning of holy scripture.

Clear Distinction

When Paul speaks of our faith in Christ and of the faith of Christ as distinct things, the distinction is clear and unmistakable. When he speaks of our faith, it is obvious (Romans 3:25, 28; 4:5; Galatians 3:26; Colossians 1:4). There's no ambiguity at all. In these, and the dozens of other passages like them, there is no question about whose faith Paul is referring to. He is talking about our faith. And when he draws a distinction between our faith in Christ and the faith of Christ, the distinction is equally obvious (Romans 3:21-22; Galatians 2:15-16; 3:22; Philippians 3:9).

Paul is not simply declaring our faith in Christ twice in different ways. He is not being repetitious. Not at all! When he speaks of 'the faith of Jesus Christ' he is talking about Christ's faith. When he speaks of our faith in Christ, he is talking about our faith. Both are vital. We could never be saved by our faith in Christ were it not for the faith of Christ; and we can never be saved by the faith of Christ until we have faith in Christ. Yes, we must have faith in Christ; and our faith in Christ is the result of 'the faith of Christ' as our Saviour while he was in this world.

Our Faithful Surety

'The faith of Jesus Christ', what exactly does that mean? When the Holy Spirit speaks about 'the faith of Jesus Christ', he is referring to our Saviour's faithful performance of all the Father's will as our covenant Surety, Substitute, and Redeemer. 'The faith of Jesus Christ' refers to our Saviour's fidelity as Jehovah's righteous Servant. It speaks of his faithful performance, in our place as our Substitute, of all that was necessary for the salvation of God's elect. 'The faith of Jesus Christ' refers to his faithfulness in accomplishing all that which the Father entrusted to his hands as our Mediator (Ephesians 1:12).

Faith And Faithfulness

When the Word of God speaks about 'the faith of Christ', the word 'faith' speaks both of our Saviour's trust in God as the perfect man and of his faithfulness to God as his Servant. It speaks not only of trust, but also of loyalty and fidelity.

We see a clear example of the word faith being used this way in Romans 3:3-4, 'For what if some did not believe? shall their unbelief make the faith of God without effect? God forbid: yea, let God be true, but every man a liar; as it is written, That thou mightest be justified in thy sayings, and mightest overcome when thou art judged.'

When Paul speaks here of 'the faith of God', it is obvious that he is referring to the truthfulness, veracity, fidelity, and faithfulness of God. In fact, the word commonly translated 'faith' in the New Testament is translated 'fidelity' in Titus 2:10. There, when Paul exhorted servants to be faithful in all things to their masters, 'showing all good fidelity', the word could be translated, 'showing all good faith'. It is in this sense that he uses the phrase 'the faith of Jesus Christ'. Our justification was accomplished and eternal redemption was obtained for us by Christ's faithfulness in doing all that he came here to do for us, according to the will of God (Matthew 1:21; Hebrews 10:1-14).

Our Kinsman Redeemer

As portrayed in the book of Ruth, the Lord Jesus Christ is our Kinsman Redeemer. As Boaz did for Ruth all that she could not do for herself, what we could not do for ourselves Christ has done for us as our Substitute and Saviour; as our Kinsman Redeemer. He took our place before the law of God, assumed total responsibility for us, obeyed the law perfectly, bringing in everlasting righteousness, and died under the penalty of the law, satisfying all its holy demands by his death upon the cursed tree, when he was made to be sin for us.

Redemption, as described in the law and illustrated in the book of Ruth, required two things on the part of the redeemer. First, the redeemer had to be able and willing to redeem. Second, he had to faithfully perform all that was required by the law to buy back the lost inheritance of his needy kinsman.

The one needing redemption was totally dependent upon the faithfulness of the kinsman redeemer for deliverance. Ruth laid herself down at Boaz's feet, looking to him alone for everything her soul required. And she found all in him. He would not rest until he had performed the thing.

So it was with us. The debt and penalty of our sins was one from which we could not escape. The righteousness required by God's holy law we could not perform: 'By the works of the law shall no flesh be justified'. None of our works, no matter how well intentioned, no matter how well performed, can propitiate God's justice and justify us in his sight. We desperately need and must have a Redeemer, One who is able and willing to do everything required by God's holy law and justice for us. We must have a Redeemer who is able and willing, but more, we must have a Redeemer who has actually stepped out onto the stage of time and faithfully performed all the work for us. 'Behold the Man!' Here is our mighty Boaz, the Lord Jesus Christ, the Son of God. 'But when the fulness of the time was come, God sent forth his Son, made of a woman, made under the law, to redeem them that were under the law, that we might receive the adoption of sons' (Galatians 4:4-5). Thanks be to God for 'the faith of Jesus Christ' and the redemption, justification and salvation he accomplished by his faithfulness as our Substitute and Surety!

The Verses
Look at the passages in which Paul uses this tremendous phrase, 'The faith of Jesus Christ', and rejoice in the glorious good news of the gospel – redemption obtained and justification accomplished by the faithful obedience of Christ as the sinner's Substitute.

'But now the righteousness of God without the law is manifested, being witnessed by the law and the prophets; Even the righteousness of God which is by faith of Jesus Christ unto all and upon all them that believe: for there is no difference' (Romans 3:21-22).

'We who are Jews by nature, and not sinners of the Gentiles, Knowing that a man is not justified by the works of the law, but by the faith of Jesus Christ, even we have believed in Jesus Christ, that we might be justified by the faith of Christ, and not by the works of the law: for by the works of the law shall no flesh be justified'. (Galatians 2:15-16).

'But the scripture hath concluded all under sin, that the promise by faith of Jesus Christ might be given to them that believe' (Galatians 3:22).

'And be found in him, not having mine own righteousness, which is of the law, but that which is through the faith of Christ, the righteousness which is of God by faith' (Philippians 3:9).

Free Salvation
The 'righteousness of God', justification, the promise of justification unto eternal life, does not come and could never come through something we do. Never! 'Salvation is of the Lord'. It has been accomplished and comes to sinners by 'the faith of Jesus Christ' (Ephesians 1:11-12; 3:8-12). It cost our Saviour dear; but the salvation he gives is a totally free salvation. In him 'we have obtained an inheritance, being predestinated according to the purpose of him who worketh all things after the counsel of his own will: That we should be to the praise of his glory, who first trusted in

Christ.' The Father trusted his darling Son as our Surety from eternity and he was faithful to that trust.

Truly, the riches of Christ are 'unsearchable riches'. By his faithful obedience unto death in our room and stead, every sinner who trusts him has been made completely worthy of God's everlasting approval in heaven's eternal glory, and shall have it. Let us give thanks to our great God for such grace by such a Saviour (Colossians 1:12-14). The life we now have and enjoy in Christ, that eternal life which is God's free gift to us, comes to us 'by the faith of the Son of God' (Galatians 2:19-20).

Our Faith In Christ

Does all of this mean that sinners must not be called upon to believe in Christ? Does this mean that 'faith in Christ' is unnecessary? Of course not. Our 'faith in Christ' is every bit as necessary for our eternal salvation as 'the faith of Christ' as our Saviour. The scriptures speak just as often and just as forcefully about our 'faith in Christ' as they do of 'the faith of Christ' as our Surety and Mediator (Acts 3:16; 24:24; Romans 3:25; Galatians 3:26; Ephesians 1:15; Colossians 1:4; 2:5).

We call upon sinners everywhere to believe on the Lord Jesus Christ, and do so with this word from God Almighty. This is a sure thing. It is sure and certain. 'He that believeth on the Son hath everlasting life' (John 3:35). We say to sinners everywhere exactly what Paul said to the Philippian jailor when he came trembling and fell down at the apostle's feet crying, 'What must I do to be saved?' 'Believe on the Lord Jesus Christ, and thou shalt be saved' (Acts 16:30-31).

If you trust Christ, you now live 'by the faith of the Son of God' who loved you and gave himself for you. You have redemption, righteousness, justification, and eternal life. You have everything included in that magnificently huge word 'Salvation!' It was all obtained for you by 'the faith of Jesus Christ'. Even your faith in him, and mine, were obtained for us by 'the faith of Jesus Christ'. No wonder Paul speaks as he does in 1 Corinthians 1:30-31. 'Of him are ye in Christ Jesus, who of God is made unto us wisdom, and righteousness, and sanctification, and redemption: that, according as it is written, He that glorieth, let him glory in the Lord.'

For ye are all the children of God by faith in Christ Jesus. For as many of you as have been baptised into Christ have put on Christ. There is neither Jew nor Greek, there is neither bond nor free, there is neither male nor female: for ye are all one in Christ Jesus. And if ye *be* Christ's, then are ye Abraham's seed, and heirs according to the promise.

(Galatians 3:26-29)

Chapter 19

Read: Galatians 3:26-29

Faith Alone

Salvation comes to sinners, in its entirety, by faith in Christ, by faith alone, without the works of the law. Is that, or is it not the doctrine of holy scripture? 'For ye are all the children of God by faith in Christ Jesus.' Paul took the Galatians at their word. Because they professed faith in Christ, he charitably assumed that their profession was genuine. Therefore, he says, 'Ye are the children of God by faith in Christ'.

Paul is not suggesting that our adoption into the family of God is the result of our believing, not at all. It is just the other way around. Our faith in Christ is the result of our adoption. We were predestinated by God into the adoption before the foundation of the world (Ephesians 1:4-5). It was our adoption that sent the Holy Spirit to us in effectual, regenerating grace. Our adoption in election was the cause of Christ's atonement and the Spirit's call (Galatians 4:3-7; 1 John 3:1).

Baptised Into Christ

Paul is not implying in verse 27 that there were some in the church who were baptised and some who were not, or that there were some Christians who submitted to the gospel ordinance of immersion in the name of Christ and some who did not. His language here is simply that there might be some of them, who though baptised in water, yet did not know Christ. John Gill explains the text correctly, saying, 'Those who are truly and rightly baptised, who are proper subjects of it, and to whom it is administered in a proper manner, are baptised into Christ.'

Neither is Paul saying that by baptism we are brought into union with Christ, but into communion with him. When baptism is an act of faith in and obedience to Christ, believers are baptised in the name of Christ, by the authority of Christ, according to the doctrine of Christ, in obedience to the command of Christ, into the body of Christ, and in hope of the resurrection with Christ.

And all who have truly been baptised into Christ have put on Christ, both before we were baptised and when we were baptised. Before we were baptised we put him on as the Lord our righteousness by faith. We put him on as our robe of righteousness. When we were baptised we put on Christ by public profession, declaring him to be our Lord and King, declaring ourselves to be his voluntary servants forever, resolving to walk with him in the newness of life. 'The allusion', Gill suggests, 'is to the priests putting off their common clothes, and then bathing or dipping themselves in water, and putting on the garments of the priesthood before they entered on their service.'

Paul is not teaching that we get to be in Christ by the act of water baptism, or that God's elect are mysteriously baptised into Christ by the Holy Spirit. The Word of God nowhere teaches either of those things. The simple meaning of this statement is that all who are rightly baptised, that is baptised as believers, looking to Christ alone for all grace and salvation were baptised into Christ and have put on Christ symbolically, professing themselves to be his. All who are immersed in the waters of baptism as believers thereby publicly confess that they are his and that they are one with him.

Believer's baptism is that which our Lord Jesus commands of all his disciples. It is 'the answer of a good conscience toward God' (1 Peter 3:21). Baptism is rightly performed and its end properly answered when a person, being conscious that it is the ordinance of Christ and his duty to submit to it, does so upon profession of his faith in Christ in obedience to his command; confessing him as Lord and Saviour, and symbolically confessing his union with Christ in his death, burial, and resurrection as our Substitute (Romans 6:3-4; Colossians 2:11-12). By this public confession of faith, all who are baptised are united in one body, the body of Christ, in one cause, the glory of Christ, and to one another. It is this union of faith in the body of Christ, by this 'one baptism', that Paul uses in Ephesians 4:3-6 as a reason why we should ever endeavour 'to keep the unity of the Spirit in the bond of peace'.

One In Christ
Now all who are in Christ are one in him (v. 28). In Christ all social, economic, racial barriers are dissolved. The only place in the world where race and place make no difference is in Christ; in his church. Grace alone can make sinful men and women truly one. God's elect really are truly one in Christ.

In verse 29 the apostle brings his argument to a tremendous conclusion 'And if ye be Christ's', nothing else really matters. If you belong to Christ by the Father's election, the Son's redemption, the Spirit's call, and your own faith in him, if you believe on the Son of God, all is well. If not you're going to hell. 'And if ye be Christ's, then are ye Abraham's seed'. This is what that means: if you believe on the Lord Jesus Christ, you are the object of God's love, the recipient of his grace, and 'heirs according to the promise'. If you believe on the Lord Jesus Christ, you are God's forever and he is yours forever! You are heirs of God and joint heirs with Jesus Christ, 'according to the promise', according to the promise of eternal life which God, who cannot lie, made to his Son before the world began!

The Children Of God
Under the legal Mosaic dispensation there were many distinctions. The Jews were distinguished, above all nations of the world, as God's chosen people, to whom alone he had given the revelation of his Word. Masters were more highly favoured than servants. And men were more greatly honoured than women, even in the worship of God. But with the coming of this new, gospel dispensation, all these things were changed.

This change was very difficult for many in the early church to accept, just as it is difficult for many of our day to accept. For many it is very difficult to realize that God no longer blesses the nation of Israel above other nations in the world. They cannot accept the fact that Israel as a nation has been forever cast off by God because of her unbelief. Many suppose that Israel is still the chosen nation of God.

For others, it is extremely difficult to accept the fact that all of God's children are equally his sons and daughters. Some suppose that the Christians of the gospel age will have a peculiar advantage over the believers of the Old Testament. Others are of the opinion that some Christians will have greater blessings in heaven than their redeemed brethren.

These erroneous opinions arise because of a failure to understand that all the blessings of God in Christ Jesus are free grace gifts procured for all of the elect by the blood of the Saviour. Our standing before God is not one of merit, but of grace. Our rewards are not because of our efforts, but by Christ's obedience unto death as our Substitute. They are things earned and bought for us by our Redeemer. This is true of saints in the Old Testament as well as those of the New. The reward of Abraham's faith is Jesus Christ, and he alone is the reward of our faith.

All believers are the children of God. We all have one heavenly Father. We are all redeemed by one great Redeemer. We all have one Elder Brother – Christ. We are all born again, sealed and indwelt by one Holy Spirit, our blessed Comforter. All who are taught of God live by 'one faith'. We are all married to one Husband – the Lord Jesus Christ. All believers make up one singular body of Christ, 'the fulness of him that filleth all in all'. We are one church universal (John 10:16; Ephesians 5:25; Hebrews 12:23).

Paul tells us that we are 'the children of God'. We are God's children by adoption (Galatians 4:6-7; Ephesians 1:5; 1 John 3:1). Every believer possesses all the rights and privileges of full-grown sons. We were adopted as sons in eternity in electing love, by the free and sovereign grace of our God, and brought into the enjoyment of adoption when God the Holy Spirit gave us faith in Christ.

We are 'the children of God by faith in Christ Jesus'. Here Paul's emphasis does not lie in the eternal act of God, but in our receiving God's gracious gift by faith. Faith does not make us God's children; it simply receives the gift of sonship (John 1:12). The Holy Spirit bears witness with our spirits that we are the sons of God when he gives us faith in Christ (Galatians 4:6). In adoption we receive the title 'sons of God'.

Faith in Christ does not make us the children of God. That is God's work alone. God the Father predestinated his elect to the adoption of children, giving us all the blessings of adoption in the covenant of grace, before the world began. God the Son, our all-glorious Christ, made a way for us to receive and enjoy this incalculable boon of grace by redeeming us at Calvary. Because we were adopted in eternity and redeemed at Calvary, God the Holy Spirit, as the Spirit of adoption, giving us faith in Christ, declares our sonship and thereby declares our freedom from the law.

As we have seen, Paul compares the Jews of the Mosaic age to children still under a schoolmaster, and believers in this gospel age to children who have reached the age of maturity. We are no longer children under the law as our schoolmaster, but full-grown children, led and taught by the Spirit of God. Our Lord Jesus said, quoting Isaiah 54:13, 'They shall be all taught of God' (John 6:45; Jeremiah 31:34). Being taught of God, we no longer need the law as our schoolmaster (Hebrews 8:10; 10:16).

One Church

The church of God is one. All true believers are one body in Christ. We ought always to defend and uphold the local assembly. It is the privilege and duty of God's people to be a part of a New Testament church. But we must never exalt any local church on earth to that glorious position of the church universal. All of God's children, of every age and time, are members of the church, which is his body; the family of God (Ephesians 1:22-23). In Jesus Christ we are one. This is what our Saviour prayed for and what he accomplished when he tore down the middle wall of partition between us. If we are one in Christ with all other believing men and women we ought to behave as one.

In this age of 'political correctness' and 'multiculturalism' almost everyone gives lip-service to the notion that all men are one and pretends that he is free of prejudice. But it is nothing more than lip-service. Every nation in the Western world has tried, for the past fifty years, to legislate social oneness, abolishing racial and social barriers between men. But it has not worked. Though almost everyone pretends otherwise, the barriers are bigger and the racial and social prejudices in society are worse than ever.

There is only one place in the universe where the colour of a person's skin, the measure of his wealth or poverty, the amount of his education or lack of education, is absolutely irrelevant. That place is the church and kingdom of God. This passage does not tell us that these distinctions cease to exist when a sinner is converted by the grace of God. They do exist. Black people do not cease to be black when God saves them; and white people do not cease to be white. Men do not cease to be males when they are born of God; and women do not cease to be females. What Galatians 3:26-29 does teach is this; in Christ those things that naturally separate people no longer matter. In Christ we are all one. In Christ all the social, racial, sexual, and even continental distinctions lose all significance (Colossians 3:11).

All God's elect are one with Christ and one in Christ. All are equal before God in him. All are accepted in the Beloved; only in the Beloved; fully in the Beloved, and equally in the Beloved. And all have an equal inheritance in him, secured by the blood with which he obtained eternal redemption for us.

In this third chapter of Galatians Paul is showing us the advantages of this gospel dispensation over the Mosaic age. Under the gospel dispensation we enjoy a clearer revelation of divine grace and mercy than the Jews did under the Old Testament economy. More than this, we are also freed from the state of bondage under the law and the terror it imposed. In the gospel age we are no longer treated as children who are minors, but as full-grown sons. And being sons of full age, we are granted greater freedoms and privileges than those of the old dispensation. In the verses before us Paul shows us our privileges as the children of God.

No Social Distinctions

There are certain duties to be performed in the body of Christ. Because of this, there are some distinctions in performance. Pastors are given to be spiritual teachers and rulers in the church (Ephesians 4:11; Hebrews 13:7, 17). Deacons are given to serve the carnal, material needs of the church. Each member, Jew and Gentile, male and female, black and white, has his proper function in his own realm of responsibility. Yet, there are no class distinctions to be permitted in the body of Christ. In Christ the old worldly lines of separation are all blotted out. All who are in Christ are one in Christ and equal before God, possessing one character, accepted in one way, belonging to one family, under one head – Christ, and equally entitled to all the blessings of grace and privileges of sonship through him. All God's church is one person, as it were, 'one new man' (Ephesians 2:15), of which Christ is the head. All, without regard to race, are blended into one whole. That is the meaning of Paul's words in verse 28, 'There is neither Jew nor Greek, there is neither bond nor free, there is neither male nor female: for ye are all one in Christ Jesus.'

Abraham's Seed

Since we are Christ's, the Father's gift to him, the purchase of his own blood, his by the power of his grace, making us willing to give up ourselves to him; since Christ dwells in our hearts by faith, all who are born of God are 'Abraham's seed' (v. 29). Obviously, faith in Christ does not make us Abraham's natural seed. Rather, we are Abraham's spiritual seed, the seed that should come, to whom the promises were made, (Galatians 3:16, 19). All who believe on the Lord Jesus Christ make up that one 'holy nation' and 'royal priesthood' (1 Peter 2:5-9) called, 'the Israel of God' (Galatians 6:16). Throughout the whole world God owns no other nation as his own.

Being Abraham's seed, we are 'heirs according to the promise'. All who are born of God are the children of the promise, which are counted for the seed. All who are born of God are the promised seed, the redeemed seed (Psalms 22:30; Isaiah 53:10-11; Hebrews 2:10), and the righteous seed (Romans 9:7-8). They are all, according to the promise made to Abraham and his spiritual Seed, heirs of the blessings of the grace of life, and of the eternal inheritance, 'heirs of God and joint-heirs with Christ'.

All the blessings of God bestowed upon Christ as our Mediator and covenant Head, when he ascended to glory after his resurrection, belong to all who are in him. In Christ, by his blood atonement and the imputation of his righteousness, we are made worthy of this great honour. Yes, our great God has made us 'meet to be partakers of the inheritance of the saints' (Colossians 1:12).

The foundation of this union of believers is the blood of Christ (1 Corinthians 3; Ephesians 2). If we are one in reality, let us demonstrate oneness in Spirit (Philippians 2:1-4). May God our Father give us grace to 'walk worthy of the vocation wherewith (we) are called, With all lowliness and meekness, with longsuffering, forbearing one another in love; Endeavouring to keep the unity of the Spirit in the bond of peace. There is one body, and one Spirit, even as ye are called in one hope of your calling; One Lord, one faith, one baptism, One God and Father of all, who is above all, and through all, and in you all' (Ephesians 4:1-6).

Blest be the tie that binds
Our hearts in Christian love!
The fellowship of kindred minds
Is like to that above.

Before our Father's throne
We pour our ardent payers;
Our fears, our hopes, our aims are one,
Our comforts and our cares.

We share our mutual woes,
Our mutual burdens bear;
And often for each other flows
The sympathizing tear.

When we asunder part
It gives us inward pain;
But we shall still be joined in heart,
And hope to meet again.

John Fawcett

Now I say, That the heir, as long as he is a child, differeth nothing from a servant, though he be lord of all; But is under tutors and governors until the time appointed of the father. Even so we, when we were children, were in bondage under the elements of the world: But when the fulness of the time was come, God sent forth his Son, made of a woman, made under the law, To redeem them that were under the law, that we might receive the adoption of sons. And because ye are sons, God hath sent forth the Spirit of his Son into your hearts, crying, Abba, Father. Wherefore thou art no more a servant, but a son; and if a son, then an heir of God through Christ.

(Galatians 4:1-7)

Chapter 20

Read: Galatians 4:1-7

Adoption Accomplished

In the passage before us the Holy Spirit has given us an inspired commentary on that statement made by the apostle John, 'Beloved, now are we the sons of God'. Here Paul is asserting the great truth of our adoption into God's family and all the privileges associated with our adoption. In the Old Testament, before Christ came, God's people were like minor children, under the law of Moses as a schoolmaster. Now that Christ has come, fulfilled the law, and given us his Spirit, the Spirit of adoption, the church in this gospel age is as children who have come of age and entered into their maturity. We have entered into 'the glorious liberty of the children of God' (Romans 8:21), which shall be fully enjoyed in the resurrection.

There are many who try to place a yoke of legal servitude upon the people of God, which none of us can bear. The apostle Paul was anxious that we should serve God, but not as fearful slaves. Rather, he would have us to serve God as loving sons. Here he is showing us that we are no longer under the bondage of the law, but in the liberty of the gospel. Let us then forsake the law and cling to Christ. Poet William Cowper wrote:

No strength of nature can suffice
To serve the Lord aright;
And what she has she misapplies,
For want of clearer light.

How long beneath the law I lay
In bondage and distress!
I toiled the precept to obey,
But toiled without success.

Then, to abstain from outward sin,
Was more than I could do;
Now if I feel its power within,
I feel I hate it too.

Then all my servile works were done
A righteousness to raise;
Now, freely chosen in the Son,
I freely choose His ways.

What shall I do, was then the word,
That I may worthier grow?
What shall I render to the Lord?
Is my inquiry now.

To see the law by Christ fulfilled,
And hear His pardoning voice,
Changes a slave into a child,
And duty into choice.

Our obedience to Christ should arise from a spirit of adoption within our hearts causing us to love the Saviour. The apostle clearly tells us that service done out of legal constraint, grudgingly, is accounted as no service at all. If we could but apprehend the privileges that are ours as a result of our being adopted into the family of God, we would never cease to marvel and serve the Lord with gladness. 'Behold what manner of love the Father hath bestowed upon us that we should be called the sons of God' If we are the sons of God we ought to live in the liberty of sons, magnifying the grace of God. We ought never to entangle ourselves with the yoke of bondage suitable only for servants.

God graciously adopted all his elect into his family, taking us into
union with Christ before the world began, and thus declaring us to be his
sons (Ephesians 1:3-4). At Calvary the Lord Jesus Christ actually made us
accepted as sons. And in regeneration and effectual calling the Holy
Spirit gives us the nature of the sons of God. Here Paul teaches us that
our adoption is an accomplished fact and that we ought to live in the
joyous comfort of it. Hymnwriter Isaac Watts put it into verse:

> Behold what wondrous grace
> The Father hath bestowed;
> On sinners of a mortal race,
> To call them sons of God!
>
> If in my Father's love,
> I share a filial part,
> Send down Thy Spirit, like a dove,
> To rest upon my heart.

Sons, Not Servants

Paul tells us that we are no longer under the law that was our schoolmaster
and tutor (vv. 1-2). It was the schoolmaster's work to care for and instruct
his master's children until the time of their maturity. Once the child came
of age he would receive his inheritance. Until he reached adulthood, the
child was as a servant in his father's house, under complete subjection to
the schoolmaster, though he was a son. The schoolmaster would often
punish the child because of disobedience.

The schoolmaster, as we have seen, represents the law. The law deals
with men as a schoolmaster. It is a letter that kills (2 Corinthians 3:6). It is
the strength of sin (1 Corinthians 15:56). It is the ministration of death (2
Corinthians 3:7). Yet, in the Old Testament the people of God were subject
to the law in this manner for a season.

Though the law was never given to the Gentiles, the same is true of
unbelieving men and women in this gospel age, because the law (its moral
commandments) is written upon the hearts of all men by creation (Romans
2:14-15), condemning all by a guilty conscience. As John Calvin wrote,
'The elect, though they are children of God from the womb, yet, until by
faith they come to the possession of freedom, they remain like slaves
under the law, but from the moment they know Christ, they remain no
longer under this bondage.'

How long are men under the bondage of the law? 'Until the time appointed of the Father'. The legal dispensation continued until the time of God's appointment ended it, with the coming of our all-glorious Saviour. When Christ comes to the hearts of his elect, by the power of the Holy Spirit at the time appointed by the Father, the sons of God receive the earnest of their inheritance (Galatians 1:15, 16; Ezekiel 16:8, 9, 11, 12, 14; Isaiah 42:16).

Hope Revealed

Next Paul tells us that the incarnation of Christ revealed the hope of liberty from the law for all the sons of God. Until Christ came we were children, but children under bondage to the law. As long as the heir is a minor, he has no advantage over a slave. Though, as a son, he owns the entire inheritance, he is subject to tutors and governors until the time set by his father for his freedom: 'Even so we, when we were children, were in bondage under the elements of the world' (v. 3).

The church was in a state of infancy from the coming up out of Egypt until the coming of the Messiah (Hosea 11:1, 3). The Old Testament church was in servile, fearful bondage to the law. All that was revealed was revealed only in type and shadow and prophecy. There was no way of free access to God. The church of the New Testament, or gospel dispensation, is the church of mature age. We are no longer 'in bondage under the elements of the world'.

All of God's elect, though they are chosen sons of God, are also in bondage by nature (Ephesians 2:1-3). When Paul says, we were by nature 'children of wrath, even as others', he is not suggesting that God's elect were the objects of his wrath, but wrathful children. That is to say, before we trusted Christ, we were under the sense of guilt and of wrath, condemned by the law in our own consciences. We were governed and controlled by the 'elements of the world', by the dread and fear of the law (1 Timothy 1:9-10). We walked according to the course of this world. In our rebellion and unbelief, we were by nature 'children of wrath', 'alienated and enemies in our minds by wicked works' (Colossians 1:21).

'The Adoption Of Sons'

God adopted his elect in union with Christ before the world began. In the counsel of peace and the covenant of his grace it was agreed that Christ would reconcile them to the Father. So, at the appointed time, Christ came. When the time arrived that was fixed by God the Father in eternal predestination, God sent his Son into the world, made of a woman, made subject to the law, so that he might redeem God's sons from the bondage of the law. Once the law was fulfilled and satisfied by Christ, the way was open for all God's adopted children to experience and enjoy all their rightful heritage of grace.

Fulness Of Time

The words, 'the fulness of the time', are full of instruction. The time was fixed and set by God in eternal predestination. Indeed, there is a time set by God in his eternal purpose for all things that come to pass in this world. And everything is accomplished exactly according to God's purpose, precisely at his appointed time. Nothing comes to pass before its time; and nothing comes to pass after its time. Our great God never gets in a hurry and never comes too late. He works all things according to his own timetable. Christ came into the world at the appointed time agreed upon in eternity (Genesis 49:10; Daniel 9:24; Mark 1:15; Ephesians 1:10).

A brief look at history will reveal the fact that God was sovereignly arranging all things for the coming of his Son. The Jews had been carried into the Babylonian captivity and delivered by the hand of God, just as he had promised. Afterward, they were never again given over to open idolatry. Ezra and the scribes compiled the scriptures and taught them. Synagogues were established for teaching the scriptures throughout the known world. All these things prepared the way for Christ's entrance into the world.

Through the conquests of Alexander the Great, Greek became the language of the world. God raised up the Roman Empire and the Romans built roads everywhere. They formed a strange system of taxation that required every man to return to his hometown to pay taxes. Perhaps you ask, 'What do these things have to do with preparing the world for Christ's incarnation at the precise time it came to pass?' Compare just two passages of holy scripture with one another, and you will see God's arranging purpose (Micah 5:2; Luke 2:1-7).

Christ Sent

The fact that the Father sent forth the Son out of heaven implies the Son's eternal pre-existence with the Father. Though he is One with and altogether equal with the Father in his eternal deity, the Son of God voluntarily subjected himself to the Father's will as our Surety, that he might redeem and save his people (Hebrews 10:5-14). In infinite love for us our Father sent his Son to redeem us with his own blood. In that same infinite love the Son willingly came here to redeem us by the sacrifice of himself (John

3:16; Romans 5:8; 1 John 3:16; 4:9-10). In Philippians 2 the apostle Paul uses the example of Christ's voluntary subjection to the Father's will as an inspiration for believers to willingly surrender themselves to the will and glory of God (Philippians 2:5-11). The apostle Peter uses it to stir our hearts to patience in suffering (1 Peter 2:21-24).

Our Redeemer's human body and soul were made of a woman (v. 4; cf. Genesis 3:15; John 1:14; Romans 1:3; Philippians 2:7; Hebrews 2:14), without the aid of man. He was conceived of the Holy Spirit (Matthew 1:21-25). God the Holy Spirit formed and prepared a human body for the Son of God in the womb of a virgin (Hebrews 10:5), that he might perform all the work of redemption for us as a perfect man who had no sin (2 Corinthians 5:21). Being made of a woman, the infinite God became our near kinsman, to whom the right of redemption belongs (Leviticus 25:24-32; Ruth 4:4; Jeremiah 32:7).

Note too, that the Son of God was made subject to the law. He who gave the law at Sinai made himself to be under the law that he might perfectly fulfil all its obligations for his people, thereby establishing the righteousness of God and bringing in everlasting righteousness for us. He was made under and perfectly obeyed all the law, civil, ceremonial, and moral. He would not allow one jot or tittle of the law to fall to the ground, but fulfilled it completely, establishing a righteousness for his people that exceeds the righteousness of the Scribes and Pharisees (Matthew 5:17-20).

From the beginning of his incarnation until the end of his earthly life, the Lord Jesus was making for us a perfect record; a record that stands opposite our names in the record books of God in heaven as a reason why we should and must enter in. Christ kept the commandments for us, which we could not keep. By his blood poured out unto death under the wrath of God as our Substitute, our blessed Saviour cancelled the penalty of the law; and by his obedience, he fulfilled the law. In the light of Christ's accomplished life and death as our Substitute, the Holy Spirit declares, 'Christ is the end of the law' (Romans 5:19; 2 Corinthians 5:21; Romans 10:4; Acts 13:39).

We did not send for Christ; but God sent Christ for us (Isaiah 59:16; 63:5; 1 John 4:10). As it was in redemption, so it is in regeneration. It is God who comes to us in grace that causes us to come to him in faith. It is not us coming to God in faith that causes him to come to us in grace. John Ryland Jr. wrote:

> Sovereign Ruler of the skies, ever gracious, ever wise;
> All my times are in thy hand, all events at thy command.

To Redeem

The purpose of Christ in coming into this world in human flesh was the redemption of his people. This was the mission upon which he was sent by the Father as his Righteous Servant (Isaiah 53:11). This was the work he came to perform (Matthew 1:21; 20:28; 1 Peter 1:18-20; 1 Timothy 1:15). This was the thing the Father entrusted to his Son as our Surety (Ephesians 1:12). Of him it was written, 'He shall not fail' (Isaiah 42:4); and he did not fail. All his people were redeemed from the curse of the law by his one great sacrifice for sin (Galatians 3:13; Ephesians 1:7).

All this was done 'that we might receive the adoption of sons'. It was not possible for chosen sinners, though loved of God with an everlasting love, to enter into heaven as the sons of God and be accepted of him, except upon the ground of righteousness established and justice satisfied by the blood of Christ (Romans 3:24-26). And now that Christ has redeemed them, it is impossible for any of them to miss their predestined inheritance, not only because God's purpose is sure; but, also, because justice demands the salvation of all for whom Christ died. All the redeemed shall be brought to receive the adoption of sons at God's appointed time. The death of Christ secured for the elect all the blessings of grace (Romans 8:32-39; 2 Corinthians 8:9).

Because You Are Sons

We did not become God's children by believing on the Lord Jesus Christ. God the Holy Spirit came to us in grace and gave us faith to trust our Saviour because we were adopted as the children of God from eternity. At God's appointed time, every chosen child shall be made the recipient of God's saving grace and given the Spirit of adoption in the new birth. This is what Paul declares in verses 6 and 7, 'And because ye are sons, God hath sent forth the Spirit of his Son into your hearts, crying, Abba, Father. Wherefore thou art no more a servant, but a son; and if a son, then an heir of God through Christ.'

Chosen sinners come to know their election and adoption as the children of God, only as God sends his Spirit into their hearts in the saving operations of his grace, giving them faith in Christ. At the time of love, God sends his Spirit and causes his adopted sons to gladly receive the adoption of sons. When he creates faith in us, he gives us the right in our own consciences to be called the sons of God, enabling us to lift our hearts to heaven and call God himself our Father! 'Behold, what manner of love the Father hath bestowed upon us, that we should be called the sons of God: therefore the world knoweth us not, because it knew him not. Beloved, now are we the sons of God' (1 John 3:1-2). John Gill says,

This is a privilege that exceeds all others. It is better to be a son than to be a saint. Angels are saints, but not sons. They are servants. It is better to be a child of God than to be redeemed, pardoned, and justified. It is great grace to redeem from slavery, to pardon criminals, and justify the ungodly; but it is another and a higher act of grace to make them sons; and which makes them infinitely more honourable, than to be the sons and daughters of the greatest potentate upon earth; yea, gives them an honour which Adam had not in innocence, nor the angels in heaven, who though sons by creation, yet not by adoption.

To be called a son of God is the most noble title in heaven or earth. If we are sons, we should not live like slaves in bondage, under the terror of the law. Let every sinner who believes on the Son of God constantly enjoy all the privileges of full-grown sons in the family of God. Soon, we shall know fully and perfectly what Paul meant when he spoke of 'the glorious liberty of the children of God'.

Howbeit then, when ye knew not God, ye did service unto them which by nature are no gods. But now, after that ye have known God, or rather are known of God, how turn ye again to the weak and beggarly elements, whereunto ye desire again to be in bondage? Ye observe days, and months, and times, and years. I am afraid of you, lest I have bestowed upon you labour in vain. Brethren, I beseech you, be as I am; for I am as ye are: ye have not injured me at all.

(Galatians 4:8-12)

Chapter 21

Read: Galatians 4:8-12

'I Am Afraid Of You'

The last words of the Apostle Paul to Timothy, his son in the ministry and the young pastor of the church at Ephesus, were in the form of a charge. Those words form the charge and make up the binding oath of every faithful gospel preacher. In those words the Holy Spirit makes an unmistakable assertion of the duties of those who labour in the gospel.

'I charge thee before God, and the Lord Jesus Christ, who shall judge the quick and the dead at His appearing and His kingdom; preach the Word; be instant in season, out of season; reprove, rebuke, exhort with all longsuffering and doctrine. For the time will come when they will not endure sound doctrine; but after their own lusts shall they heap to themselves teachers, having itching ears; and they shall turn away their ears from the truth, and shall be turned unto fables. But watch thou in all things, endure afflictions, do the work of an evangelist, make full proof of thy ministry' (2 Timothy 4:1-5).

Paul was as good as his word. He loved the souls of God's people and was faithful to them, proving himself to be the servant of Jesus Christ. He was watchful over the souls of men. He did the work of an evangelist. He carefully declared all the counsel of God, when it was popular to do so and when it was unpopular to do so. When the people of God erred, he was faithful and longsuffering, reproving their backslidings, rebuking their sins, and exhorting them to repentance. For all of this, he was abused, criticised, misunderstood, misrepresented, afflicted, and imprisoned. But he was, nonetheless, faithful to his calling; and when no man stood with him, notwithstanding, the Lord stood with him and strengthened him.

That is what is involved in the work of the ministry. The greatest blessing that God can give to any community is a faithful gospel preacher and a church wherein the gospel is freely proclaimed and boldly upheld. And the most terrible curse that can be brought upon any society of men is for God to stop the mouths of his servants. How clearly this is proven both in the Word of God and in history.

The Apostle Paul was, in the broadest sense of the term, a man of God. His work in the gospel was truly a labour of love. He had gone, at great sacrifice to himself, into the region of Galatia preaching the gospel of God's redeeming grace and many were brought to Christ. As a result of his faithful labours, a gospel church was formed in Galatia. But after he left, the Galatians became influenced by Judaism and began to heap to themselves teachers after their own lusts. These teachers pampered their 'itching ears', caring more for their popularity and good name than for the souls of men. Soon, the Galatians would no longer stand for the sharp, but loving rebukes of Paul. He had become an enemy to them. Yet, he remained faithful to their souls. He loved them. Therefore, in the passage before us we see this broken hearted, loving preacher pleading with the erring children of God to repent of their evil ways and return to Christ.

The Galatians seemed ready to sacrifice all the blessings of the gospel: Full redemption by the blood of Christ, the indwelling of the Holy Spirit giving them the assurance of sons before the Father and free access to heaven, and eternal glory. They seemed ready to give all of this up and return to their former state of slavery. For this, Paul's heart was breaking. And now he pleads with their very souls.

Once Idolaters

Paul knew that perhaps the surest way to win the hearts of these believers back to Christ and his gospel was to remind them of what Christ had done for them. Therefore, Paul reminds the Galatians of what they were before God, by his free-grace, called them. God had saved them out of heathen idolatry: 'Howbeit then, when ye knew not God, ye did service unto them which by nature are no gods' (v. 8). Let us be reminded of what God has done for us by his grace (1 Corinthians 6:9-11).

Men by nature are ignorant of God. Paul does not here teach that men have no knowledge of God at all, but that they have no proper, saving knowledge of him. All men by nature know that there is a God (Romans 1:19-20); and the law of God is written in their hearts (Romans 2:14-15). They suppress this knowledge in unrighteousness (Romans 1:18). Rebellion against that which they know and can see clearly of the revelation of God in creation, renders all men without excuse. And while this revelation can never save them, their refusal to acknowledge God (Romans 1:21) compounds and aggravates their condemnation. All men are by nature ignorant of the glory of God revealed in Christ (Ephesians 2:12). They are blinded by Satan (2 Corinthians 4:4).

Yet, all men have a consciousness of God from which they cannot escape. Man is both a spiritual and a physical creature. Therefore, he must have an object of worship. Yet, all are so depraved and blind to all things spiritual that they turn to some creature of their own hands and worship it (Romans 1:25; 1 Thessalonians 1:9). Men delight to have a god after their own image. It may be a physical object, or it may be a mental concept. Such idols are, as Paul puts it here, 'no gods' (v. 8). Not only are they not gods, they are nothing (Acts 19:26).

These Galatians had been delivered from heathen idolatry by the grace of God. And now they were despising God's free-grace and returning to the doctrines of men. For this, Paul sharply rebukes them, 'But now, after that ye have known God, or rather are known of God, how turn ye again to the weak and beggarly elements, whereunto ye desire again to be in bondage? Ye observe days, and months, and times, and years. I am afraid of you, lest I have bestowed upon you labour in vain' (vv. 9-11).

Knowing God

Salvation is knowing God (John 17:3). It is the result of being known of God (Isaiah 53:11). Paul asserts that those who were born of God and taught of God at Galatia knew God. This saving knowledge of God is the promise of the New Covenant (Jeremiah 31:33-34). This knowledge of God is the knowledge of Christ (John 6:44-46; 1:14, 18; 2 Corinthians 4:6; Hebrews 1:3). It is knowing God as he is revealed in Christ. It comes to chosen, redeemed sinners by divine revelation, by the irresistible power and grace of the Holy Spirit through the preaching of the gospel (2 Corinthians 4:4-7). Paul brought the knowledge of God to these Galatians by the preaching of the gospel (Isaiah 52:7; Romans 10:15).

They knew God because they were 'known of God'. Those words are full of instruction. Paul is saying, 'You were actively known by God before there was any action on your part to win his knowledge.' God's knowledge of us is more than a bare, factual acquaintance of our existence and actions. It is an active, loving, eternal knowledge (John 10:14; 2 Timothy 2:19; Exodus 3:12, 17; Nahum 1:7; John 10:28; Romans 8:28-29). God's knowledge of his elect is particular (Matthew 7:21-23), distinguishing (Romans 8:29-30), and eternal. His knowledge of us is his everlasting love for and delight with us in Christ. All our acquaintance with God begins with him. We know him because he first knew us.

'Beggarly Elements'

Paul was shocked that those men and women who had experienced such rich and bounteous grace at the hands of God would now turn from the riches of Christ (Ephesians 1:18) to the 'beggarly elements' of the law. Therefore, he gives them this sharp, but loving rebuke – 'How turn ye again to the weak and beggarly elements, whereunto ye desire again to be in bondage?'

These 'weak and beggarly elements' are the vain traditions of sinful men, the religious ideas and principles that sinful men come to by nature as a means of finding favour with God. Jewish legalists and pagan idolaters alike are subject to them. They are the attempts of lost religionists to obtain salvation by something they do. Specifically, the Galatian saints, Gentiles to whom the law was never given, were being seduced into law observance by Jewish teachers who claimed to be followers of Christ.

Paul used words of scorn, words that were sure to offend the Judaisers and hopefully shame those who were being influenced by them. He speaks of all those ordinances of divine worship in the Old Testament, which have now been fulfilled by Christ, as 'weak and beggarly elements'.

The law is weak, so weak that it is utterly incapable of helping anyone. It cannot give life. It is a ministration of death. It cannot give joy. It cannot give peace. It cannot give comfort. It cannot produce righteousness. It cannot bring salvation. The law is beggarly, too. It lies in the observation of poor things (meat and drinks and holy days), in comparison with Christ, in whom we have grace and mercy and life. The law is only a shadow of the riches of grace and glory revealed in Christ. Serving the law is nothing more than bondage and will-worship (Colossians 2:18-23).

Martin Luther wrote, 'People who prefer the law to the gospel are like Aesop's dog who let go of the meat to snatch at the shadow in the water … The law is weak and poor, the sinner is weak and poor: two feeble beggars trying to help each other. They cannot do it. They only wear each other out. But through Christ a weak and poor sinner is revived and enriched unto eternal life.'

'Ye observe days, and months, and times, and years' (v. 10). Paul's obvious reference is to the Old Testament law requiring the Jews to observe certain holy days and the sabbath days prescribed in the Mosaic age (Colossians 2:16). The Judaisers were trying to impose these things upon Gentile believers, to whom such laws were never given. Legal ritualism and human tradition are the ruin of religion. They numb the soul and harden the heart.

All human religion is freewill, works religion, and inherently legalistic and ritualistic. It substitutes the choice and works of man and the bondage of the law for a living, saving knowledge of God, and eternal life in Christ. It forfeits the life of liberty in the Spirit by faith in Christ alone. It looses the glorious liberty of free justification by faith in Christ, a life ruled, animated, and motivated by grace, love, and gratitude. Christ has delivered us from all forms of legalism by his grace. Let us ever cling to him, refusing to be 'entangled again with the yoke of bondage' (Galatians 5:1).

Having found that life that is worthy to be called life, why would anyone think of giving it up to go back to the bondage and futility of the law? The question is rhetorical, of course. The reason should be obvious. The human heart, as Calvin put it, is an 'idol factory'. Charles Simeon wrote, 'The human mind is very fond of fetters, and is apt to forge them for itself.' Sin makes fools of us all.

Paul's Fear

True gospel preachers are men who labour in the work of the gospel for the souls of men and the glory of God. They labour in the study of the scriptures and in prayer, under the burden of the Lord Jesus Christ (1 Timothy 4:12-15).

Paul knew that the servant of God never labours in vain (Isaiah 49:5; 2 Corinthians 2:14-16). What he is referring to in verse 11 is those who were following the Judaisers back to Moses. If they persisted in mixing legal ceremonies and human works with the grace of God and the work of Christ to make God's grace and Christ's redemptive work effectual, they would prove that for them his labour had been in vain. Any such mixture is a frustration of grace and damning (Galatians 2:21; 5:1-4).

In verse 12 Paul calls upon the Galatian believers and us, in love and tenderness, to turn from their backsliding ways and return to the worship and service of the Saviour. He says, 'I want you to be like me, free from the bondage of the law'. Reckon yourselves to be dead to the law, which has been fulfilled by Christ. Count these things as loss and rubbish for Christ (Philippians 3:7-11).

Paul, with respect to all things spiritual, became as they – as though he were a gentile. They are both alike in Christ: chosen in him, redeemed in him, perfected in him and free in him. 'Ye have not injured me at all'. They had not injured Paul by their behaviour, but only themselves. His feelings for them had not changed. Rather, their feelings toward him had changed (Galatians 4:16). Paul wanted them to cling to Christ alone, as he did (Galatians 6:14). He would have us renounce all personal righteousness for Christ, 'And be found in him, not having our own righteousness, which is of the law, but that which is through the faith of Christ, the righteousness which is of God by faith.'

Multitudes forsake Christ and the gospel of God's free grace in him, while claiming to uphold and defend it. They even do so without knowing it. They introduce works (self-salvation) into their 'gospel' and make it another gospel, but are thoroughly convinced that their new works 'gospel' is the gospel of God. These Gentile believers at Galatia, I am sure, did not think they had fundamentally shifted the foundation of their faith. They did not think they were returning to their former bondage. They did not imagine that they were abandoning the faith they had embraced, when by their baptism they professed faith in Christ. They would have vigorously denied that they had in any sense turned their backs on the knowledge of God. They did not see that their embracing Jewish ceremonies was nothing but idolatry, and the same thing as embracing the human traditions and barbaric religious rituals of their idolatrous ancestors. They never dreamed that their law observance was a repudiation of the gospel. They thought they would be more holy, more spiritual, stronger Christians by keeping the law. Paul had to tell them what a catastrophic mistake they were making, how immense the error was; and he had to do so with such blunt force that they could not misunderstand him. They would never have imagined it otherwise.

The scriptures teach us that vast multitudes of people will be surprised on the Day of Judgment to discover that their religion, with all their religious works and ceremonies, will be as a millstone around their necks to drag them forever down to hell (Matthew 7:21-23). Let us not be numbered among them (Romans 4:16; 11:6; Colossians 2:6, 8, 16-23).

Hymnwriter James Proctor prefaced his hymn, 'Nothing, either great or small', with these words:

> Since I first discovered Jesus to be the end of the law for
> righteousness to every one that believeth, I have more than once
> met with a poor sinner seeking peace at the foot of Sinai instead

of Calvary, and I have heard him again and again in bitter disappointment and fear groaning out, 'What must I do?' I have said to him, 'Do, do? What can you do? What do you need to do?'

> Nothing, either great or small;
> Nothing, sinner, no;
> Jesus did it, did it all,
> Long, long ago!

> When He, from His lofty throne,
> Stooped to do and die,
> Everything was fully done;
> Hearken to His cry –

> 'It is finished!' Yes indeed,
> Finished every jot.
> Sinner, this is all you need.
> Tell me, is it not?

> Weary, working, plodding one,
> Why toil you so?
> Cease your doing, all was done
> Long, long ago!

> Till to Jesus' work you cling
> By a simple faith,
> Doing is a deadly thing.
> Doing ends in death!

> Cast your deadly 'doing' down,
> Down at Jesus' feet.
> Stand in Him, in Him alone,
> Gloriously complete!

Ye know how through infirmity of the flesh I preached the gospel unto you at the first. And my temptation which was in my flesh ye despised not, nor rejected; but received me as an angel of God, even as Christ Jesus. Where is then the blessedness ye spake of? for I bear you record, that, if it had been possible, ye would have plucked out your own eyes, and have given them to me. Am I therefore become your enemy, because I tell you the truth? They zealously affect you, but not well; yea, they would exclude you, that ye might affect them. But it is good to be zealously affected always in a good thing, and not only when I am present with you. My little children, of whom I travail in birth again until Christ be formed in you, I desire to be present with you now, and to change my voice; for I stand in doubt of you.

(Galatians 4:13-20)

Chapter 22

Read: Galatians 4:13-20

The Flattery Of False Teachers

God's saints in this world are often compared to sheep. Pastors are called 'shepherds' because it is their responsibility to tend the sheep. God's people are sheep. Like sheep they must be guided, protected, and cared for. They frequently leave the prescribed path. They are easily led astray. They are in danger because of deceptive wolves. It is the duty of God's appointed shepherds to feed his lambs, to protect them from the dangers they face, instruct them in the way of righteousness, and to faithfully restore them when they fall, when they turn aside, or when they are taken in a snare.

The Galatian saints were foolishly turning aside to Judaism, the works of the law, being taken in the snare of Satan's messengers of self-righteousness. They had been flattered into thinking that their good works could supplement the free-grace of God in Jesus Christ. And they had foolishly accepted this doctrine of will-worship to the great dishonour of Christ and the gospel, and to the grief and anguish of the man who first brought the gospel to them. Paul had been the instrument of their conversion and he loved their souls. He was a faithful shepherd to their souls. Therefore, he sharply rebuked them for their sin. Rather than loving Paul for his faithfulness to God and to their souls, the Galatians were treating him as though he were their enemy.

Paul would not allow their abuse of him to hinder his love and faithfulness to them. In verses 8-11 he had sharply reproved them. Here, he makes an urgent, intensely personal plea, appealing to them as one who loved them and as one they had once received 'as an angel of God' to their souls. He writes as one who is in agony because he cannot endure the thought that a people, who at one time had treated him with so much sympathetic consideration and received the gospel preached by him with such enthusiasm, were continuing to wander farther and farther away from the truth. Therefore, he lovingly pleads with them as a parent to his children.

'As I Am'

In verse 12 Paul again addresses the Galatians as his 'brethren' in Christ, taking them at their word. They professed to be his brethren, they professed faith in Christ and though they had gone so far backward and appeared to have departed from the faith, yet Paul hopes the best concerning them. His hopes are truly born of God. Because he tenderly loved them and cared for them, he wanted them to be as he was, completely free from the tyranny and bondage of the law. He wanted them to reckon themselves dead indeed to the law (Galatians 2:19). He wanted them to forever relinquish the observance of sabbath days, Mosaic ceremonies, and personal righteousness according to the law, counting all but dung for Christ and his righteousness (Colossians 2:16-23; Philippians 3:7-14).

Anxious lest he should do more harm than good, Paul carefully shows the Galatians that his heart is with them, that he loves them as himself, as one with him. He wants them to know that his sharp rebukes have come, not from a man who despises them but from one who loves them. Commenting on this phrase, Martin Luther wrote:

> Like Paul, all pastors and ministers ought to have much sympathy for their poor straying sheep, and instruct them in the spirit of meekness. They cannot be straightened out in any other way. Over-sharp criticism provokes anger and despair, but no repentance. And here let us note, by the way, that true doctrine always produces concord. When men embrace errors, the tie of Christian love is broken.
>
> At the beginning of the Reformation we were honoured as the true ministers of Christ. Suddenly certain false brethren began to hate us. We had given them no offence, no occasion to hate us. They knew then as they know now that ours is the singular desire to publish the Gospel of Christ everywhere. What changed

their attitude toward us? False doctrine. Seduced into error by the false apostles, the Galatians refused to acknowledge St. Paul as their pastor. The name and doctrine of Paul became obnoxious to them. I fear this Epistle recalled very few from their error.

Paul knew that the false apostles would misconstrue his censure of the Galatians to their own advantage and say: 'So this is your Paul whom you praise so much. What sweet names he is calling you in his letter. When he was with you he acted like a father, but now he acts like a dictator.' Paul knew what to expect of the false apostles and therefore he is worried. He does not know what to say. It is hard for a man to defend his cause at a distance, especially when he has reason to think that he personally has fallen into disfavour.

Paul is saying, 'I am as you are, and you are as I am with respect to things spiritual'. We are alike in Christ, chosen in him, and redeemed by him. We are equally regenerated by his Spirit. We are all the children of God by faith in Christ. We are no more servants, but sons. We are all equally his free men. Therefore, be as I am, free in Christ.

Paul has shown them how that their doctrine injures the character of God; the work of Christ who fulfilled the law, the gospel of God's grace; and their own souls; but he wanted them to know that they had not injured him. Their rejection of Paul was not injury to him (v. 12). It was rather a rejection of Jesus Christ, whose servant Paul was (1 Samuel 8:6-7; Exodus 16:8). They must not imagine that the things he wrote in this epistle were written out of resentment. Paul desired that the Galatians be bound to him as their faithful and loving pastor. He acted toward them as though he and they were one. Above that, Paul wanted these Galatians once again to be bound to Jesus Christ (Galatians 2:20; 6:14; Philippians 3:7-10).

'An Angel of God'

When he first came among them, the Galatians had received Paul 'as an angel of God, even as Jesus Christ'. They received him as God's messenger to their souls, as though Christ himself spoke to them by him. Indeed, that is exactly what God's servants are to his people. Faithful pastors are described as God's angels to his churches (Revelation 1-3), through whom God speaks to chosen sinners by the gospel (2 Corinthians 5:20). But things had changed. The Galatians were now beginning to treat Paul as an enemy (vv. 13-16).

When he first preached the gospel of God's free and sovereign grace in Christ to them, he did so in much weakness, humility, persecution and bodily afflictions. They were to be commended for receiving the gospel and God's messenger to them. Wherever he preached the gospel both Jews and Gentiles were enraged against him. All the influential and religious people of his day denounced him. But the Galatians were different. That was greatly to their honour. And Paul does not neglect to praise them for it. This praise Paul bestows on none of the other churches.

Paul's Infirmity

When he speaks of the infirmity of his flesh he does not mean some physical defect or carnal lust, but the sufferings and afflictions he endured in his body. Paul tells us what these infirmities were in 2 Corinthians 12:9-10, 'And he said unto me, My grace is sufficient for thee: for my strength is made perfect in weakness. Most gladly therefore will I rather glory in my infirmities, that the power of Christ may rest upon me. Therefore I take pleasure in infirmities, in reproaches, in necessities, in persecutions, in distresses for Christ's sake: for when I am weak, then am I strong.'

He speaks in a similar manner in 2 Corinthians 11:23-25, 'Are they ministers of Christ? (I speak as a fool) I am more; in labours more abundant, in stripes above measure, in prisons more frequent, in deaths oft. Of the Jews five times received I forty stripes save one. Thrice was I beaten with rods, once was I stoned, thrice I suffered shipwreck, a night and a day I have been in the deep.'

These are the afflictions he is talking about when he speaks of his 'infirmity of the flesh'. He reminds the Galatians how he was always in peril at the hands of the Jews, Gentiles, and false brethren, and how he suffered hunger and want.

Now, the afflictions of the believers always offend people. Paul knew this and, therefore, has high praise for the Galatians, because they over looked his afflictions and received him like an angel. Our Saviour said, 'Blessed is he, whosoever shall not be offended in me' (Matthew 11:6). It is no easy thing to confess him as Lord and Saviour who was a reproach of men and despised of the people and the laughing stock of the world (Psalms 22:7-8; Matthew 5:11-12; 27:39, 43). To prize Christ, so spitefully scorned, spit upon, scourged, and crucified, more than the riches of the richest, the strength of the strongest, the wisdom of the wisest, he calls 'blessed'.

Paul had both those outward afflictions and inward, spiritual afflictions. He speaks of them in 2 Corinthians 7:5, 'Without were fightings, within were fears'.

In his letter to the Philippians he speaks of the restoration of Epaphroditus as a special act of mercy from God, 'lest I should have sorrow upon sorrow'. He commends the Galatians for not being offended at him in the past, for receiving him as 'an angel of God, even as Christ Jesus'. They received him with all that reverence, respect, and high esteem, veneration, and affection, that might have been given to an angel sent down from heaven to bring them the gospel; as one that had his mission and commission from God.

They had received Paul 'even as Christ Jesus', as his ambassador, as representing him, as speaking to them in his stead, as if Christ himself had been personally present as man among them. They could not have shown greater respect to him. The Galatians did not look upon Paul and his infirmities as offensive things. Far from it. They were so glad to hear the gospel of Christ from his lips that had it been possible they would have plucked out their own eyes and given them to him. By reminding them how much they had loved him and how highly they had honoured him before the invasion of the legalists, he tenderly urges them to so receive him now.

They were so happy in Christ and so thankful to have heard the gospel of God's free grace to sinners in him that they counted the man who preached the gospel to them as their dearest friend. Now that the law-preachers had influenced them, they had not only turned from the gospel of Christ alone, but had become Paul's enemies. A more passionate appeal is not to be found in all of Paul's writings than this, 'Am I therefore become your enemy because I tell you the truth?' They treated him as an enemy because he preached that believers are complete in Christ and have no need to be circumcised, to keep sabbath days, and to live under the yoke of bondage.

Fake Devotion
In verse 17 Paul speaks of the false teachers at Galatia as contemptuously as possible, by not even mentioning their names. By omitting their names, he is saying that such wicked men as those who preach righteousness by the works of the flesh must not have even their names transmitted to posterity, much less their doctrine.

These false preachers were courting the saints of God, pretending great love and concern for them, but it was all beguiling flattery. Satan's messengers soft soap people 'with good words and fair speeches', to deceive the simple (Romans 16:18). They pretend great love for others, but are motivated by nothing but love for themselves. Their god is their own belly. By promoting law righteousness, they speak flatteringly to men of their righteousness, giving them an excuse to be proud of their superiority over others in the matter of righteousness, while pretending meekness before God.

They are enemies of the cross, enemies of God, and enemies to the souls of men (Philippians 3:18-19). They seek to use the souls of men for themselves. The Judaisers at Galatia were trying to exclude and isolate the saints from Paul and the other true apostles, so that they might follow them and make them appear successful (2 Peter 2:1-3). Their zeal and enthusiasm was not to turn the Galatians to Christ, but to win popular applause unto themselves. To that end they were willing to make merchandise of men's souls.

In verse 18 the Apostle is looking for some consistency of profession from the Galatian believers. Paul is saying, 'When I was present with you, you loved me and received me as an angel of God to your souls. The fact that I am now absent from you should not cause your attitude toward me to change. Though I am absent in the flesh, I am with you in spirit. You ought not reject me or my doctrine, by which you received the grace of Christ and his Holy Spirit, because of the evil influence of those wicked men.'

Paul's Travail

It appears that when Paul was present with them, they were devoted to him and to the gospel, but when he left, their affection to him and to the gospel he preached cooled (v. 19). They turned to other teachers who convinced them that Paul had abandoned them. Nothing could have been further from the truth.

Paul speaks in the tender, affectionate language of a father to his sons calling them 'My little children'. They were, he hoped, sons of God and were still babes in Christ. Therefore, the term 'little children' was appropriate. But they were also Paul's children. He was the instrument God used to bring them to faith in Christ.

Then Paul compares himself to a woman giving birth. All his pains, sufferings, and labours in preaching the gospel are compared to the sorrows of a woman in travail of labour. At such a time, a woman is concerned about just one thing. She considers her pain and suffering worthwhile if she can give birth to a living, healthy child. Paul's concern was not for himself, but for them. All he was concerned about and dedicated to in prayer, preaching, and suffering was that Christ might be formed in them.

'Until Christ Be Formed In You'

To have Christ formed in you is to be saved, to be a new creature in Christ Jesus. In the new birth we are made 'partakers of the divine nature' (2 Peter 1:4). 'Christ in you' is the hope of glory (Colossians 1:27). A form of religion, with its laws, ordinances, and ceremonies, is not eternal life. A form of morality, with its laws and commandments, is not eternal life. A form of religious profession, with its decisions, baptisms and creeds, is not eternal life. Eternal life is knowing God and Jesus Christ, whom he has sent (John 17:3). Eternal life is, as Henry Mahan put it, having, 'the life of Christ, the presence of Christ, the Spirit and mind of Christ and the very glory of Christ begotten, created and formed in us (Galatians 2:20). Until this is done and unless this miracle of grace is accomplished, our religion is vain. It is no more than that of the Pharisees of old, of whom Christ said, 'They neither know me nor my Father'. Salvation is Christ in you; the hope of glory is Christ in you; the life of God is Christ in you (1 John 5:11-12)'.

Paul's Doubt

Paul wanted to be present with them (v. 20). He wanted to speak to them face to face, and be assured that his concerns were ill-founded. But their concern about law obedience, circumcision, sabbath days, and ceremonies made him fearful that they did not know Christ at all. Therefore, he writes, 'I stand in doubt of you'.

It is significant to note that Paul never expressed such doubt regarding any other congregation. Nothing, not even the immorality and divisions in the Corinthian church, caused the apostle to express doubt concerning the genuineness of their professed faith in Christ. But when men and women embrace self-righteous works religion, when they turn again to the weak and beggarly elements of the law, it becomes obvious that they never knew the grace of God and do not trust Christ (Galatians 5:1-4). When professed believers appear to be turning away from Christ and the gospel of God's free and sovereign grace in him, there is grave reason to stand in doubt of their professed faith in Christ.

Tell me, ye that desire to be under the law, do ye not hear the law? For it is written, that Abraham had two sons, the one by a bondmaid, the other by a freewoman. But he who was of the bondwoman was born after the flesh; but he of the freewoman was by promise. Which things are an allegory: for these are the two covenants; the one from the mount Sinai, which gendereth to bondage, which is Agar.

(Galatians 4:21-24)

Chapter 23

Read: Galatians 4:21-24

Two Covenants

In the preceding chapters of this epistle the Apostle Paul has clearly established the doctrine of justification by faith. He has shown that the law was given for the purpose of shutting sinners up to the grace of God in Jesus Christ for their justification. It has been his aim throughout the book to bring God's children to enjoy the Spirit of adoption, who has set us free from the bondage of the law, by bringing us to faith in Christ. Now, Paul proceeds to a deeper and fuller teaching of the scriptures.

Ishmael And Isaac

In Galatians 4:21-31 Paul explains the teaching of holy scripture regarding the two covenants of works and grace. Using Abraham's two sons, Ishmael and Isaac, and their mothers, Hagar and Sarah, as an allegory, the Apostle shows us that these two distinct covenants operate by two distinct principles: the flesh and the Spirit. The covenant of works, he shows us, always brings bondage, and the covenant of grace, liberty. Paul's message is crystal clear. The covenant of works and the covenant of grace are distinct and mutually exclusive.

In these verses the Holy Spirit gives us the spiritual meaning of the historical relation of Sarah and Hagar, as recorded in Genesis 16 and 21. He tells us that the things recorded in those two chapters of Genesis were, by God's design, an allegory – an earthly picture of gospel truth. Robert Hawker reminds us:

> We can never be sufficiently thankful to God the Holy Ghost for giving himself the spiritual meaning of those records; for never, untaught of God, could it have entered into the mind of man, that matters of so important a nature were veiled under that covering. We might, and should no doubt, have read the history of both again and again, as the different characters are there stated in the holy scripture, and have considered the whole an interesting memoir in the family of the patriarch Abraham, in that early age of the world; but to have supposed that it had so vast a reference to ourselves, and that in the son of Sarah was intended to show the election of grace; and in the son of the bond-woman Hagar was meant what the apostle calls 'the rest' (Romans 11:7), such a spiritual apprehension of the subject, untaught of God, would have been for ever impossible, (as indeed it is now, without the same divine instruction,) and must have been unknown.

The doctrine here revealed is essential to a proper understanding of the gospel. God deals with men only in covenant relationships. You may ask, 'What is a covenant?' A covenant is a promise made upon the fulfilment of stipulated conditions. The covenant of works was initiated in Eden and later more fully revealed at Sinai. It says, 'Do this and live'. This is the law. The covenant of grace was initiated in eternity and gradually revealed in many promises to God's elect. It is fully realised in the person and work of Christ, the Surety of the covenant (Hebrews 7:22). It declares that Christ has done all.

The Word of God plainly teaches these two covenants. The covenant of works was that agreement made between God and Adam, and it included all of Adam's posterity. God promised Adam life and happiness, on the condition that he would perfectly keep his commandments; and God threatened Adam with death if he broke his commandments (Matthew 19:17; Luke 10:28; Hosea 6:7).

The covenant of grace is an agreement made between the persons of the Sacred Trinity. It is the agreement of salvation for God's elect made in eternity by God the Father, God the Son, and God the Holy Spirit. It was agreed that the race should fall in Adam and be redeemed by Christ (Isaiah 53:10; Hebrews 8:6). The covenant of works stood between God and Adam. Adam fell and now it is hopelessly broken. The covenant of grace stands forever established upon Christ's blood and righteousness. The covenant of works said, 'Do, man, or die!' The covenant of grace says, Christ has done all that men may live.' All the conditions of the covenant of grace were forever and perfectly fulfilled by Christ. Every sinner, looking to Christ as his Saviour, can say with David, 'Although my house be not so with God; yet he hath made with me an everlasting covenant, ordered in all things and sure' (2 Samuel 23:5).

My God! The covenant of Thy love
Abides forever sure;
And, in its matchless grace, I feel
My happiness secure.

What though my house be not with Thee,
As nature could desire!
To nobler joys than nature gives
Thy servants all aspire.

Since Thou, the everlasting God,
My Father art become,
Jesus, my Guardian, and my Friend,
And heaven my final home –

I welcome all Thy sovereign will,
For all that will is love;
And when I know not what Thou dost,
I wait the light above.

Thy covenant in the darkest gloom
Shall heavenly rays impart,
And when my eyelids close in death,
Sustain my fainting heart.

No Mixture

The God of Glory is the God of grace. His grace is free, everlasting, and boundless. How men ought to love His grace! Yet, men are forever shunning his grace and clinging to the law. Men, by nature, prefer the covenant of works to the covenant of grace. Some do not deny grace, but simply mix it with the law. But any mixing of the two is a denial of grace (Romans 11:6; Galatians 5:1-4). Even among those who are born of God, there is a terrible, evil inclination toward works. How often we find ourselves foolishly looking within, looking to our works, our experiences, and our feelings as a basis for assurance and peace! The result is always bondage.

It is God himself who has made that vast distinction between law and grace. The two covenants are as different as east and west, as light and dark, as fire and water. The law is death; grace is life. This distinction lies at the very heart of the gospel. One of the most difficult things in the world is to see the difference between law and grace, between my doing something for righteousness and salvation and another doing everything in my place for the totality of my acceptance with the holy Lord God. Even those who are clear sighted enough to realise that justification must be all of grace, are, yet, very often deluded into thinking that they are sanctified by the keeping of the law, and, thus, make themselves more acceptable to God. Somehow, we tend to think that rituals and ceremonies and good works will give us merit and favour with God. But this can never be. We are accepted before God in our Covenant Head, the Lord Jesus Christ, and in the covenant he is everything to God's people. 'For of him are we in Christ Jesus, who of God is made unto us, wisdom, and righteousness, and sanctification, and redemption'. Christ is everything in the matter of salvation. We cannot make too much of our Saviour or ascribe too much to him. He is the sum total of the covenant of grace. It is written, 'I will ... give thee for a covenant of the people, to establish the earth, to cause to inherit the desolate heritages; that thou mayest say to the prisoners, Go forth' (Isaiah 49:8-9). In Christ, by his obedience and death as the Surety of the covenant and Representative of his elect, the temporary covenant of works (the law of condemnation and death) has been permanently supplanted by the everlasting covenant of grace through Jesus Christ.

A Question For Legalists

There were many in Paul's day, as there are many in our day, who attempted to bring God's saints back under the bondage of the law, while professing to trust Christ as their Saviour. We have seen this throughout the book of Galatians. Few would claim to perfectly obey the law. Rather, they profess that they sincerely live by the law and obey it to the best of their ability. That is the problem. Doing our best will never do for righteousness. Our best efforts will never please God. So Paul raises a question in verse 21 that needs to be answered. It is not a mere rhetorical question. 'Tell me, ye that desire to be under the law, do ye not hear the law?'

The question is just this: Do you who seek to make yourselves righteous, who seek acceptance with God, who seek assurance and peace before God by your obedience to the law, do you not hear what the law really says? The law never speaks peace or pardon, but declares us all to be guilty (Romans 3:19, 20). It sentences us to wrath and condemnation. The law does not minister life, but death (2 Corinthians 3:7). The law does not require a sincere effort of obedience, but perfect obedience (Galatians 3:10). Do you really want to be under the yoke of bondage and death? Do you really want to be under the law?

Edgar Andrews points out the fact that, 'Paul is using 'the law' here in two different senses. His meaning is, 'You who desire to be under the law of Moses, do you not hear (or heed) the Mosaic scripture?' Of course, there is no sleight of hand intended. Paul is simply pointing out that the Sinaitical law forms part of a larger body of Scripture from the hand of Moses, namely the Pentateuch. Had the Galatians seen Moses' law in the context of all Moses' writings, implies Paul, they would have rejected the Judaisers' advances.'

The Judaisers at Galatia, like legalistic work-mongers today, interpreted the law very narrowly. The Judaisers with whom Paul contended applied only the ten commandments, circumcision, and selected holy days to believers in the gospel age. Their followers today, with rare exception, make only the ten commandments applicable, altering the laws regulating sabbath keeping to suit themselves. By such a narrow interpretation and application of the law, they take it totally out of the context of the Old Testament, particularly the five books of the Old Testament written by Moses (Genesis through Deuteronomy), commonly referred to as 'the law'. Thereby, they ignore and refuse to hear and heed what the law says. While professing to love and honour the law, they would destroy the law.

The message of the law is exactly the same as the message of the gospel – salvation by Christ! The whole Word of God is the declaration of redemption, grace, and salvation by Christ (Luke 24:27; John 5:39; Hebrews 1:1-14). Paul shows us in verses 22-24 that this is the case, using Sarah and Hagar and their two sons, Isaac and Ishmael (by divine inspiration) as an allegory portraying the gospel and the covenants of works and of grace. These two women and their sons were not merely people who lived long, long ago. They were, by the design and purpose of God, typical of spiritual truths. They were living parables (an allegory), demonstrating the futility of works and the efficacy of God's free grace in Christ.

Two Sons

'For it is written, that Abraham had two sons, the one by a bondmaid, the other by a freewoman' (v. 22). Actually, Abraham had many sons (Genesis

25:1-4); but Ishmael and Isaac were specifically intended to be illustrations of works and grace. Ishmael was born of a slave, Sarah's handmaid, Hagar. As such, he was but a servant himself and not the heir. Isaac was born of Sarah, Abraham's wife, who was a free woman, one who was joined to Abraham in a family relationship. That made Isaac a free man, a son, and the heir.

Paul uses this allegory to show us that all who are in bondage to the law are slaves, the spiritual descendants of the bondwoman, Hagar. Those who enjoy the liberty of grace are free in Christ, spiritual descendants of the freewoman, Sarah. Hagar and her son, Ishmael, owned nothing. They had none of the privileges belonging to Sarah and her son, Isaac, who possessed all things by virtue of their relationship to Abraham.

Paul's doctrine is obvious. Those who seek to obtain righteousness by works, even by trying to obey God's holy law, are mere slaves. Though they follow after righteousness, they cannot attain 'to the law of righteousness ... For they being ignorant of God's righteousness, and going about to establish their own righteousness, have not submitted themselves unto the righteousness of God. For Christ is the end of the law for righteousness to every one that believeth' (Romans 9:31-10:4). But all who come to God by faith in Christ, without the deeds of the law, inherit all things in Christ.

Though Abraham was an old man, and his wife Sarah, was an old woman, whose womb had been barren, the Lord promised Abraham a son (Genesis 13:16; 15:4-6). Though everything seemed to be against it ever happening, Abraham believed God's promise (Romans 4:18-22). But, as the years passed and they grew older, it seemed increasingly unlikely that the child of promise would ever be born without Abraham and Sarah doing something to make it happen.

Mixing Faith And Works

Sarah came up with an idea. She suggested, and Abraham agreed to it, that the Lord would fulfil his promise in a way that involved their own effort, by giving God a hand. Sarah gave her handmaid, Hagar, to Abraham as his mistress for a night. Their faith wavered. They mixed human reason with divine revelation, and, as is always the case, the wisdom of the flesh flew in the face of divine revelation and was a denial of the promise of God. Therefore, Paul tells us that, 'he who was (born) of the bondwoman was born after the flesh' (v. 23).

Abraham and Sarah did not abandon God's promise altogether. They simply decided that God needed their help to fulfil his promise. And their help produced Ishmael, a slave who caused unceasing pain and trouble as long as he was in the house. That is precisely the error of all who attempt to mix law and grace, the works of the flesh and the work of God, in the matter of obtaining righteousness before God. Every attempt to obtain the promise of God by human effort (law obedience, religious ceremony, good works, decisions, etc.) is doomed to failure and only produces bondage and trouble.

Isaac, on the other hand, was born of 'the free woman' Sarah, and was born 'by promise' (v. 23). He was not conceived normally by the flesh in a natural way, but was born when the promise of God was fulfilled miraculously in his parents' old age. His father was nearly 100 and his mother was 90 years old and barren (Romans 4:19). They were simply too old to have children. 'With men this was impossible; but with God all things are possible' (Matthew 19:26). Had it been possible for Isaac to have been born in a natural way, no faith would have been involved and no righteousness imputed to Abraham. But Isaac was born because Abraham believed God. He not only believed that God would give him a son, he believed that God would give him his Son (the Seed of woman who would crush the serpent's head and bring the blessing of God's salvation); and God declared him righteous (Romans 4:20-22).

Being the seed of promise, Isaac was a type and picture of our Lord Jesus Christ's incarnation (Galatians 3:16-18). His birth also illustrates the new birth. Every child of God is, like Isaac, 'born after the Spirit' (Galatians 4:29). Our Saviour said, 'That which is born of the flesh is flesh; and that which is born of the Spirit is spirit' (John 3:6). The new birth is not the work of the flesh, but of the Spirit, a sovereign, irresistible, unaided work of God's grace, according to covenant promise (Ezekiel 36:25-27). As Isaac, not Ishmael, was Abraham's heir, so all who are born again by God's free grace are 'heirs of God and joint-heirs with Christ' (Romans 8:17). Commenting on this John Gill states,

> Isaac was born out of the common order and course of nature; his conception and birth were owing to the promise and power of God, and to his free grace and favour to Abraham. This son of promise was a type of the spiritual seed of Abraham, whether Jews or Gentiles, the children of the promise that are counted for the seed; who are born again of the will, power, and grace of God, and are heirs, according to the promise, both of grace and glory, when they that are of the law, and the works of it, are not.

An Allegory

In verse 24 the Apostle tells us that 'which things are an allegory: for these are the two covenants; the one from the mount Sinai, which gendereth to bondage, which is Agar.' Paul does not mean for us to understand that these events of history just happen to illustrate what he is teaching. By divine inspiration, he is telling us they came to pass by God's intention and purpose to teach us these things. The purpose of God in bringing them to pass and recording them in the book of Genesis was to convey to us a picture of the distinction between the old covenant of works and the new covenant of grace.

We cannot understand the Bible correctly if we fail to see the constant distinction it makes between these two covenants. God established the old covenant of works in the garden with Adam and gave it to Israel through Moses at Mount Sinai. The new covenant, the covenant of grace and promise, was established in eternity with Christ, our Surety, the Surety of the covenant (Hebrews 7:22), and was ratified in time by the shedding of his blood at Calvary (Hebrews 9:11-28). This new covenant is seen in God's covenant with Abraham and was spoken of in prophecy by David, Jeremiah, and Ezekiel (Psalms 89; Jeremiah 31; Ezekiel 36; cf. Hebrews 8:10-13; 10:16-22).

In the old covenant of law and works God laid all responsibility upon the shoulders of men. It was a load that no man can carry. In the new covenant the Lord God laid upon his own darling Son the full weight of responsibility, making him alone totally responsible for the salvation of his people. Looking upon Christ as our Surety as the Lamb slain from the foundation of the world, trusting to him the whole of his glory and the whole of our salvation, the Lord God declared the whole work of redemption and grace done in that covenant before the world began (Ephesians 1:3-14; Romans 8:28-30).

This new covenant of life and grace, redemption and peace, though the first made, was the last revealed. Though made in eternity, it is called the 'new covenant' because it is always new and never old. The covenant of law and works is set before us in Genesis 2, where God commanded Adam to do something and threatened him with death, declaring that in the day he broke his covenant he would surely die. The new covenant, the covenant of grace, is set before us in Genesis 3 after the fall, when God promised to send his Son, the Seed of woman, to crush the serpent's head and save his fallen children. By slaying an innocent victim and clothing Adam and Eve with the skins of the slaim victim, God even pictured how the covenant would be fulfilled by Christ's vicarious death and righteousness. This covenant of grace was gradually revealed in greater fulness in God's covenant with Noah, his covenant with Abraham, Isaac, and Jacob, and his covenant with David. But we see it fully accomplished in the finished work of our Lord Jesus Christ.

While children of the bondwoman groan in bondage, trying to work themselves into the favour of God, every believer, every child of the free woman, walks at liberty and rejoices in the free, immaculate, immutable, indestructible grace of God, singing with David, 'Although my house be not so with God; yet he hath made with me an everlasting covenant, ordered in all things, and sure: for this is all my salvation, and all my desire, although he make it not to grow' (2 Samuel 23:5).

> With David's Lord and ours,
> A covenant once was made,
> Whose bonds are firm and sure,
> Whose glories ne'er shall fade;
> Signed by the Sacred Three in One
> In mutual love, ere time begun.
>
> Firm as the lasting hills
> This covenant shall endure,
> Whose potent shalls and wills
> Make every blessing sure;
> When ruin shakes all nature's frame
> Its jots and tittles stand the same.

For this Agar is mount Sinai in Arabia, and answereth to Jerusalem which now is, and is in bondage with her children. But Jerusalem which is above is free, which is the mother of us all. For it is written, Rejoice, thou barren that bearest not; break forth and cry, thou that travailest not: for the desolate hath many more children than she which hath an husband. Now we, brethren, as Isaac was, are the children of promise. But as then he that was born after the flesh persecuted him that was born after the Spirit, even so it is now. Nevertheless what saith the scripture? Cast out the bondwoman and her son: for the son of the bondwoman shall not be heir with the son of the freewoman. So then, brethren, we are not children of the bondwoman, but of the free.

(Galatians 4:25-31)

Chapter 24

Read: Galatians 4:25-31

Hagar And Sarah

Paul has stated that the history of Sarah and Hagar recorded in the book of Genesis is an allegory. In verses 21-24 he showed us that their sons, Isaac and Ishmael, represented the two covenants revealed in holy scripture. Ishmael represented the covenant of works (law) and Isaac the covenant of grace. Here he continues to explain the allegory, showing us the difference between the two covenants. As Isaac and Ishmael represent the two covenants, their mothers represent two Jerusalems.

Two Jerusalems

There are but two religions in the world: works and grace. The one system declares that salvation is obtained by what man does for God. The other declares that salvation is obtained by what God does for man. These two systems are here represented by two Jerusalems.

Hagar signifies Mount Sinai, or is a figure of the law given on that mount. She represents the covenant revealed and given to Israel on Mount Sinai. Therefore, Paul tells us that she 'answereth to Jerusalem which now is, and is in bondage with her children'.

Being a bondwoman, she represented that state of bondage the Jews were in at the time. They were, at the time, in a state of civil, moral, and

legal bondage. They were in civil bondage to the Romans. They were in
moral bondage to sin, to Satan, to the world and the lusts of it. And they
were in legal bondage to the law, 'the yoke of bondage' (Galatians 5:1).
John Gill described their state very clearly.

> They were in bondage under the elements or institutions of
> it, such as circumcision, a yoke which neither they, nor their
> forefathers could bear, because it bound them over to keep the
> whole law; the observance of various days, months, times, and
> years, and the multitude of sacrifices they were obliged to offer,
> which yet could not take away sin, nor free their consciences
> from the load of guilt, but were as an handwriting of ordinances
> against them; every sacrifice they brought declaring their sin
> and guilt, and that they deserved to die as the creature did that
> was sacrificed for them. And besides, this law of commandments,
> in various instances, the breach of it was punishable with death,
> through fear of which they were all their life long subject to
> bondage. They were also in bondage to the moral law, which
> required perfect obedience of them, but gave them no strength to
> perform; showed them their sin and misery, but not their remedy;
> demanded a complete righteousness, but did not point out where
> it was to be had. It spoke not one word of peace and comfort, but
> all the reverse. It admitted of no repentance. It accused of sin,
> pronounced guilty on account of it, cursed, condemned, and
> threatened with death for it, all which kept them in continual
> bondage.

True Religion Versus Legal Religion

Though there were exceptions, on the whole, the Jerusalem that then was
sought righteousness before God by their own works; by their 'obedience'
to the law of God. This only aggravated their bondage. Their obedience
was a mercenary obedience, not the obedience of a son, but of a slave. It
was not the obedience of love, but of fear. Such people, whether they
acknowledge it or not, are in bondage. Hagar represented Jerusalem, not
the geographic or political city Jerusalem, but that which it portrayed –
Judaism, the religious system of legalism, self-righteous, works religion.
Paul is telling us here that the covenant of works gives birth to a people
who live continually in spiritual bondage. Hagar represents all legal
religion, all self-righteous works religion.

Sarah, on the other hand, represents all true religion. She represents the covenant of grace. 'But Jerusalem which is above is free, which is the mother of us all' (v. 26). Here Paul describes the covenant of grace and life in Christ our Mediator, Representative, and sin-atoning Saviour. The kingdom of Christ is from heaven above, not from Sinai. The righteousness set forth and given in this covenant is found in his obedience, not in ours. Redemption is found in his sacrifice and his satisfaction, not in legal obedience and religious ceremonies. In the covenant of grace we have access to and acceptance with the holy Lord God through Christ, our great High Priest, not through an earthly priesthood or by our own merit (Hebrews 10:10-22). This covenant is free from the curse and bondage of the law and is the mother of every believer, Jew and Gentile. 'Jerusalem which is above' (the church of Christ) is 'the mother of us all' in the sense that she embraces all who trust Christ. We are born of grace. 'For by grace are ye saved through faith; and that not of yourselves: it is the gift of God: not of works, lest any man should boast' (Ephesians 2:8-9).

God's Church
'Jerusalem which is above' is the church and kingdom of Christ. Christ's church and kingdom lives by covenant grace. The apostle John uses the same imagery in describing God's church. He writes, 'I John saw the holy city, new Jerusalem, coming down from God out of heaven, prepared as a bride adorned for her husband ... And he carried me away in the spirit to a great and high mountain, and showed me that great city, the holy Jerusalem, descending out of heaven from God, Having the glory of God: and her light was like unto a stone most precious, even like a jasper stone, clear as crystal ... And the city had no need of the sun, neither of the moon, to shine in it: for the glory of God did lighten it, and the Lamb is the light thereof. And the nations of them which are saved shall walk in the light of it: and the kings of the earth do bring their glory and honour into it. And the gates of it shall not be shut at all by day: for there shall be no night there. And they shall bring the glory and honour of the nations into it. And there shall in no wise enter into it any thing that defileth, neither whatsoever worketh abomination, or maketh a lie: but they which are written in the Lamb's book of life' (Revelation 21:2, 10, 11, 23-27).

The church is called Jerusalem because the name signifies peace. The church and kingdom of God is under the government and rule of Christ the Prince of peace. God's saints are children of peace. We have been given peace and are called to peace, and by faith in Christ enjoy peace with God. The gospel of Christ is the gospel of peace. The covenant of grace, of which Paul is speaking, is the covenant of peace. Jerusalem, the object of God's choice, the palace of the great King, the place of divine worship, was compact together, and well fortified. As such, it stands in Scripture as a picture of the church and kingdom of our God.

As Hagar and Sarah gave birth to two distinct sons (a slave and an heir), the covenant of works and the covenant of grace give birth to two distinct nations (a nation of bondmen and a nation of free born sons). It is impossible for anyone to belong to both nations at the same time. Edgar Andrews writes, 'We cannot simultaneously be under the law and under grace. We are either children of the earthly Jerusalem, in bondage to a fruitless religion of works; or we are children of the heavenly Jerusalem, and enjoy the glorious liberty of the children of God. We are either slaves like Ishmael, or heirs like Isaac.'

Bondage

Paul tells us that Hagar 'is in bondage with her children'. What is this bondage? How are all who seek righteousness by the law brought into bondage? How are men brought into bondage by the law? They are in bondage because they set about to do that which cannot be done. They pursue righteousness by the works of the law, but never attain it. The law requires men to work for reward; but they can never do the work. The law demands both righteousness and satisfaction for sin, but man can produce neither. Everything man does, both regenerate men and unregenerate men, is tainted by sin and can never satisfy the law, which requires perfection (Leviticus 22:21; Galatians 3:10). Being ignorant of God's righteousness, they go about to establish their own righteousness, refusing to trust Christ, refusing to submit to the righteousness of God in Christ. They simply cannot grasp the fact that 'Christ is the end of the law for righteousness to every one that believeth' (Romans 9:31-10:4). Consequently, they can never rest. They can never cease from their work. They are doomed to endless bondage and slavery.

Every religion that teaches sinners to perform works of any kind to obtain righteousness is a prison. To quote Edgar Andrews, 'This is true, even if the work required is to "believe", or "trust", or "commit", or "surrender".' Such things are just as truly 'works' as circumcision, sabbath keeping, penances and pilgrimages. Legalism tells sinners to work for grace. The gospel of Christ declares that grace comes freely. Good works follow God's operations of grace. They do not cause them (Ephesians 2:8-10). 'It is God which worketh in you both to will and to do of his good pleasure' (Philippians 2:13). He does not wait for you to do something for him.

Do not make the mistake that most do in thinking that the bondage of legalism refers only to those who seek justifying righteousness by works. It also applies to those who seek righteousness and holiness in sanctification by their own works. In fact, that is precisely what Paul is dealing with in Galatians 3 and 4 (Galatians 3:1-3, 10). Sanctification, like justification, is the free gift of God's grace in Christ, enjoyed by faith, without works (1 Corinthians 1:30-31; Hebrews 10:10, 14).

Even true believers can bring themselves into bondage by such ignorance, as is evidenced by this epistle. Throughout the six chapters of this book Paul treats the Galatians as believers, as we have seen (3:1-3, 26-29; 4:6-9; 5:7-10, 13; 6:1). He regarded them as believers who were being confused and led astray by false doctrine, the false doctrine of works righteousness. We seek to honour God our Saviour in all things, ever striving against sin, not to attain righteousness before God, but because our great and gracious God has made us righteous in Christ (1 Corinthians 6:9-11, 19-20; 10:31).

Freedom

'But Jerusalem which is above is free, which is the mother of us all' (4:26). The heavenly Jerusalem, the church of Christ, is founded on the covenant of promise, which has its fulfilment in the new covenant ratified by the blood of Christ. 'For it is written, Rejoice, thou barren that bearest not; break forth and cry, thou that travailest not: for the desolate hath many more children than she which hath an husband' (4:27).

Paul here quotes from Isaiah 54:1, promising the continual enlargement of God's church and kingdom in this world until all Israel (all God's elect) is saved in fulfilment of his covenant purpose (Romans 11:26-27). Sarah's inability to give birth to Isaac was no hindrance to God fulfilling his promise. Rather, her inability was the very thing that demonstrated that God alone could fulfil the promise. So it is with us. If the Lord God left salvation, in any measure, to us, none could ever be saved. But that which is impossible with man is possible with God. Where sin abounds, grace much more abounds (Romans 5:20). By God's free and sovereign grace 'Jerusalem which is above' shall be a city fully inhabited (Revelation 21:10-17).

'Now we, brethren, as Isaac was, are the children of promise' (4:28). Believers are the children of promise, as Isaac was. As Isaac was promised to Abraham, we were promised and given to the Lord Jesus Christ (Ephesians 1:3, 4; John 6: 37-39). As Isaac was conceived and born by the power of God, we are born spiritually by God's omnipotent grace (John

1:12,13; Ephesians 1:19-20; Colossians 2:12). As Isaac was the heir of Abraham, we are heirs of God and joint-heirs with Christ (Romans 8:16,17).

The inhabitants of this city of grace, 'Jerusalem which is above', are 'the children of promise', being born of God in fulfilment of the covenant of promise in Christ. We are free from the law, no longer subject to its requirements or its penalties. That does not mean that God's saints are a lawless people. We are under a new law, the rule and law of Christ (1 Corinthians 9:21; Galatians 6:2). It is written in our hearts (Jeremiah 31:31-33). In all things we are motivated by the love of Christ (2 Corinthians 5:14). The Son of God has made us free; and we are free indeed (John 8:36).

Ishmael The Persecutor

'But as then he that was born after the flesh persecuted him that was born after the Spirit, even so it is now' (4:29). Ishmael, the son of the flesh, mocked and persecuted the son of promise (Genesis 21:9). Nothing has changed. False prophets, teaching righteousness by works, trying to bring God's saints back under the yoke of legal bondage, mock and deride, slander and persecute all who trust Christ alone for righteousness. Salvation by works and salvation by grace are mutually exclusive. Legalists are threatened by grace, just as Ishmael was threatened by Isaac. He was not threatened by anything Isaac did, but by the mere fact that Isaac lived as Abraham's free born son. And legalists are not threatened by anything God's people do. Believers do not mock and persecute others. Legalists are threatened by the mere fact that we live in this world as God's free born children, walking in the liberty of grace.

Ishmael Cast Out

Grace and works, as stated above, are mutually exclusive. Therefore Paul writes, 'Nevertheless what saith the scripture? Cast out the bondwoman and her son: for the son of the bondwoman shall not be heir with the son of the freewoman' (4:30). This was God's command to Abraham (Genesis 21:10-12). Ishmael, the child of flesh, the fruit of Abraham's works, had to be cast out along with the mother who produced him, and cast out by Abraham. God would not allow Ishmael to be an heir with Isaac, the true son. He will not allow any mixture of works and grace (Romans 11:6). We must cast aside the filthy rags of our own righteousness, if we would wear the righteousness of Christ. All systems of works and human merit must be forsaken from our hearts. Works religion must be cast out of our churches. We must have 'no fellowship with the unfruitful works of darkness' (Ephesians 5:11). The heirs of God are the children of grace in Christ Jesus. The self-righteous, those who seek righteousness by works, those who are part Christ and part flesh, part grace and part works advocates, cannot be heirs with children of promise.

'So then, brethren, we are not children of the bondwoman, but of the free' (4:31). There can be no marriage of law and grace. Believers are not hybrids or mongrels. We are the children of free grace and heirs of all that God promised his sons and daughters in the covenant of grace before the world began, 'heirs of God and joint-heirs with Christ'.

Stand fast therefore in the liberty wherewith Christ hath made us free, and be not entangled again with the yoke of bondage. Behold, I Paul say unto you, that if ye be circumcised, Christ shall profit you nothing. For I testify again to every man that is circumcised, that he is a debtor to do the whole law. Christ is become of no effect unto you, whosoever of you are justified by the law; ye are fallen from grace.

(Galatians 5:1-4)

Chapter 25

Read: Galatians 5:1-4

The Blessed Liberty Of Grace

In this chapter the Apostle Paul urges every believer to stand firm in the blessed liberty of the gospel, the liberty of grace, and urges us never to abuse that liberty. We must stand fast in, hold to, defend, and maintain 'the liberty wherewith Christ hath made us free'. The liberty we have in Christ is too precious to lose or take for granted. It is the liberty of grace, salvation, and life in him. Every believer, every saved sinner, every heaven born soul is free in Christ. Because 'we are not children of the bondwoman, but of the free' (Galatians 4:31), because Christ has made us free, we must continually stand fast in the blessed liberty of grace.

Paul's exhortation in verse 1 could not be urged with more pressing arguments than those given in verses 2-4. All who attempt to make themselves holy before God by the works of the law have made Christ and his redemptive work meaningless to themselves and have fallen from grace altogether (vv. 2-4). Works salvation is not simply a doctrinal error; it is an utter denial of the gospel of Christ. To embrace it is to embrace 'another gospel' (Galatians 1:6-9).

Made Free

'Stand fast therefore in the liberty wherewith Christ hath made us free' (v. 1). It is Christ who has made us free, and Christ who keeps us free. He has made us free by his obedience unto death as our Substitute and by the gift of his grace in the new birth. He keeps us in the blessed liberty of grace as he keeps us looking to him alone for righteousness, acceptance with God, assurance, and peace. Yet, it is our responsibility to continually look to him, to continually trust him, and refuse to be entangled with the oppressive yoke of legal bondage. What is this 'liberty wherewith Christ hath made us free'?

It Is Liberty From The Law's Bondage
Believer's are not under the law. This fact cannot be stated more emphatically, or more constantly than it is throughout the New Testament. Every reference to the law of God as it relates to believers declares that we are dead to it and it to us, because Christ has fulfilled it for us (Romans 6:14-15; 7:1-4; 8:1-4; 10:4; Galatians 3:24-25; Colossians 2:8-17; 1 Timothy 1:8-10). There is not a single passage to be found in the New Testament in which believers are motivated by law to do anything. 'Christ is the end of the law'. No, he did not destroy the law. He fulfilled it, finished it, and brought it to an end. He was made under the law, that he might fulfil it for us. Now, he is free from the law. And we are free from the law in him, in exactly the same sense and to exactly the same degree. We are free from the curse of the law (Galatians 3:13-14), the condemnation of the law (Romans 8:1), and from the covenant of the law (Galatians 4:24-31). Martin Luther wrote, 'In the stead of sin and death, he giveth unto us righteousness and everlasting life; and by this means he changeth the bondage and terrors of the law into liberty of conscience and consolation of the gospel.'

Almost all who profess to believe that salvation is by grace agree that we are free from the ceremonial law, that we are free from circumcision, feast days, sacrifices, and all the burdensome, carnal rites and ceremonies of the Mosaic dispensation. But many try to impose upon us the rules of the moral law (the ten commandments), vainly attempting to divide the moral law from the ceremonial law. Such a division does not exist in the Word of God. Those who would teach us to live by the moral law, were they consistent, must also demand that we observe and keep all the carnal ordinances of the ceremonial law. It is impossible to keep a sabbath day without a sacrifice! (Read and see what the law says – Numbers 28:9-10.)

I do not suggest or imply that believers are free to violate God's law. The Word of God does not teach that and believers do not live in rebellion to the law. However, the Word of God does teach, and I do assert, that all who are born of God are free from the yoke, bondage, curse, and rule of the law. We do not mind repeating Philip Bliss's fine verses:

Free from the law – O happy condition!
Jesus hath bled, and there is remission.
Cursed by the law and bruised by the fall,
Christ hath redeemed us once for all.

Now are we free – there's no condemnation!
Jesus provides a perfect salvation.
'Come unto Me' – O hear His sweet call!
Come – and He saves us once for all.

Children of God – O glorious calling!
Surely His grace will keep us from falling.
Passing from death to life at His call,
Blessed salvation – once for all!

Liberty From Sin

We are not free from the being of sin, nor from the indwelling of it, nor from the temptation to it, but from the dominion and damning power of it (Romans 6:11, 18; 1 John 3:5). The Lord God imputed all our sins (past, present, and future) to Christ and punished him for them to the full satisfaction of justice. Christ, by his one offering for sin, has purged our sins and put them away forever. That means that God will never impute sin to any for whom Christ was made to be sin. Thus, we say with David, 'Blessed is the man to whom the Lord will not impute sin' (Romans 4:6-8).

Liberty Of Life

Spiritual, eternal life is ours in Christ (Ephesians 2:1, 5-6; 1 Peter 1:23-25; Revelation 20:6). Being made partakers of the first resurrection, we shall be made partakers of resurrection glory when Christ comes again. That is to say, as surely as Christ has given us spiritual life, he will raise our bodies to life and immortality at the last day (1 Corinthians 15:53-58; 1 Thessalonians 4:13-18). We 'shall be delivered from the bondage of corruption into the glorious liberty of the children of God' (Romans 8:21).

With this liberty of life in Christ comes freedom from the fear of death. Christ has destroyed the power of death by dying in our place and rising again. Since all of God's elect were partakers of flesh and blood, under the dominion of death, Christ became a man to suffer and die for us. It was not possible for our Representative to satisfy the claims of divine justice against us unless he lived and died in our nature. By his substitutionary death on the cursed tree and his triumphant resurrection, the Son of God destroyed the power of Satan and the power of the grave over us. We are now more than conquerors in him. Why then should we fear death?

The Lord Jesus delivers us from the fear of death by removing our sin. 'The sting of death is sin.' It is sin that causes men torment in death. But in Christ we have no sin. In him we are fully forgiven. By his blood our sins are washed away. If we are born of God, we are in Christ; 'and in him is no sin' (1 John 3:1-5). Be sure you have the forgiveness of sin by faith in Christ, and fear death no more. To die forgiven, 'accepted in the Beloved', is not really to die at all. It is simply the departure out of this world into the Father's house. The Son of God declares, 'Whosoever liveth and believeth in me shall never die' (John 11:26).

The law of God held us in bondage to the sentence of death and condemnation; but 'Christ hath redeemed us from the curse of the law' (Galatians 3:13). 'Christ is the end of the law for righteousness to everyone that believeth' (Romans 10:4). He is the end of the law's power to condemn. In the book of God's holy law there is no legal claim of condemnation upon any believer. Christ satisfied that claim for us. Why then should we fear? If I am in Christ, I am dead to the law (Romans 7:4; 8:1-4).

The Lord Jesus Christ delivers us from the fear of death by changing the character of death. For the unbeliever death is a horrible thing. For the unbeliever, anything short of death is mercy. But, for the believer death is a great blessing. John Trapp wrote, 'To those that are in Christ death is but the day-break of eternal brightness; not the punishment of sin, but the period of sin. It is but a sturdy porter opening the door of eternity, a rough passage to eternal pleasure.'

Why should Israel be afraid to cross the swelling Jordan into the land of promise with the ark of God before them? The fact is, believers do not die in the sense that others do (John 11:25-26). To the ungodly, death is the penalty of sin; but to the believer, it is just a change of location. Death to the wicked is the execution of justice; but to the believer it is a deliverance from sin. To the worldling, death is the beginning of sorrows; but to the believer, it is admission into glory. To the rebel, death is imprisonment; but to the believer, it is freedom.

Liberty Of Sonship

Moreover, the Lord Jesus has given us free access to the throne of grace (Hebrews 4:16), free use of the gospel ordinances, freedom to use all things for his glory, and freedom from the fear of death and of judgment. This is Paul's admonition — do not allow anyone to entangle you with any system of works religion. We are free in Christ, because we are complete in Christ (Colossians 2:9-10).

Stand Fast

Paul uses a term borrowed from the battlefield in verse 1. He says, 'Hold your ground. Stand fast.' Your freedom in Christ is under constant assault. As those who have been set free from the shame, drudgery, shackles and misery of slavery, we must never allow anyone to bring us back under the yoke of bondage.

'Be not entangled again with the yoke of bondage.' The yoke of bondage is the yoke of legal slavery (Galatians 2:4). Those who are under the yoke of slavery to the law are under an unbearable yoke (Acts 15:10), and are condemned to the futile pursuit of righteousness by their own obedience. They can never find rest. The Lord Jesus calls for sinners to come to him and take upon them his easy yoke and light burden, assuring all who come that they shall find rest for their souls in him (Matthew 11:28-30).

Here is Christ's word to lost, ruined, guilty sinners: 'Come unto me, all ye that labour and are heavy laden, and I will give you rest.' There is no salvation to be had, but by coming to Christ. There can never be any true, peaceful, satisfying rest for our souls, except we come to Christ, trusting him alone as our Lord and Saviour; trusting his blood as our only atonement and his obedience as our only righteousness. Only Christ can give weary sinners rest.

Here is the Master's word to us all, both to the unbeliever and the believer; 'Take my yoke upon you, and learn of me; for I am meek and lowly in heart: and ye shall find rest unto your souls.' In all circumstances of life we find rest unto our souls only as we voluntarily submit to the rule and dominion of the Son of God as our Lord and King. The only way to find rest is to willingly slip our necks under his yoke. When we do and only when we do, we will find that his yoke really is easy and his burden really is light. I bid you now, whatever your circumstances, take the Master's yoke upon you, and find rest unto your soul. Take upon you the yoke of his grace, bowing to him as your Lord (Luke 14:25-33). Take upon you the yoke of his doctrine, his gospel, bowing to him as your Prophet (Jeremiah 6:16). Take upon you his yoke of providence, trusting him as your God and Saviour (Psalms 31:1, 5, 7, 15). Only in this way do we find rest for our souls.

'Come unto me, all ye that labour and are heavy laden, and I will give you rest. Take my yoke upon you, and learn of me; for I am meek and lowly in heart: and ye shall find rest unto your souls. For my yoke is easy, and my burden is light.' The call of the gospel is a call to rest, the blessed rest of faith in Christ. It is this rest that the Old Testament sabbath day pointed to and typified. All things relating to sabbath law in the Old Testament pointed to the necessity and blessedness of that rest of faith which believers enjoy in Christ (Hebrews 4:9-10). 'It is', wrote Edgar Andrews, 'to die with him, to rise with him, to walk with him and to reign with him. It is to be cleansed by his blood, led by his Spirit, taught by his Word, strengthened by his power, filled with his love ... A bird, released from captivity, is free to soar above the mountains, rove the land and cross the oceans. There are no limits to its odyssey. So there is no limit to the liberated soul. It is free to explore the "breadth and length and depth and height; and to know the love of Christ, which passes knowledge," free to be "filled with all the fulness of God" (Ephesians 3:18-19).'

'If Ye Be Circumcised'

Christ must be trusted as our only, all-sufficient Saviour. True faith looks to Christ alone. If we add anything, even the most solemn religious duties, to the obedience and blood of Christ to obtain God's favour, to improve our standing in God's favour, or to keep God's favour, whether it be circumcision, baptism, Bible reading, praying, church attendance, or doing good for others, we do not fully trust Christ alone as our Redeemer and Saviour (v. 2). Such proud self-righteousness is an utter contempt of Christ. He profits us nothing because we are, rather than submitting to the righteousness of God in Christ, going about to establish our own righteousness (Romans 10:3).

A Debtor

That person who seeks righteousness to any degree by his own works and religious exercises does not trust Christ alone and, therefore, is a debtor to keep the whole law perfectly (v. 3). 'Tell me, ye that desire to be under the law, do ye not hear the law?' (Galatians 4:21). The law demands perfect, complete obedience. 'For as many as are of the works of the law are under the curse: for it is written, Cursed is everyone that continueth not in all things which are written in the book of the law to do them' (Galatians 3:10).

Fallen From Grace

Keep this verse (v. 4) in its context. Remember to whom it is written and for what reason. Paul is addressing himself to those people, whoever and wherever they may be, who try to merit God's favour by something they do; who have one eye on Christ and one eye on their own works. Such people, while professing to believe in salvation by grace, have departed from it altogether. You have fallen from the gospel of the grace of God and embraced another gospel. Christ is become of no effect to you.

Paul is not suggesting that such people once were saved, but now are lost again. Those who are saved by grace, those to whom Christ gives eternal life 'shall never perish'. These people never truly had the grace of God. They only claimed to have it. They never truly walked in grace. They merely professed to walk in grace. Those who depart from the faith never had faith. Works and grace are mutually exclusive (Romans 11:5-6). Joseph Hart writes:

> How can ye hope, deluded souls,
> To see what none e'er saw,
> Salvation by the works obtained
> Of Sinai's fiery law?
>
> There ye may toil, and weep, and fast,
> And vex your heart with pain;
> And, when you've ended, find at last,
> That all your toil was vain.
>
> That law but makes your guilt abound;
> Sad help! and (what is worst),
> All souls that under that are found,
> By God himself are curs'd

For we through the Spirit wait for the hope of righteousness by faith. For in Jesus Christ neither circumcision availeth any thing, nor uncircumcision; but faith which worketh by love.

(Galatians 5:5-6)

Chapter 26

Read: Galatians 5:5-6

The Hope Of Righteousness

Paul has fully demonstrated the fact that the justification of God's elect is free and complete, that it is entirely detached from and is in no way connected with our own obedience to the law, and is received by faith alone. In the opening verses of this chapter he calls for all who know this righteousness, for all who trust the Lord Jesus Christ, to stand fast in the blessed liberty of grace. That liberty is the perfect and complete freedom Christ has, by himself alone, obtained for us by his obedience and death as our sin-atoning Substitute. He has, as the great Head and Surety of his church, redeemed us from the curse of the law, being made a curse for us.

Free In Christ

Therefore, 'the law of the Spirit of life in Christ Jesus hath made me free from the law of sin and death' (Romans 8:2). We are free in Christ. Let us cherish and stand fast in that blessed liberty our Saviour has obtained for us. He has, as our Surety and Representative, answered every demand of God's holy law and justice. He has paid our debt for every sin, suffered our penalty for every breach of God's law, and thereby completely satisfied divine justice for us. As our Surety, he has magnified the law and made it honourable (Isaiah 42:21). Upon the basis of his finished work of righteousness and redemption, he says 'to the prisoners, Go forth; to them that sit in darkness, Show yourselves' (Isaiah 49:9). 'We are not under the law, but under grace' (Romans 6:15). Robert Hawker says,

The whole church of God, therefore, and every individual soul of that church, is delivered from the curse of the law: from guilt, from sin, from the accusations of Satan, the alarms of conscience, unbelief, and all the whole train of evils of a fallen state. And it is the privilege of all the church of God to behold themselves in Christ, perfectly holy in him. For Christ and his church being one, what Christ is in God's sight so must the church be. And, as God hath declared himself well pleased in him, the church is included in this view, and is 'holy and without blame before him in love'.

Sinners Still

Every child of God is freely, fully, completely holy in Christ before God. We are eternally 'accepted in the Beloved' (Ephesians 1:6). 'He was manifested to take away our sins; and in him is no sin' (1 John 3:5). Yet, we are (in ourselves) sinners still. We still carry within us the body of sin and death. In the new birth God the Holy Spirit created a new nature within us, but our old, Adamic nature is unchanged. That old nature is altogether unholy. All that is evil in the world is in us by nature. We feel the assaults of sin. We groan and mourn under the weight of inward corruption. We are ever at war within ourselves. As Paul stated it, we delight in the law of God after the inward man; but we constantly find that when we would do good evil is present with us, and we cannot do the things we would (Romans 7:14-23).

Christ has freed us from all the condemnation due to sin, but not yet from its inward corruption. He has freed us from the penalty due to our sins, but not yet from the sorrow of sin. Christ has conquered sin, death, hell, and the grave for us, and has made us more than conquerors in him. Yet, so long as we are in the world, we must struggle against sin in our members. We know, by constant, painful experience the horrible evil that is within us.

Yet, in the teeth of all the wickedness that is in us and that which is done by us the Spirit of God calls for us to 'Stand fast therefore in the liberty wherewith Christ hath made us free.' The terrors of the law have nothing to do with the sinner who is justified by God's free grace through the redemption that is in Christ Jesus. It is written, 'If any man sin, we have an advocate with the Father, Jesus Christ the righteous: and he is the propitiation for our sins' (1 John 2:1-2). 'There is therefore now no condemnation to them which are in Christ Jesus' (Romans 8:1).

This 'liberty wherewith Christ hath made us free' is unspeakable, blessed liberty. It is written, 'Where the Spirit of the Lord is, there is liberty' (2 Corinthians 3:17). It is this liberty given by Christ through the indwelling of his blessed Spirit that causes God's saints in this world to 'rejoice in hope of the glory of God'. Knowing that we are freely, fully, completely justified by Christ, by faith in him we have peace with God and confidently anticipate the glory that awaits us (Romans 4:25-5:5).

Through The Spirit
'For we through the Spirit wait for the hope of righteousness by faith' (v. 5). We who believe in Christ by the gift, grace, power, and operations of God the Holy Spirit do not look for and expect heaven and eternal happiness through any law-work performed by us, but through the righteousness of Christ received by faith, under the influence and testimony of the Spirit of God.

It is God the Holy Spirit whose office and work it is to convince chosen, redeemed sinners of the righteousness of God brought in for sinners by the obedience and death of our all-glorious Christ (John 16:8-11). When he reveals Christ, he works faith in the heart by convincing God's elect of their own sin, of righteousness established, brought in for them and imputed to them by Christ's obedience in life, and of judgment (condemnation) finished by his obedience unto death.

Until God the Holy Spirit has revealed Christ in us and convinced us of his righteousness, causing us to cast aside all our own imaginary righteousness, being satisfied and delighted with Christ and his righteousness, we can never know this blessed liberty. But when the Spirit of God comes in saving power and grace and reveals Christ in the heart, the chosen, redeemed sinner is delighted to cast off all his carnal hopes and trust Christ alone as 'The Lord our Righteousness'. Then, ceasing from all our works, we rest with full assurance of faith and 'rejoice in hope of the glory of God'. This is the meaning of our Saviour's words in John 16:14, 'He shall glorify me: for he shall receive of mine, and shall show it unto you.'

The Hope Of Righteousness
'For we through the Spirit wait for the hope of righteousness by faith'. When Paul speaks here of 'the hope of righteousness', he is not referring to the righteousness of Christ imputed to us by which we are justified, as if our justification and righteousness before God is something yet to be hoped for, or as if to imply that we are not yet complete in Christ (Colossians 2:9-10). Not at all. Our righteousness before God was established, wrought

out, and brought in by Christ, who is the end of the law for righteousness. It is revealed in the gospel from faith to faith, being revealed and applied to God's elect by the Holy Spirit. It is put upon us and imputed to us by the Father. This righteousness is something that is the present possession of all who believe on the Son of God. It is written, 'Ye are justified in the name of the Lord Jesus' (1 Corinthians 6:11). Christ is made of God unto us righteousness (1 Corinthians 1:30). Righteousness before God is not something we have in hope, but in hand.

The righteousness of faith is not something we hope to have in the future, but something we have already received. It is called 'the righteousness of faith', not because faith performed it, or established it, but because faith receives it from God (Romans 5:1-10). This is that righteousness in which we stand and in which we shall ever be found.

'The hope of righteousness' is the confident, eager, assured hope and expectation of eternal glory with Christ, secured to us by that perfect righteousness that is ours in Christ. Because the righteousness of Christ is ours, because we are assured of that fact by the indwelling Spirit of God by whom the love of God is shed abroad in our hearts, we are assured of our inheritance of eternal glory with Christ as the children of God. In fact, the Holy Spirit is himself the seal and pledge of that inheritance (2 Corinthians 1:21-22; Ephesians 1:13-14; 4:30).

The only basis, foundation, and assurance of our hope is the righteousness of Christ. We know that none but those who are perfectly righteous shall enter into heaven (Revelation 21:27). Because Christ is our righteousness and we are made the righteousness of God in him, we eagerly wait for our eternal inheritance upon the ground of justice as well as grace. John Gill wrote,

> Waiting for it supposes it to be certain, real, solid, substantial, valuable, and worth waiting for; which, when possessed, will be with the utmost pleasure, and be abundantly satisfying; and that the persons that wait for it have knowledge, and at least hope of interest in it; and do highly value and esteem it, having their hearts set on it, and looking with contempt on the things of time and sense, in comparison of it.

Faith And Love

'For in Jesus Christ neither circumcision availeth any thing, nor uncircumcision; but faith which worketh by love' (v. 6). In Christ law-work means nothing. Everything Paul says about 'circumcision' is equally applicable to everything men attempt to join with Christ for righteousness. Though circumcision was the solemn ordinance of God in the Old Testament, those who observe that rite or do anything else to obtain righteousness before God are saying that Christ is not enough, that he has not fulfilled all righteousness, and that his obedience and death were meaningless. They do, in effect, make Christ to be of no effect. They have totally departed from the gospel of the grace of God. Like the Jews of old, they, being ignorant of the righteousness of God in Christ, go about to establish their own righteousness and refuse to submit to Christ alone for righteousness. They have not yet learned the sweet meaning of that blessed assertion of the gospel; 'Christ is the end of the law for righteousness to everyone that believeth' (Romans 10:3-4).

In the church and kingdom of God the only thing that matters is faith in Christ, that faith that God the Holy Spirit has wrought in and given to every believer, that faith that constantly works and operates upon the basis of the love of God shed abroad in our hearts by the Holy Spirit. 'The love of Christ constraineth us' (2 Corinthians 5:14). This is the fruit of the Spirit (Galatians 5:22-23).

Faith in Christ shows its existence by love to God and to men. Faith is not a mere intellectual assent to revealed truth. It is that which reaches the heart and controls the affections. Faith is not dead, but operative. It is manifest in kindness and affection (Romans 12:10). Religion without Christ, all law based (works based) religion, leaves the heart cold and hard, judgmental and harsh, constantly stirring up strife and division, causing its adherents to look down their noses at others and say, 'Stand by thyself, come not near to me; for I am holier than thou' (Isaiah 65:5). Faith in Christ causes men to know themselves, and that makes them esteem their brethren better than themselves in love. Faith causes saved men and women to be gracious, kind, long-suffering, forbearing, forgiving, and charitable in attitude and in deed. As James puts it, 'Pure religion and undefiled before God and the Father is this, To visit the fatherless and widows in their affliction, and to keep himself unspotted from the world' (James 1:27).

The love of God shed abroad in our hearts in Christ, not the law given at Sinai, is the believer's rule of life. We 'have not received the spirit of bondage again to fear'. We no longer require the rule of fear. We 'have received the Spirit of adoption, whereby we cry, Abba, Father' (Romans 8:15). The Holy Spirit working teaches us to love our God and one another. Nothing inspires devotion like liberty. Find a child who is thoroughly happy, and you will see a child who seeks to please his parents, one who looks upon his duties as light, easy, and delightful things. Find one who is miserable, and you will see one whose every duty is like an iron chain upon him. Law is bondage and death. Grace is liberty and life. 'Walk in the Spirit and ye shall not fulfil the lust of the flesh' (Galatians 5:16). If you attempt to live by the law, you cannot do otherwise. 'If ye be led of the Spirit, ye are not under the law' (Galatians 5:18).

Ye did run well; who did hinder you that ye should not obey the truth? This persuasion cometh not of him that calleth you. A little leaven leaveneth the whole lump. I have confidence in you through the Lord, that ye will be none otherwise minded: but he that troubleth you shall bear his judgment, whosoever he be. And I, brethren, if I yet preach circumcision, why do I yet suffer persecution? then is the offence of the cross ceased. I would they were even cut off which trouble you.

(Galatians 5:7-12)

Chapter 27

Read: Galatians 5:7-12

Troublers Of Israel

The church of our Lord Jesus Christ is 'a habitation of God, through the Spirit'. It is His kingdom of righteousness and peace. Yet, there have always been those who would do everything in their power to destroy the peace and joy of God's people by taking their hearts and minds away from the true worship of God in Spirit and truth, and fixing them upon some external object or ceremony. They are troublers of Israel, who impede the progress and worship of the church of God by their corrupting influence.

The church of the Old Testament had many such troublers. The one who stands out most conspicuously in my mind is that wicked King Ahab. You will remember how that Ahab kept Israel in constant turmoil by his childish peevishness and constant sin. He hindered the worship of Israel, and turned them aside from worshipping Jehovah, the God of grace and mercy, to worship the works of their own hands. But in those dark days God had his prophet, whom he had preserved for the comfort, protection, instruction, and preservation of his church. That godly old prophet was Elijah. Elijah was a marvellous man. He was as bold as a lion in the cause of God. He was a man of righteousness and great faith.

Are you not surprised when you read of the meeting of Elijah and Ahab face to face, and how that ungodly king charged the prophet of God with being the one 'that troubleth Israel' (1 Kings 18:17)? Indeed, we would all be surprised, were it not for the fact that this has always been the case. Those who trouble God's people with their wicked ways are always the ones who turn upon God's servants, who uphold the way of truth, and charge them with disturbing the peace of the saints. Thus, Ahab so charged Elijah, Israel so charged Moses, Hananiah so charged Jeremiah, Haman so charged Mordecai, and Zedekiah so charged Micaiah.

But this was not only true throughout the history of the Old Testament church. It was also true of the church in the New Testament. There are several examples of this in the New Testament; but we will limit our thoughts in this study to the ones exhibited in our text. The apostle Paul was the most zealous, self-sacrificing, and successful of all the apostles of Christ. Yet, he was incessantly charged by false teachers with inconsistency and troubling the church. This was exactly what had happened in the church at Galatia.

These troublers of Israel had come to Galatia after Paul left that region, and began to pervert the gospel of Christ. They were not teaching anything directly contrary to the facts of the gospel. They were, in fact, teaching the very same thing that Paul taught – that Christ, the Son of God, died for our sins, was buried, and rose again on the third day. They taught that salvation is by the grace of God in Christ. But, along with the message of grace, these false teachers were saying that it was also necessary for a man to be circumcised and keep the law of Moses in order to truly be a Christian.

Thus, they perverted the gospel. In doing this they had taken away the peace, joy, and comfort the Galatians had enjoyed in the grace of God. Instead of worshipping God in Spirit and in truth as free sons, they had been brought to 'observe the days, and months, and times, and years' of the Jewish calendar as slaves in bondage to the law. And in order to buttress their weak, legalistic position, and deceive many into their persuasion, they said that Paul himself had taught this doctrine. In the passage before us Paul takes these troublers of Israel and their legalistic doctrines to task.

Up to this point he has been addressing the saints at Galatia, and has expressed his confidence that they would recover from their error (v. 10). But here he condemns those false teachers who had led them astray from 'the simplicity that is in Christ' (2 Corinthians 11:3). Those who, by their false teachings and corrupt practices, defile the church of God shall most assuredly bear the judgment of God.

Hindered In The Race

The Apostle goes back in his mind for the fourth time (Galatians 1:8-9; 3:2-3; 4:9, 12-15) to the time when the Galatians had heard the gospel from his lips and had accepted Christ as their Saviour and Lord. But someone had hindered them in their race. He says, in verse 7, 'Ye did run well'. Then he asks, 'Who did hinder you that ye should not obey the truth?'

Paul characteristically compares the Christian life to the famous Isthmian races (1 Corinthians 9:24; Philippians 3:13-14; 2 Timothy 4:7-8). There is a cloud of witnesses in heaven urging us on in this race, 'Wherefore seeing we also are compassed about with so great a cloud of witnesses, let us lay aside every weight, and the sin which doth so easily beset us, and let us run with patience the race that is set before us, Looking unto Jesus the author and finisher of our faith; who for the joy that was set before him endured the cross, despising the shame, and is set down at the right hand of the throne of God. For consider him that endured such contradiction of sinners against himself, lest ye be wearied and faint in your minds. Ye have not yet resisted unto blood, striving against sin' (Hebrews 12:1-4).

These witnesses are the saints of God who have gone before us. There is a course of work set before us. It is the course of faith in Christ. The race must be run patiently and perseveringly. Christ our Saviour has run the race before us, leaving us an example to follow; and he will carry us through to the end and crown us in the end. Let us ever look to and focus our hearts on him. 'He that endureth to the end shall be saved', (Matthew 10:22, 1 Peter 5:4; Revelation 2:10).

When the Galatians first professed faith in Christ, they ran well. They were steadfast in the gospel and zealous for the glory of God. They were devoted to Christ and increasing in the knowledge of Christ. They ran cheerfully after him, and ran in the old paths of gospel truth (Jeremiah 6:16). But they had been 'hindered', checked in their course, and beaten back.

'Who did hinder you'? Paul and his fellow labourers in the gospel encouraged them to go forward, and did everything in their power to assist them. Those who hindered them were the false teachers who did all they could to turn them to another gospel, to turn them away from the truth.

'Who did hinder you that ye should not obey the truth?' Paul is talking about the truth that is in Christ, the truth of the gospel. Specifically, he is talking about the righteousness of God, the righteousness of complete, free justification in and by Christ. The question is really rhetorical. Paul is speaking with indignation against the work-mongers who had been the means of hindering the Galatians in the pursuit of Christ, in the pursuit of that holiness that is found only in Christ, 'without which no man shall see the Lord' (Hebrews 12:14). His purpose is to both condemn the legalists and to recover God's saints from their error.

'This persuasion cometh not of him that calleth you' (v. 8). The Galatian believers had come to Christ as poor, needy, helpless sinners, finding all in him (1 Corinthians 1:30). They had been turned back to the law, looking for righteousness in their own obedience to the commands of the law. Who persuaded them to make such a blunder? It was not God who called them by his grace. It was not Christ who fulfilled all righteousness for them. And it was not the Holy Spirit who had revealed the gospel to them, convincing them of the righteousness of God in Christ. Those who had hindered them were false apostles, the messengers of Satan who transform themselves into angels of light and preachers of righteousness attained by human effort (2 Corinthians 11:2-3, 13-15). The Galatians had been encumbered by those legalists who bound them with the fetters of the law, so that they could not run with liberty in the course of the gospel.

'This persuasion cometh not of him that calleth you' (v. 8). Edgar Andrews writes, 'What persuasion? Clearly, the Judaisers' idea that to follow Christ one must submit to the law of Moses. This doctrine, avers the apostle, does not come from God (the one who calls them). He only calls men 'in the grace of Christ' (1:6), never by the works or religious observances of men.' Professor Andrews continues …

> Here is a most valuable test, which can be applied to all or any teaching purporting to be Christian. Any belief or 'persuasion' which does not testify to 'the grace of Christ', is not from God. Here are twin pillars of the truth, namely the person and work of Christ, and the grace of God in Christ. They support and underpin all truly Christian teaching. No matter how attractive or pious a doctrine may appear, it is not to be received as coming from God unless it passes this double test namely:
>
> 1. Does it make Christ central, and glorify him?
> 2. Does it exalt the grace of God, over against the activity of man?
>
> Whether it be instruction in salvation, in worship, in service, or in living for God, its precepts are only to be received if they flow from the grace of Christ. Had the Galatians applied this test

to the teachings of the Judaisers, they would soon have realized that they detracted from Christ's perfect, finished and sufficient work of atonement.

The Lord Christ has called us to liberty. He brought us out from the bondage of the law. He gave us freedom. He continues calling us to liberty. The law bogs us down with doubts and fears. Christ urges us to serve with liberty. Legalistic teachings are inconsistent with the grace of God. Heed not their calls, but that of Christ.

> Day by day His sweet voice soundeth,
> Saying, Christian, follow Me.
> Cecil F. Alexander

A Little Leaven

The work-mongers might reply by saying, 'We do not teach that believers are to obey the whole law, and we certainly do not teach that salvation comes by our obedience to the law. We are simply saying that there is still a sense in which believers are to live under the rule of the law; and that all who would live in true righteousness are to keep the commandments, observe the sabbath day, and certain of the Mosaic rituals, like circumcision. Surely, anyone who opposes that must be a promoter of licentiousness.' To such Paul says that a little error, especially regarding salvation by grace alone and righteousness in Christ alone, is like leaven in a lump of dough. It soon runs through everything, corrupts the whole gospel, and nullifies the work of Christ. It must be stamped out immediately and completely.

Our Lord said to his disciples, 'Beware of the leaven of the Pharisees' (Matthew 16:6). In verse 9 Paul is talking about the same thing. A few corrupt principles corrupt the whole body of truth. The leaven of legalism had already begun to work among the Galatians, and Paul was afraid that they might become attached to it and abandon the truth (Galatians 4:10-11). A few corrupt people can corrupt the whole body of a congregation (1 Corinthians 5:6). Therefore, they must be avoided (Romans 16:17). These false teachers must not be tolerated.

Confidence In You

What Paul says in verse 10 regarding the saints at Galatia can be said with regard to all who truly trust the Lord Jesus Christ: 'I have confidence in you through the Lord, that ye will be none otherwise minded.' He had spoken to them sharply; but he was confident that, once they saw how utterly inconsistent legalism is with the grace of God, they would abandon it and those who taught it altogether. He was confident that God who had begun the good work of grace in them would perform it to the end. God will not allow his elect to perish in the error of the wicked. He will not allow the believer to abandon Christ and his gospel.

Sure Judgment
As sure as Paul was of the certain preservation of God's elect from the damning influence of the wicked Judaisers at Galatia, he was equally emphatic in declaring that those who preached another gospel, a gospel of works, must bear the wrath and judgment of God, 'But he that troubleth you shall bear his judgment, whosoever he be ' (v. 10). Those who corrupt the churches of Christ shall bear the judgment of God in this world and in that which is to come (1 Corinthians 3:16-17).

The Offence Of The Cross
The false teachers at Galatia charged Paul with duplicity. They said in one place Paul preaches circumcision (on one occasion he had Timothy circumcised as a matter of expediency), and in another place he opposes it. Paul had Timothy circumcised (Acts 16:1-5) in an unsuccessful attempt to be conciliatory to the Jews, not to make Timothy righteous or more spiritual. The fact is, those who oppose the gospel of God's free, sovereign, absolute grace in Christ, claiming to be promoters of righteousness, never hesitate to slander any who preach free grace, hurling accusations against them that they know are not true.

Paul's response is simple and pointed. He asks in verse 11, 'If I preach circumcision (law obedience) why do your legalistic teachers relentlessly oppose me?' They opposed him because the cross of Christ is now, ever has been, and ever will be an offence to work-mongers. Lost religious people do not object to the teaching that Christ is the Son of God, the Saviour of sinners, the Lord our Righteousness, and our sin-atoning Substitute. They only object to that which offends their own self-righteousness: the plain revelation that Christ alone is our consummate, all sufficient Saviour, and that all who believe are complete in him, 'who of God is made unto us wisdom, and righteousness, and sanctification, and redemption' (1 Corinthians 1:30).

Cut Off
The Apostle is making a play on the words. He desired that the Judaisers would cut themselves off. It is as though he said, 'I wish these agitators,

these troublers of your souls, obsessive as they are about circumcision, would go all the way and castrate themselves! Since the Judaisers, who were upsetting the Galatians, believe a little physical mutilation is of spiritual value, then, let them cut even more radically. Let them be like the pagan priests of Cybele and make eunuchs of themselves.' He wanted the Judaisers cut off from the Galatian church altogether (v. 12). This may seem severe to some; but it was most truly an act of love. Paul would rather have a few corrupt false teachers suffer the wrath and judgment of God, than see the entire assembly be destroyed by their doctrine. John Gill wrote,

> These words are a solemn wish of the apostle's with respect to the false teachers, or an imprecation of the judgment of God upon them; that they might be cut off out of the land of the living by the immediate hand of God, that they might do no more mischief to the churches of Christ: this he said not out of hatred to their persons, but from a concern for the glory of God, and the good of his people.

For, brethren, ye have been called unto liberty; only use not liberty for an occasion to the flesh, but by love serve one another. For all the law is fulfilled in one word, even in this; Thou shalt love thy neighbour as thyself. But if ye bite and devour one another, take heed that ye be not consumed one of another.

(Galatians 5:13-15)

Chapter 28

Read: Galatians 5:13-15

'A More Excellent Way'

These verses begin a very important passage that extends into the opening verses of chapter 6. In this section of Galatians Paul gives us much needed, clear, and practical instruction about walking in the Spirit in the blessed liberty of faith in Christ. Here he tells us that this liberty is the liberty of love. The life into which believers have been delivered is a life of love.

There are two great evils to which our fallen human nature is constantly drawn, evils that must be consciously avoided. The one is the horrid evil of legalism. The other is the equally horrid evil of licentiousness. Both are evil products of the flesh. Paul has devoted the larger part of this epistle to the Galatians to the task of exposing and denouncing the legalistic, self-righteousness, and arrogance of the Judaisers who ever attempt to bring God's saints under the oppressive yoke of legal bondage. Now he turns to the subject of licentiousness.

It may appear to be a strange paradox to many that legalism, when it is most prominent, produces licentiousness; paradoxical perhaps, but it is not a self-contradiction. Legalism is the mother of malice, strife, heresy, and slander. Who was ever more legalistic than the Pharisee? He prayed three times a day. He fasted twice in a week. He gave tithes of all that he had. He kept the sabbath. He ate no unclean thing. He was a legalistic moralist! But who was ever more licentious than the Pharisee? He slandered the Son of God. He tried to trick the Saviour into speaking against the law of Moses and against Caesar. It was a band of religious legalists who took a woman in the act of adultery to be condemned, but left their fellow Pharisee in his tent unaccused. Religious legalists took up stones to slay the Lord Jesus. They crucified the Lord of glory to satisfy their own lusts. It is not at all surprising therefore that Paul brings in a solemn warning against licentiousness right upon the heels of such strong condemnations of legality. We are free in Christ; but our freedom in Christ is not a license to sin. Rather, our freedom in Christ is the blessed liberty of love.

A Better Way

Paul has shown the excellence of the gospel. He has thoroughly denounced all possibility that sinners can be justified by works. He has shown us that once a person is justified by the free grace of God in Christ, he is not then sanctified and made perfect by his own efforts. He asks in chapter 3 verse 3, 'Are ye so foolish? Having begun in the Spirit, are ye now made perfect by the flesh?' Paul has shown us that our entire standing before God is the result of his free-grace and not the result of human merit.

Now, lest anyone should say, 'Shall we then continue in sin that grace may abound?' (See Romans 6:1-22) Paul gives a solemn warning against licentiousness. He tells us that our liberty in Christ is not licentiousness, but love. We are free from the bondage of the Mosaic law. And, being made free from the law, we are now free to live by the law of Christ. Believers are not antinomians, though legalists love to hurl that slanderous accusation against us. We do not live by the carnal rule of the Mosaic law, but by the law of love to Christ. In all things, 'the love of Christ constraineth us' (2 Corinthians 5:14). Legalistic duties can never fulfil the law, but love does. We have been brought under the law to Christ. What is the law of Christ? It is the law of love. Love not only fulfils the law, as legalism never can, but it also prevents the bitter strife that legalism produces.

This is what Paul has called, 'a more excellent way' (1 Corinthians 12:31-13:13). Love is the law of Christianity. The commandment of Christ is love. The fruit of the Spirit is love. Faith works by love. The joy of heaven is love. Peace on earth is love. That which sanctifies our every deed is love. Tongues are nothing without love. Prophecy is nothing without love. Understanding is nothing without love. Faith is nothing without love. Self-sacrifice is nothing without love. The charter, the continuance, and the consummation of Christ's kingdom is love. 'God is love.' God's people reflect that love. Wherever God is there is love. Wherever love is absent, God is absent. Joseph Swain put it nicely,

How sweet, how heavenly is the sight,
When those that love the Lord,
In one another's peace delight,
And so fulfil His Word.

When each can feel his brother's sigh,
And with him bear a part;
When sorrow flows from eye to eye,
And joy from heart to heart.

When free from envy, scorn, and pride,
Our wishes all above,
Each can his brother's failings hide,
And show a brother's love.

When love, in one delightful stream,
Through every bosom flows;
And union sweet, and dear esteem,
In every action glows.

Love is the golden chain that binds
The happy souls above;
And he's an heir of heaven who finds
His bosom glow with love.

'Called Unto Liberty'

Whenever religious legalists hear or read about the blessed liberty God's saints have in Christ from the law of Moses, red flags immediately arise in their minds. When we assert, in Bible language, that 'Christ is the end of the law', that 'we are not under the law, but under grace', and 'ye are dead to the law', they are terrified that such gospel declarations will lead people professing godliness to live in licentiousness. Because they know that they are ruled and motivated by legal threats and rewards, because their religion is nothing more than mercenary duty, they presume the same is true of God's children. Shall we, therefore, refuse to assure God's saints of their liberty in Christ? Perish the thought! Instead of that, Paul asserts, 'Brethren, ye have been called unto liberty' (v. 13). Then he gives us this admonition, 'only use not liberty for an occasion to the flesh'. We must take care that we do not use (or abuse) our liberty in Christ to indulge the lusts of the flesh.

Paul again calls the Galatian saints 'brethren'. He does so to express his own affection for them and to remind them (and us) of their relationship to one another in Christ, a loving family relationship. Then he reminds us that we have been called to liberty by the effectual grace and power of God the Holy Spirit.

The work-mongers at Galatia were frustrating the grace of God by their doctrine (Galatians 3:21). They taught that the rule of the Mosaic law was still in effect, that men and women make themselves righteous by their obedience to the law, and, thereby, taught that the sacrifice of Christ and the grace of God were meaningless (Galatians 5:1-4). Paul here reminds us that Christ has given all who trust him freedom from the law, calling us to liberty. Our liberty in Christ includes freedom from condemnation by the law and from the consciousness of guilt because of sin (Romans 8:1). Christ has freed us from the carnal ordinances and ceremonies of the law (Colossians 2:16-23). He has freed us from the oppressive rule of the law (Romans 6:14-15; 7:4; 10:4). And he has given us the liberty of access to and assured acceptance with God as his own dear children (Galatians 4:6-7; Hebrews 10:19-22).

'An Occasion to the Flesh'

The corrupt, depraved nature of fallen, unregenerate men is so base and vile that it finds encouragement to licentiousness in the goodness, mercy and grace of God in Christ. The sweet, blessed doctrines of grace revealed in the gospel (unconditional election, everlasting love, free justification, the non-imputation of sin, immutable grace, absolute security in Christ, etc.), though the very source and inspiration for all true godliness, are perverted and abused by ungodly religionists and made to be a covering and excuse for evil. This was the doctrine of Balaam and the Nicolaitans, which our holy Saviour hates (Revelation 2:14-15).

Paul's comments here are not addressed to lost religionists. They are addressed to the saints of God. Believers are no longer in the flesh (Romans 8:9), and do not live after the flesh (Romans 8:12-13). Yet the flesh, the old nature of the flesh, is in us and is constantly at war against us (Galatians 5:17). That old nature that is in us is prone to the same evils that the unregenerate practice. That makes Paul's admonition needful. We must not give in to the flesh. We must take care that we do not indulge the flesh, abusing the liberty that is ours in Christ to gratify the lusts of the flesh. Christ's free men must not give way to such evil lusts. To do so is both to bring reproach upon our Saviour and upon the gospel of the grace of God. Let us, rather, 'adorn the doctrine of God our Saviour in all things' (Titus 2:10). John Berridge wrote:

> To Jesus some will pray,
> Yet not with single eye;
> They turn their eyes another way,
> Some creature help to spy.
> In darkness such are held;
> And bound in legal fear;
> A double eye is in the child,
> The heart is not sincere.

Our liberty in Christ is abused, or used as an occasion to the flesh whenever we begin to live for the gratification of our fleshly lust. In this context Paul is particularly telling us that we must not excuse, or attempt to justify any conduct that injures our brethren. 'To use this liberty as an excuse to indulge the old nature is', wrote Edgar Andrews, 'a contradiction in terms. Any who do so have not understood the meaning of Christian liberty, for liberty and lawlessness are bitter enemies, not companions.'

Christian liberty is not a spring board, or incentive for the sinful human nature to assert itself. The doctrine of Christ is a 'doctrine according to godliness' (1 Timothy 6:3-5). It is freedom to walk with and serve our God. We are free to use all things lawfully, but we are not to be in bondage to any (1 Corinthians 6:12). And our liberty must never be so pressed as to become a stumbling block to a weaker brother (1 Corinthians 8:9, 13). We are to use this liberty for the good of men and the glory of Christ; not to gratify ourselves (1 Corinthians 9:12, 19, 22; 1 Corinthians 10:23, 24, 31; 11:1).

'By Love Serve'

Gospel liberty and the service of the saints go hand in hand. Faith works by love. Our Saviour commands us to love one another. Our profession of faith in Christ and our family relation to one another in Christ, the grace of God that we have experienced, and the love of God revealed to us in the sacrifice of his own dear Son for us all teach us to devote ourselves to and serve one another in love. Throughout the New Testament good works are set before us, not as deeds by which we attempt to show how good, devoted, and holy we are (which is ever the practice of Pharisees), but by acts of kindness, love, and mercy: visiting the fatherless and the afflicted, giving a cup of cold water, bearing one another's burdens, etc..

Let every child of God make it his goal in life to help his brothers and sisters in Christ in their pilgrimage through this world. That is what it is to serve one another by love. Believers ought always to pray for one another, sympathise with one another's needs, and provide for one another's needs. We ought to be forgiving, forbearing, and longsuffering with one another, patient, kind, and gentle toward one another. We are to think well of and speak well of one another, each esteeming his brother and sister in Christ better than himself (Philippians 2:1-4). Love is a debt we owe to one another (Romans 13:8). If we were more concerned about loving and less concerned about being loved, that would put an end to resentment, strife and division, envy, malice, and feuds in the church of God.

Our Example

The love Paul is speaking of here is not mere human affection. It is the love of God revealed to us in Christ and shed abroad in our hearts by the Holy Spirit. The great example of serving one another by love that is held before us in the Book of God is Christ himself (John 13:13-15; Ephesians 4:32-5:2; 1 John 3:16-17). He said, 'I am among you as he that serveth'. He came into the world in the form of a servant (Philippians 2:7). When he arose from supper, he put a towel around his waist, poured water into a basin, and washed his disciples feet (John 13:4-5). The Prophet called the Messiah a Servant (Isaiah 42:1; 50:4-11; 52:13-53:12).

What is this love? It is a deep affection, but more than affection. Love is devotion, self-sacrificing tenderness, genuine care, and a readiness to help. It is free, spontaneous giving and forgiving. William Hendriksen tells us that, 'When Paul warns the Galatians not to turn freedom into an opportunity for the flesh, but through love to be serving one another, he is placing service over against selfishness ... Vice can only be conquered by virtue, which is the Spirit's gift, man's responsibility.'

> Saviour, give me grace that I may
> Love Your people as I ought,
> Ever serve them, and defend them,
> And with care offend them not.
>
> May the grace You have imparted,
> In relieving me of woe,
> Make me kind and tender-hearted;
> Give me grace Your grace to show.
>
> As You laid down Your life, Saviour,
> For the people that You love,
> Help me to my own life lay down
> For my brethren, whom I love.

The Law Fulfilled By Love

Paul, by divine inspiration, reduces the whole Mosaic system to one commandment, 'Thou shalt love thy neighbour as thyself' (v. 14). Legalists take great offence at this, saying that such a view of the law makes every man a law unto himself and gives no real direction for life. Nothing could be further from the truth. The law of love is the new commandment of the gospel (Ephesians 5:2; 1 Thessalonians 4:9; James 2:8, 1 Peter 1:22; 1 John 3:23; 4:21). This love is not natural to men. It is the fruit of the indwelling Spirit making manifest the fact that Christ dwells in us (Galatians 5:22; 1 John 3:9-24). Pastor Henry Mahan wrote,

> When I consider what I can do, should do and am required to do in word, thought and deed toward others, it is all fulfilled in the word 'love' (Matthew 7:12). My love for the Lord will control my personal conduct and behaviour, and my love for others will control my public conduct where others are concerned. As far as a man loves aright, so far he fulfils the law.

Who Needs My Help?

'Thou shalt love thy neighbour as thyself.' What more needs to be said? If I want to know how I ought to love my neighbour, I need only to ask, 'How do I love myself?' When I am in trouble, or danger, or need of any kind, I welcome the help of others who are able to help. We do not need a book of instructions to teach us how to love our neighbour. All we need to do is look to our own enlightened hearts. If any ask, as the lawyer in Luke 10, 'Who is my neighbour?' the answer is given in the parable that followed his question. My neighbour is anyone who needs my help (Luke 10:25-37). Let us so love our neighbours, especially our brothers and sisters in Christ. But our responsibility (our great privilege of love) reaches beyond the household of faith. We are to love all men, even those who despise and abuse us. My neighbour is anyone with whom God in his providence brings me into contact, anyone I can help in anyway, even though he hates me and is my enemy (Matthew 5:43-48). My neighbour is especially my brother in Christ.

Most people talk glibly about love and boast that they practice it, but love is a rare, very rare, thing in this world. Love is more than a feeling, a sentiment, or an emotion. To love my neighbour is to serve him. We are to 'by love serve one another'. Love is not merely putting up with people, or refraining from injuring them. It is doing them good (Galatians 6:10). To serve one another in love is to instruct the erring, comfort the afflicted, raise the fallen, and help one another in every possible way. If I love my neighbour, I bear his burdens, and forgive his offences. I am patient with his infirmities, weaknesses, and ignorance, and am long-suffering with him in all things.

Love forgives the unforgiving, is patient with the impatient, merciful to the unmerciful, and kind to the mean-spirited. Love makes children honour their parents and parents to be patient with unruly children, causes husbands to be patient with nagging wives and wives to be patient with obstinate husbands. If I love my neighbour as myself, I will not defraud him, betray his trust, lie to him, cheat him, slander him, or reveal his faults, weaknesses, and failures to others.

'By Love Serve One Another'

These things are not regarded as good works by most people; but they are the very things our God speaks of as good works. They are such excellent things that the unregenerate cannot possibly estimate them at their true value. The religious legalist vainly imagines that good works are the observance of rituals, ceremonies, holy days, dress codes, dietary laws, fastings, and countless other things seen, approved of, and applauded by men. Their religion is street corner and market place religion. Nothing more. While they strenuously observe the outward duties of religious laws and customs, they are filled with violence and hatred. What greater example of this horrid spirit of legalism could be found than in the fact that those very men who crucified the Lord of glory because of their envy and hatred insisted that his body be taken down from the cross (John 19:31) lest their sabbath day be polluted? The Old Testament as well as the New is replete with examples that show how highly our God values love. When David and his men had no food they ate the showbread, though the law forbade them to eat it. Our Saviour's disciples broke the legal sabbath law when they plucked ears of corn and ate it as they followed the Master, resting in him who is our Sabbath. The Lord Jesus himself broke the sabbath day, as far as the Jews could see, by healing the sick on the sabbath day. In all these things, we are taught that the holy Lord God calls for mercy, not sacrifice.

The law itself was designed to teach us this blessed doctrine, 'Thou shalt love thy neighbour as thyself'. Therefore, Paul urges us to serve one another by love. He says to them and to us, 'If you want to do good works and honour God's holy law, "by love serve one another". The world is full of people who need your help'. Yet, those who teach that righteousness comes by works never mention such things.

A Needed Warning

In verse 15 Paul is saying, 'If you are critical, unforgiving, unkind, and filled with bitterness and strife, you will destroy the unity and peace of God's church. Love is the cement that binds us together and enables us to live and labour together in peace' (Ephesians 4:1-7; Colossians 3:12-14).

In the church at Galatia, as in countless churches today, there was much strife and division, backbiting and slander, bitterness, and jealousy. The fact that Paul gives us the warning in the context of Galatians 5 tells us that the root cause of these evils is the carnal, fleshly spirit of legalism and self-righteousness. One of the problems with living by law is the fact that once the explicit duties of the law have been fulfilled in the mind of the legalist, he vainly imagines that he is 'holier' than other people and sets himself up as a judge over them. Those who walk in the Spirit (i.e. those who live by faith in Christ) do not fulfil such lusts of the flesh. They know themselves to be sinners in constant need of mercy, whose only hope before God is the blood and righteousness of Christ. If we truly know that, if truly we have experienced the grace of God and know something of the evil of our own hearts, we will esteem our brothers and sisters better than ourselves, and 'by love serve one another'.

Let us hear and heed Paul's warning, 'If ye bite and devour one another, take heed that ye be not consumed one of another'. Here people, church members at that, are pictured in the act of rushing upon one another as wild beasts. Strife and divisions are always carnal and ungodly (1 Corinthians 3:3). It is not strange to see dogs and wolves biting and devouring sheep; but it is unthinkable that sheep should bite and devour one another. 'He that soweth discord among brethren' is an abomination to the Lord. Strife and division destroy the peace of churches (1 Corinthians 3:17). It is by these things that we quench the Spirit of God and destroy our usefulness in the cause of Christ (Ephesians 4:30).

Four Helpful Comments

Here are quotations taken from the writings of four men on this fifteenth verse. Each is helpful.

> Christian churches cannot be ruined but by their own hands; but if Christians, should be helps to one another and a joy to one another, be as brute beasts, biting and devouring each other, what can be expected but that the God of love should deny his grace to them, and the Spirit of love should depart from them, and

that the evil spirit that seeks the destruction of them all should prevail? (Matthew Henry)

Strife, contention, bickering, detraction, and the biting of hard, unjust words will rend a church in pieces quicker than all the assaults of men and devils from outside. (G. S. Bishop)

How distressing, how mad it is that we, who are members of the same body, should be leagued together, of our own accord, for mutual destruction! (John Calvin)

When faith in Christ is overthrown peace and unity come to an end in the church. Diverse opinions and dissensions about doctrine and life spring up, and one member bites and devours the other, i.e. they condemn each other until they are consumed. To this the scriptures and the experience of all times bear witness. The many sects at present have come into being because one sect condemns the other. When the unity of the spirit has been lost there can be no agreement in doctrine or life. New errors must appear without measure and without end. For the avoidance of discord Paul lays down the principle: Let every person do his duty in the station of life into which God has called him. No person is to vaunt himself above others or find fault with the efforts of others while lauding his own. Let everybody serve in love. (Martin Luther)

Do Not Grieve The Holy Spirit

For the glory of God our Saviour, for the furtherance of the gospel, and for the sake of our brethren, let us endeavour to keep the unity of the Spirit in the bond of peace by our conduct toward one another (Ephesians 4:2-3). Let us ever take care that we do not grieve the Holy Spirit of God by treating the objects of God's love with contempt (Ephesians 4:30-5:1-2). May God give us grace to love and serve one another, taking no offence at anything done to us by others. If another person will not walk in peace, but insists upon stirring up strife and division in the family of God, for the sake of Christ and his kingdom and the gospel of his grace, we must simply avoid them (Romans 16:17; 2 Thessalonians 3:6, 14-15).

Read Paul's words of wise instruction one more time and ask God the Holy Spirit who inspired them to graciously apply them to your heart, for Christ's sake. 'For, brethren, ye have been called unto liberty; only use not liberty for an occasion to the flesh, but by love serve one another. For all the law is fulfilled in one word, even in this; Thou shalt love thy neighbour as thyself. But if ye bite and devour one another, take heed that ye be not consumed one of another.'

This I say then, Walk in the Spirit, and ye shall not fulfil the lust of the flesh. For the flesh lusteth against the Spirit, and the Spirit against the flesh: and these are contrary the one to the other: so that ye cannot do the things that ye would.

(Galatians 5:16-17)

Chapter 29

Read: Galatians 5:16-17

My Soul's Greatest Trouble

Believers are men and women with two distinct, separate, warring natures: the flesh and the spirit. When God saves a sinner he does not renovate, repair, and renew the old nature. He creates a new nature in his elect. Our old, Adamic, fallen, sinful nature is not changed. The flesh is subdued by the spirit; but it will never surrender to the spirit. The spirit wars against the flesh; but it will never conquer or improve the flesh. The flesh is sinful. The flesh is cursed. Thank God, the flesh must die! But it will never be improved.

This dual nature of the believer is plainly taught in the Word of God. It is utterly impossible to honestly interpret this portion of Paul's epistle to the Galatians, the seventh chapter of Romans, and 1 John 3 without concluding that both Paul and John teach that there is within every believer, so long as he lives in this world, both an old Adamic nature that can do nothing but sin and a new righteous nature, that which is born of God, that cannot sin, that can only do righteousness. The Holy Spirit's work in sanctification is not the improvement of our old nature, but the maturing of the new, steadily causing the believer to grow in the grace and knowledge of Christ and bring forth fruit unto God.

Every believer knows the duality of his nature by painful, bitterly painful experience. Ask any child of God what he desires above all things and he will quickly reply, 'That I may live without sin in perfect conformity to Christ, perfectly obeying the will of God in all things.' But that which he most greatly desires is an utter impossibility in this life. Is it not so with you? Though you delight in the law of God after the inward man, there is another law of evil in your members, warring against you. You would do good; but evil is always present with you, so that you cannot do the things that you would. Even your best, noblest, most sincere acts of good, when honestly evaluated, are so marred by sin in motive and in execution that you must confess, 'All my righteousnesses are filthy rags' (Isaiah 64:6).

It is this warfare between the flesh and the spirit more than anything else that keeps the believer from being satisfied with life in this world. Blessed be God, we shall soon be free! Soon, very soon, we shall be going home, and when we have dropped this old robe of flesh we shall be perfectly conformed to the image of him who loved us and gave himself for us!

Faith In Christ

If we would overcome the horrible propensity of our flesh to evil, if we would avoid biting and devouring one another like mad dogs, we must live not by the carnal rule of the law, which only stirs up sin, but by the gracious rule of the Holy Spirit. The believer's life in this world is often compared to a journey. The word 'walk' is used in holy scripture as a synonym for 'live' (Mark 7:5; Romans 4:12; 6:4; 8:1). Paul is talking in verse 16 about God the Holy Spirit. To walk in the Spirit is to live by faith in Christ. Those who walk in the Spirit walk with God, as Enoch did, trusting Christ alone for acceptance with the Holy Lord God. All who walk in the Spirit, all who trust Christ, have the witness and testimony of God within them that they please God, being accepted of God in Christ (Hebrews 11:5-6; 1 John 5:10-13; Ephesians 1:3-6). This is what Paul declares in Romans 8:1-4. 'There is therefore now no condemnation to them which are in Christ Jesus, who walk not after the flesh, but after the Spirit. For the law of the Spirit of life in Christ Jesus hath made me free from the law of sin and death. For what the law could not do, in that it was weak through the flesh, God sending his own Son in the likeness of sinful flesh, and for sin, condemned sin in the flesh: That the righteousness of the law might be fulfilled in us, who walk not after the flesh, but after the Spirit'.

However, Paul does not say that by walking in the Spirit the flesh shall not be in us, or that the lust of the flesh will no longer burn within us. He says that living by faith in Christ, as we walk 'in the Spirit', we 'shall not fulfil the lust of the flesh' (v. 16). This is not stated as a possibility, but as a certainty. Believers do not live by the evil dictates of the flesh, but by the gracious rule of the Spirit. This is stated as a matter of fact. Paul is not here telling us that we might not fulfil the lust of the flesh if we can manage, by self-discipline and self-denial, to yield ourselves to the influence of the Holy Spirit. Rather, he is telling us that if we live by faith in Christ, if our lives are ruled by the Spirit of God, we 'shall not fulfil the lust of the flesh'. Paul's subject has not changed. He is talking about God's ongoing work of grace in the believer. He is telling us, as Edgar Andrews states, 'that the law and the flesh are co-conspirators against grace and the Spirit'.

The Emnity Of Flesh And Spirit
As he uses it in verse 17, the word 'flesh' does not refer to the physical body in which we live in this world, but to our fallen, corrupt, Adamic nature, the old man that still exists in saved sinners. It is that internal principle of corruption, 'the carnal mind', that is ever 'enmity against God' (Romans 8:7). The flesh is flesh, nothing else, just sinful flesh. It can do nothing but evil. 'The Spirit' is the internal principle of grace in regenerate men and women. It refers to the Holy Spirit who dwells in us. This is 'Christ in you, the Hope of glory' (Colossians 1:27). This is that holy thing born of God that cannot sin (1 John 3:9). John Gill says;

> The flesh, or the old man, the carnal I, in regenerate persons, wills, chooses, desires, and loves carnal things, which are contrary to the Spirit or principle of grace in the soul ... The Spirit or the new man, the spiritual I, wills, chooses, desires, approves, and loves spiritual things, such as are contrary to corrupt nature ... They are as contrary to one another as light and darkness or fire and water. They continually war against one another.

Because the flesh ever lusts against the Spirit and the Spirit against the flesh, 'ye cannot do the things that ye would'. The believer would do perfectly good. That is our desire. Yet, we cannot do that which is good, because sin dwells within us. Our old nature of flesh would do nothing but sin, that which we hate. But the Spirit of Christ reigning within keeps the flesh from having its way (Romans 7:15-17, 22, 23).

Two Armies

This is the lamentation expressed by God's church in the Song of Solomon (6:13). 'What will ye see in the Shulamite (Solyma[1])? As it were the company of two armies.' She is saying, 'There is nothing in me but conflict and confusion. In my heart two armies are at war. If you look upon me, you will see a raging battle, good fighting evil, light contending with darkness. I am a house divided against itself'. This is a true and accurate description of the people of God. All of God's elect experience constant warfare within, constant conflict between the flesh and the Spirit, so long as we live in this body of flesh. This conflict, this warfare causes us so much pain and trouble.

These inward conflicts are facts in every believer's life. The believer's life is not all sweets. It is not all joy and peace. Faith in Christ brings some bitter conflicts, which cause God's child much pain, much toil, and many tears. The struggles between the flesh and the Spirit are evident enough to all who are born of God. To the unbelieving, unregenerate religionist, true Christians are confusing paradoxes. We are the happiest and the most mournful people in the world. We are the richest and the poorest people on earth. We are men and women who possess perfect peace; yet, we are always at war.

We see traces of this conflict throughout the Song of Solomon (1:5; 3:1; 5:2). We see these inward conflicts throughout the Psalms of David (Psalms 42; 43; 73). We see them dealt with and explained in Romans 7:14-25, and here in Galatians 5:16-18. And we see these terrible inward conflicts in our own daily experience of grace.

The people of God throughout the centuries have had the same struggles that we now have. John Bunyan wrote a book about his conflicts of heart and soul, which he titled, 'The Holy War'. Richard Sibbes wrote a similar book called, 'The Soul's Conflict'. Though we are born of God, God's saints in this world have a corrupt nature within, which would drive us to sin. Yet, we have within us a righteous nature, which would draw us into perfect conformity and union with Christ. Between these two forces of good and evil there is no peace (1 John 3:7-9).

---

[1] Solomon chose his bride and espoused her to himself, giving her his name. 'Shulamite' should be translated 'Solyma'. The Hebrew word is the feminine of the name 'Solomon'. The Lord Jesus Christ has made us so thoroughly one with himself that he has given us his Name. He is our Solomon, and we are his Solyma (cf. Jeremiah 23:6 and 33:16). All that our Lord Jesus Christ is, he has made us to be by divine imputation.

Two Natures

This conflict is caused by and begins in regeneration. C. H. Spurgeon said, 'The reigning power of sin falls dead the moment a man is converted, but the struggling power of sin does not die until the man dies.' A new nature has been planted within us; but the old nature is not eradicated.

Do not think for a moment that the old nature dies in regeneration, or even that it gets better. Flesh is flesh, and will never be anything but flesh. Noah, Lot, Moses, David, and Peter, like all other believers, had to struggle with this fact. We need no proof of the fact that God's people in this world have two warring natures within beyond an honest examination of our own hearts and lives. Our best thoughts are corrupted with sin. Our fervent prayers are defiled by lusts of the flesh. Our reading of holy scripture is corrupted by carnal passions. Our most spiritual worship is marred by the blackness within. Our holy aspirations are vile. Our purest love for our Saviour is so corrupted by our love of self and love for this world that we can hardly call our love for Christ love. From time to time we have all found, by bitter experience, the truthfulness of Robert Robinson's lines:

> Prone to wander, Lord, I feel it!
> Prone to leave the God I love:
> Here's my heart, O take and seal it,
> Seal it for Thy courts above.

My Hope

I am confident that I am loved and chosen of God (Jeremiah 1:5; 31:3), redeemed by the precious blood of Christ (Galatians 2:20; 2 Corinthians 5:21), and born again by the power and grace of God the Holy Spirit (Ephesians 2:1-9). These things give me great joy, peace, and comfort. I have a good hope through grace regarding these things. I have some measure of confidence and assurance before God that these things are so, and that I am a child of God and an heir of eternal salvation. And I base that assurance upon the fact that I trust the Lord Jesus Christ alone as my Saviour (1 John 5:1, 12-13; Hebrews 11:1). Toplady writes:

> Kind Author and Ground of my hope,
> Thee, Thee, for my God I avow;
> My glad Ebenezer set up,
> And own Thou hast helped me till now.

Yet, there is a terrible struggle within my soul, a tormenting trial in my spirit, a heavy burden upon my heart. I have a new heart and a new will, a new, heaven-bent nature, created in me by the grace of God, a nature that longs for and seeks after righteousness and conformity to the Lord Jesus Christ. But I cannot do the things I would. I find a law in my members that when I would do good evil is present with me. I find in my soul iniquity, transgression, and sin far more hideous and ignominious than the most profane acts of ungodly men. I want to pray; but there is too much selfish lust in my prayers to call them prayer. I want to worship God; but there is too much pride in my worship to call it worship. I want to be completely free of earthly care, trusting God in all things, but there is too much unbelief and selfish resentment toward God's providence to call my faith, faith, or my submission, submission. The envy that is in me is enmity against God. My lack of contentment is the despising of God's providence. My worry is questioning God's wisdom and goodness. My fears are the denial of God's power. My covetousness is proud rebellion against God.

'Progressive Holiness'

I hear men talk of becoming less and less sinful and progressively holier today than they were yesterday. I hear men talking about what they call 'progressive sanctification'. Their doctrine is that God's children grow in righteousness and holiness until they are ripe for heaven. They teach that glorification is the end result of their own progressive attainments in personal holiness. If their doctrine is true, then, it is possible for men, by diligent self-denial and personal holiness, to eventually attain sinless perfection in this life.

Such doctrine, of course, is contrary to holy scripture (1 John 1:8, 10). Honesty compels me to acknowledge that such doctrine is totally contrary to all personal experience. I have, I believe, over these past 37 years grown in grace. My love, faith, commitment to Christ, and joy in the Lord have grown, increased, and matured by the grace of God. But, my sin has not diminished. My outward acts of sin are more restricted and controlled. But the inward evil of my flesh has not diminished. If anything, it is worse now than ever. Reader, is it not so with you? With aching heart, I confess my sin. Though I am redeemed, justified, and sanctified in Christ, I am still a man in the flesh, full of sin. Do you not experience the same thing? Paul did (Romans 7:14-24). This is my soul's greatest trouble. I wish it were not so, but it is. The fact is, we who believe God, we who walk in the Spirit, trusting Christ as our Saviour, are people with two natures, two principles, warring against one another continually; and those two natures are the flesh and the Spirit.

Psalm 73
A Psalm of Asaph.[1]

1 Truly God *is* good to Israel, *even* to such as are of a
clean heart.
2 But as for me, my feet were almost gone; my steps had
well nigh slipped.
3 For I was envious at the foolish, *when* I saw the
prosperity of the wicked.
4 For *there are* no bands in their death: but their strength
is firm.
5 They *are* not in trouble *as other* men; neither are they
plagued like *other* men.
6 Therefore pride compasseth them about as a chain;
violence covereth them *as* a garment.
7 Their eyes stand out with fatness: they have more than
heart could wish.
8 They are corrupt, and speak wickedly *concerning*
oppression: they speak loftily.
9 They set their mouth against the heavens, and their
tongue walketh through the earth.
10 Therefore his people return hither: and waters of a full
cup are wrung out to them.
11 And they say, How doth God know? and is there
knowledge in the most High?
12 Behold, these *are* the ungodly, who prosper in the
world; they increase *in* riches.
13 Verily I have cleansed my heart *in* vain, and washed
my hands in innocency.
14 For all the day long have I been plagued, and chastened
every morning.

---

[1] "It seems by the title that Asaph was the penman of this psalm, as it is certain that he was a composer of psalms and hymns; see 2 Chronicles 29:30, though it may be rendered, 'a psalm for Asaph,' or 'unto Asaph'; and might have David for its author, as some think, who, having penned it, sent it to Asaph, to be made use of by him in public service; see 1 Chronicles 16:7, and so the Targum paraphrases it, 'a song by the hands of Asaph." (John Gill)

15 ¶ If I say, I will speak thus; behold, I should offend
   against the generation of thy children.

16 When I thought to know this, it *was* too painful for me;

17 Until I went into the sanctuary of God; *then* understood I
   their end.

18 Surely thou didst set them in slippery places: thou
   castedst them down into destruction.

19 How are they *brought* into desolation, as in a moment!
   they are utterly consumed with terrors.

20 As a dream when *one* awaketh; *so*, O Lord, when thou
   awakest, thou shalt despise their image.

21 ¶ Thus my heart was grieved, and I was pricked in my
   reins.

22 So foolish *was* I, and ignorant: I was *as* a beast before
   thee.

23 Nevertheless I *am* continually with thee: thou hast holden
   me by my right hand.

24 Thou shalt guide me with thy counsel, and afterward
   receive me *to* glory.

25 Whom have I in heaven *but thee*? and *there is* none upon
   earth *that* I desire beside thee.

26 My flesh and my heart faileth: *but* God *is* the strength of
   my heart, and my portion for ever.

27 For, lo, they that are far from thee shall perish: thou hast
   destroyed all them that go a whoring from thee.

28 But *it is* good for me to draw near to God: I have put my
   trust in the Lord GOD, that I may declare all thy works.

Chapter 30

Read: Psalm 73

An Object Lesson

The struggle Paul is talking about in Galatians 5:16-17 is clearly displayed in the life of David and recorded, it seems, in Psalm 73, for our instruction. David, the man after God's own heart, describes before God the warfare and struggle of his own soul between the flesh and the spirit. When he looked over his own household, with all its troubles, and thought about the propriety and peace of the wicked around him, he said, 'My feet were almost gone; my steps had well nigh slipped. For I was envious at the foolish, when I saw the prosperity of the wicked … Verily I have cleansed my heart in vain, and washed my hands in innocency. For all the day long have I been plagued, and chastened every morning' (Psalms 73:2, 3, 13, 14). Then, he went into the house of God and understood their end. Then, he said, 'Thus my heart was grieved, and I was pricked in my reins. So foolish was I, and ignorant: I was as a beast before thee' (Psalms 73:21-22).

Sinner Still

Taking David's words as my own, I make the painful confession of my sin before God and before you who read these lines. It is my hope that by writing as I do in the first person, you can and will identify with what you are reading. Though I am saved by the grace of God, I am a terribly foul and sinful man, 'So foolish was I, and ignorant: I was as a beast before thee' (v. 22). I have had a few trials in my life. But the most painful, most difficult trial I have ever had to endure is one that I must endure so long as I live in this world. It is the ever-increasing realisation and awareness of my sin.

David uses three words to describe his sin before God: 'foolish', 'ignorant', 'beastly'. He says, 'I have behaved as a fool before God'. This is a very strong word. It is the same word he uses to describe the atheist in Psalm 14:1. It means 'one who forgets God and loves evil'. Yet, David uses this word to describe himself. He even intensifies his foolishness – 'So foolish was I'. Then he says, 'I have been ignorant'. My speech, my thoughts, and my actions betray my ignorance. How often we act like ignorant men and women! And David goes on to say, 'I have behaved like a brute beast before God'. This word 'beast' speaks of some hideous, monstrous, astonishingly wild creature. This is an accurate description of our flesh. The old man is a sinful, beastly, monstrous creature. John Newton wrote:

> I would disclose my whole complaint,
> But where shall I begin?
> No words of mine can fully paint
> A picture of my sin.

A Brute Beast

Like David, I most truly describe myself when I describe myself 'as a beast before' God. Like the brute beasts of the earth, I am too much attached to this world. The hog, grubbing in the mud for its roots, cares nothing for the stars. The wild ass's colt, roaming the hills, cares nothing for the angels of God. The ravenous wolf has no regard for eternity. Educate the beast, train it as well as you can, but it will have no regard for anything, but its natural appetite. How much like beasts I am! Is it not so with you? Are we not too fondly attached to the things of this world? Let us never be content with our beastly attachment to this world. But do not be so proud and foolish as to deny it.

I am like the wild beasts in this regard, too. I seem to have so little emotion and passion for heavenly things. Isaac Watts writes:

> Look how we grovel here below,
> Fond of these trifling toys;
> Our souls can neither fly nor go
> To reach eternal joys.

In vain we tune our formal songs,
In vain we strive to rise;
Hosannas languish on our tongues,
And our devotion dies.

Dear Lord, and shall we ever live
At this poor, dying rate?
Our love so faint, so cold to Thee,
And Thine to us so great?

There is a beastly deadness, coldness of heart, and apathetic indifference about everything I do. My preaching, my repentance, my Bible reading, my praying, my singing, my worship, everything is so dead! Like brute beasts, we are terribly short-sighted. Our hearts and minds are too much concerned for the things of time, and too little concerned for the things of eternity.

And we may well compare ourselves to brute beasts because of our animal like passions. I will not go far into this dark path of our painful experience. I will say only enough to make you understand that this is the common experience of God's elect. C. H. Spurgeon said, 'He that hath fellowship with God will sometimes feel the devil within him till he thinketh himself a devil.'

When we honestly look within, we will find that there is nothing lovely to be seen. We are as brute beasts before God. There is no evil of which this sinful flesh is not capable. We are evil, only evil, and that continually. Were it not for the free grace and sovereign love of God for us, we could not live with ourselves. The characteristics of beasts rage within each of us. In my flesh there still remains the pride of a lion, the lust of the horseleech, the raging anger of a bull, the envy of a wolf, and the stubbornness of a jackass.

Old Nature Unchanged

Again, let us understand that the grace of God does not change our old nature. Grace gives us a new nature. But flesh is still flesh, undiluted evil, just as evil as it was before the Lord saved us. Old Adam is still old Adam, even though Christ is in the heart. Grace conquers Adam and grace rules Adam, but grace does not change Adam. 'The flesh lusteth against the Spirit and the Spirit against the flesh.' This warfare and struggle within each of us is constant and perpetual. It will continue, until at last grace wins the victory, the flesh returns to the earth, and we are received up into glory. This is my painful, but honest confession of sin. 'So foolish was I, and ignorant: I was as a beast before thee.' This one thing I must acknowledge, 'I am carnal, sold under sin … I know that in me, (that is in my flesh,) dwelleth no good thing'.

A Believer Still

Though I am a vile, sinful man, I still trust the Lord Jesus Christ. I am a believer still. I still sing with David, 'Nevertheless I am continually with thee: thou hast holden me by my right hand. Thou shalt guide me with thy counsel, and afterward receive me to glory' (Psalms 73:23-24). I am sinful, shamefully sinful; but God is faithful, gloriously faithful. Therefore, trusting the Lord my God, I can say with joy and confidence, 'Nevertheless I am continually with thee'. Notwithstanding all my sin, God is faithful! This is a glorious fact. If you are a believer, if you are in Christ, your sins shall never be charged to you, be they ever so great, ever so many, and ever so constant! And they will never separate you from the Lord your God (Romans 4:8; 8:1; 1 John 2:1-2).

Four Pillars Of Faith

Here are four blessed pillars for your faith and mine.

1. God's Perseverance

'I am continually with thee' (Psalms 73:23). God perseveres in his grace toward us. We are one with Christ. Not until the Lord God forsakes his own dear Son will he forsake us who are in his Son. C. Paget writes:

> Near, so very near to God,
> Nearer I cannot be;
> For in the Person of His Son,
> I am as near as He.
>
> Dear, so very dear to God,
> Dearer I cannot be,
> For in the Person of His Son,
> I am as dear as He!

Our position and relationship with the eternal God is as immutable as God himself. We are continually upon his mind, before his eye, in his hand, on his heart, and in is favour. We are accepted in the Beloved. 'With His spotless garments on, I am as holy as God's own Son!'

It takes very little faith, when you think you have many graces and many virtues, to say, 'I am accepted in Christ'. But when a vile, wretched man, who knows his own evil heart and tastes the bitterness of his utter depravity, can look to God and say, 'Though I am a sinful beast before You, I trust Christ alone as my Lord and Saviour', that is faith. Only as sinners do we need a Substitute!

Our security does not depend upon our faithfulness, but upon God's faithfulness (Malachi 3:6). It does not depend upon our perseverance, but upon our God's. I want you to get this. May God help you to understand it and rejoice in it. I made this statement in a Bible conference more than 20 years ago. What an uproar I stirred! But I cannot tell you how this blessed fact comforts my soul! My relationship with the eternal God does in great measure determine what I do. But what I do does in no way determine my relationship with God.

It is good, wonderfully good, for me to look up to my Father, my God, my Saviour and say, 'Nevertheless, I am continually with thee'. But here is something even better. I could be mistaken, but when God beholds my sin and says, 'Nevertheless', he is not mistaken. Let us take a few moments to read Psalm 89:27-37, it will bless your heart.

> Also I will make him my firstborn, higher than the kings of the earth. My mercy will I keep for him for evermore, and my covenant shall stand fast with him. His seed also will I make to endure for ever, and his throne as the days of heaven. If his children forsake my law, and walk not in my judgments; If they break my statutes, and keep not my commandments; Then will I visit their transgression with the rod, and their iniquity with stripes. Nevertheless my lovingkindness will I not utterly take from him, nor suffer my faithfulness to fail. My covenant will I not break, nor alter the thing that is gone out of my lips. Once have I sworn by my holiness that I will not lie unto David. His seed shall endure for ever, and his throne as the sun before me. It shall be established for ever as the moon, and as a faithful witness in heaven. Selah.

2. Unfailing Help
Then the author speaks of God's unfailing help. 'Thou hast holden me by my right hand' (Psalms 73:23). The right hand signifies strength. For God to hold me by my right hand implies that the hand of my strength is only weakness. He holds me by omnipotent grace. He has held me. He is holding me. He will not let me go!

He may, in his wise and good providence, allow me to fall; but even when I fall, he is holding me still.

3. Divine Guidance
Third, the Psalmist sings confidently of divine guidance for the future. 'Thou shalt guide me with thy counsel' (Psalms 73:24).

According to his wise decree, God orders my steps. By his written Word, God directs my path. By his Holy Spirit, God leads me in his way (Proverbs 3:5-6).

4. Assurance Of Salvation
Then, fourth, he speaks with assurance of everlasting acceptance in glory, 'And afterward receive me up to glory' (Psalms 73:24).

Yes, old Adam will soon be sent to the grave to rot because of sin; but God will receive his own up into glory (Ephesians 5:25-27; Jude 24-25; Jeremiah 50:20; Psalms 17:15). Did you ever notice what our Lord Jesus said to Peter immediately after telling his faithful disciple that before the rising of the morning sun he would deny his Saviour three times? Here is the Master's very next word to that disciple ...

> Let not your heart be troubled: ye believe in God, believe also in me. In my Father's house are many mansions: if it were not so, I would have told you. I go to prepare a place for you. And if I go and prepare a place for you, I will come again, and receive you unto myself; that where I am, there ye may be also (John 14:1-3).

My Only Hope
My soul's only hope of eternal glory is God my Saviour; 'Whom have I in heaven but thee? and there is none upon earth that I desire beside thee. My flesh and my heart faileth: but God is the strength of my heart, and my portion for ever' (Psalms 73:25-26).

I have no hope in myself; 'My heart and my flesh faileth'. There is nothing in me, nothing done by me, and nothing felt in my heart that gives me hope or commendation before God. My only hope of salvation and acceptance with God is God himself, the Lord Jesus Christ. In simple faith, because I can do nothing else, this sinful man turns to Christ Jesus the Lord and casts himself upon a Substitute. Christ is my only Hope. And Christ is Hope enough. Christ is all the hope I have and Christ is all the hope I desire; 'Whom have I in heaven but thee?' No one. 'And there is none upon earth that I desire beside thee.' 'Christ is all' for cleansing, for pardon, for righteousness, for peace, for holiness, for sanctification, for acceptance. Jesus Christ alone is the Rock of my salvation and the Strength of my heart. He is the Rock upon which I am built. And he is the Strength, the Support, Comfort, and Assurance of my heart. God, as he is revealed in Christ, is my portion forever. Therefore, I will hope in him (Lamentations 3:21-26).

Do not ever expect to be free from sin in this world. Do not ever expect your brethren to be free from sin in this world. In the midst of your sin go on trusting the Lord Jesus Christ. He will not cast you off (1 John 2:1-2). Give praise, honour, and glory to God your Saviour. His blood is effectual. His grace is unchangeable. His love is unfailing. 'His mercy endureth forever'.

Good Effect

Without question, our heavenly Father could remove all this evil from us, but he chooses not to do so. Why? The fact is, these inward conflicts do have some good effect. Hard as they are to bear now, in heaven's glory we will look back upon these days of great evil with gratitude, and see the wisdom and goodness of God in all of our struggles with sin. Our struggles with sin help humble us and curb our pride. Our struggles with sin force us to lean upon Christ alone for all our salvation (1 Corinthians 1:30), and confess with Jonah, 'Salvation is of the Lord'. Struggling hard with sin, we find that 'Christ is all' indeed. Our struggles with sin cause us to prize the faithfulness of our God (Lamentations 3:1-27). Our struggles with sin upon this earth will make the glorious victory of heaven sweeter. And our struggles with sin make us rejoice in the fact that 'salvation is of the Lord'.

I do not doubt that in eternity we will be made to see that God wisely and graciously allowed us to fall into one evil to keep us from a greater evil, or to make us more useful in his hands. Certainly, an honest acknowledgement of the sin that is in us, and of the fact that we are never without sin (1 John 1:8-10) ought to make us gracious, kind, forgiving, and patient with one another.

Soon Over

Blessed be God, these inward conflicts will soon be over (Philippians 1:6; Jude 24-25). We shall soon drop this earthly tabernacle and shall be completely free from sin. We shall be perfect, personally perfect, at last. We shall be triumphant in the end. In that day when our God shall make all things new, the former things shall not only pass away, they shall be remembered no more! All the evil consequences of sin shall be forever removed. We shall be forever 'faultless before the presence of his glory with exceeding joy'.

Yet, so long as we live in this world we will be 'as the company of two armies'. So I give you this word of admonition 'Keep thy heart with all diligence: for out of it are the issues of life' (Proverbs 4:23). Keep your heart tender. Keep your heart in the fellowship of Christ. Keep you heart full of the Word. Keep your heart in prayer. Keep your heart full of the cross. Keep your heart full of Christ and rest your soul upon Christ. 'This I say then, Walk in the Spirit, and ye shall not fulfil the lust of the flesh.'

But if ye be led of the Spirit, ye are not under the law. Now the works of the flesh are manifest, which are these; Adultery, fornication, uncleanness, lasciviousness, idolatry, witchcraft, hatred, variance, emulations, wrath, strife, seditions, heresies, Envyings, murders, drunkenness, revellings, and such like: of the which I tell you before, as I have also told you in time past, that they which do such things shall not inherit the kingdom of God.

(Galatians 5:18-21)

Chapter 31

Read: Galatians 5:18-21

'But If Ye Be Led Of The Spirit'

What a horrid warfare rages in our souls, a warfare between the flesh and the Spirit! 'But', how good it is to read that word here, 'But'. That means the Apostle has more instruction to give us about this matter. 'But if ye be led of the Spirit', that is to say, if we are led by God the Holy Spirit, as children are led by the hand, and taught to live by faith in Christ, we 'are not under the law'.

Life Implied

The fact that we are led by the Spirit of God implies that he has given us life in Christ, that we are born of God. A dead person cannot be led. 'It also supposes some strength', John Gill wrote, 'though a good deal of weakness. Were there no spiritual strength derived from Christ, they could not be led. And if there was no weakness, there would be no need of leading.'

All who are led of the Spirit are led by him out of the paths of bondage and sin and ruin and destruction to Christ. They are led away from Sinai's fiery mount to Christ. They are led away from all creature trust in legal works and personal righteousness to Christ. We are led to him for shelter, safety, and salvation. The Spirit of God leads us to Christ's sin-atoning blood for pardon and cleansing, to his righteousness for justification and sanctification, and to his fulness for every supply of grace. He guides us into all truth and causes believing sinners to walk in the ways of faith and truth, in the paths of righteousness and holiness, looking to Christ alone as our hope before God. He leads through all the days of our pilgrimage in grace and leads at last to glory.

'Not Under Law'

Being led by the Spirit, living by faith in Christ, we have nothing to fear from the law. It is written, 'Ye are not under the law'. This is not an obscure statement, but one that is repeated numerous times in the New Testament (Romans 6:14, 15; 7:4; 10:4). God's saints in this world are not under the law. Those who are born of God, those who live by faith in Christ are not under the law.

Read it again – 'Ye are not under the law'. Being led by the Spirit of God to Christ alone for righteousness, sanctification, and redemption, we are completely delivered from and free from the law, both in fact and in our own consciences. Trusting Christ, we possess the comfortable knowledge and experience of freedom from the law, freedom from all possibility of condemnation, because we are assured of our indestructible acceptance with God by the merits of our Redeemer.

Believers do not need the law (as religious hypocrites do) to force them to the performance of legal duties and religious activity. Believers delight in the law of God after the inward man and cheerfully serve God their Saviour and one another, being constrained by the love of Christ. God's saints are not mercenaries, but volunteers. We are not motivated by fear of punishment, reward, or loss of reward. What Paul says about being led by the Spirit, and not being under the law, also implies that if you are led by the law, you are not led by the Spirit.

Life In The Spirit

What is this life that Paul is describing? Is it a 'deeper' life? Is it a 'higher' life? Is it a life that some believers enjoy, while others live as mere 'carnal Christians?' Is Paul here promoting the idea that there are class distinctions in the church and kingdom of Christ? The answer to those questions is an emphatic 'No!' The life Paul is describing in this passage is the life of faith in Christ. It is written, 'The just shall live by faith.' We do not make ourselves alive by faith in Christ. God the Holy Spirit creates life in us by his omnipotent grace. And the life he gives us in Christ is a life of faith. Just as the natural man lives by breathing, the children of God live believing Christ. Life in the Spirit is a life of faith in Christ. Those who do not live in the Spirit but in the flesh, who are not led of the Spirit but by the lusts of the flesh; those who live after the carnal mind and not after the Spirit are yet dead in sin (Romans 8:1-14).

To 'walk in the Spirit (v. 16) is to be 'led of the Spirit' (v. 18). And those who walk in and are led of the Spirit of God bear fruit by the Spirit, having 'crucified the flesh with the affections and lusts' (vv. 22-25). Paul's whole emphasis here is the work of God the Holy Spirit in us, not a work we do for God. Paul is telling us that his admonition is to use our liberty in Christ to 'by love serve one another' (v. 13), and asserts that 'all the law is fulfilled in this one word, even in this, Thou shalt love thy neighbour as thyself' (v. 14), he is not urging us to go back to the law. Rather, he is telling us that the grace of God in us writes the law of God upon our hearts (Hebrews 8:10), causing us to love one another.

'Ye Shall Not'

Remember, Paul did not say, 'Walk in the Spirit, and ye may not fulfil the lusts of the flesh'. He said, 'Walk in the Spirit, and ye shall not fulfil the lusts of the flesh' (v. 16). Verse 18 is another way of saying the same thing, 'If ye be led of the Spirit, ye are not under the law'. Then, in verses 19-21 he tells us what the works of the flesh are.

'Now the works of the flesh are manifest, which are these; Adultery, fornication, uncleanness, lasciviousness, Idolatry, witchcraft, hatred, variance, emulations, wrath, strife, seditions, heresies, Envyings, murders, drunkenness, revellings, and such like: of the which I tell you before, as I have also told you in time past, that they which do such things shall not inherit the kingdom of God.'

We do not need to look very far to see the horrible evils Paul here speaks of as 'the works of the flesh'. We find them in our own hearts. This we must confess if we are honest before God. Remember, as Paul uses this term 'flesh' he does not have reference to the physical body, but to the fallen nature of man. It is the word from which we have the word carnal. The carnal man is all that man is by nature and all that he brings with him into the world.

Our thoughts, our affections, our consciences, and our wills are all governed by sin as natural men. The flesh is the carnal mind, which is enmity against God. It will not and cannot please God (Romans 8:6-7). This carnal mind (the flesh) asserts itself in works, which are clearly opposed to the Spirit of God. They are manifestly the works of the flesh. They are manifest before God. They are manifest in the law. And they are manifest in the consciences of men.

'Works Of The Flesh'

Paul says these things are works of the flesh, whereas that produced in us by grace is the fruit of the Spirit. Paul specifically mentions seventeen different, manifest works of the flesh. These sins of humanity are common in all human beings in all ages. That which Paul describes here are evils flowing in a constant stream of vileness from the depraved hearts of depraved men. These are not things learned by bad company, but evils arising from the corrupt hearts of fallen men (Mark 7:20-23).

Sins Of Passion

Paul first mentions sins of passion. Passion is a disease of the heart that betrays itself in constant restlessness. It is never satisfied with what it possesses. They include, but are not limited to, what we commonly think of as 'sexual sins'. The sins of passion Paul names are 'adultery, fornication, uncleanness, and lasciviousness'. Adultery is the defilement of the marriage bed (Proverbs 5:18-19). Fornication is a word used to describe any illicit sexual behaviour between unmarried people. The word here translated 'fornication' is the word from which we get our English word 'pornography'. It includes incest, homosexuality, and all other forms of deviant sexual behaviour. 'Uncleanness' is a word generally used to portray any lack of chastity in thought, word, or action. Like fornication, it commonly has reference to sodomy and other perversions. 'Lasciviousness' speaks of all lustful, sensual desires and those things that lead to acts of uncleanness, such as impure words and filthy gestures. Lasciviousness is the lack of self-control that characterizes the person who gives way to lust. Society and even the religious world tolerates and promotes these evils. But they are things in direct opposition to both the law of God and the gospel of the grace of God (1 Corinthians 6:9-11).

Sins Of Profanity

Next, the Apostle speaks of sins of profanity: idolatry and witchcraft. 'Idolatry' certainly includes covetousness (Colossians 3:5). However, in this place it has specific reference to the worship of false gods and images. Idolatry is participating in such worship. Any representations of the divine being are idolatrous, including religious pictures, images, icons, etc.. The substitution of anything, or any person, for the love, adoration, and desire of the true God as he has revealed himself in Jesus Christ is idolatry. 'Witchcraft' is the use of magic to accomplish real or supposed superhuman acts. The carnal mind turns to the basest absurdities of witchcraft (fortune tellers, horoscopes, etc.), and rejects the revelation of God in holy scripture.

Sins Of Pride

Next, Paul names a long list of what might be called sins of pride. 'Hatred' is murder. G. S. Bishop wrote, 'The two extremes of nature are sensuality and murder. The pendulum swings between these. The worship of the beautiful ends in an orgy! Shechem admires Dinah and defiles her. Amnon ruins Tamar and drives her from his house in anger.'

'Variance' is fighting and quarrelling with one another. 'Emulations' are a boiling, a rising of temper because of the honour or happiness enjoyed by someone else. 'Wrath' is the violent passion that seeks revenge.

'Strife' is the disruption of peace and harmony, causing discord (James 3:14-16). 'A wrathful man stirreth up strife'. Believers appease it (Proverbs 15:18). Strife always occurs when men are moved by selfish motives, each craving honour for himself. 'He loveth transgression that loveth strife: and he that exalteth his gate seeketh destruction' (Proverbs 17:19). Strife is always the result of pride. 'He that is of a proud heart stirreth up strife' (Proverbs 28:25).

'Seditions' are schisms, factions, and divisions. Whether social, domestic, or religious, 'seditions' (schisms) are always the evil result of pride and strife. 'Heresies' are bad principles of doctrine, things that subvert the gospel. Heresy is the result of that miserable pride which sets itself up as the critic and judge of God's Word.

'Envyings' are those uneasy, grieving vexations of the mind that arise because of the good others enjoy. Envy is aroused by pride when we see someone else advancing before us. Envy destroys the soul (Proverbs 14:30). Envy caused Cain to murder Abel. Envy caused Joseph's brothers to sell him into slavery. Envy caused Korah, Dathan, and Abiram to rise up in rebellion against Moses. Envy kept the prodigal's brother out of the Father's house. Love is not envious (Galatians 5:13; 1 Corinthians 13:4).

'Murders' are acts by which one man deliberately takes the life of another in order to gratify his own hatred and wrath or attain his own ends. 'Drunkenness' is intoxication of the mind and body with drugs, alcoholic drinks, or any other means. 'Revellings' are the uncontrolled riotousness of drunks.

Then, Paul says, 'and such like'. With those words, John Gill tells us 'He shuts up the account, it being too tedious to give an enumeration of all the works of the flesh; nor was it necessary, judgment may be made of the rest by these; nor might it be so proper, since the carnal heart is but the more pleased with, and irritated by, the mention of evil things.' The law of God was given to restrain and condemn all such behaviour among men (1 Timothy 1:9-10).

Unregenerate People

At the end of verse 21 the Apostle tells us plainly that all such people are utterly without grace and life in Christ. They are unregenerate, unbelieving people. 'Of the which I tell you before, as I have also told you in time past, that they which do such things shall not inherit the kingdom of God'. Henry Mahan wrote,

> Understand that these sinful practices are characteristics of the flesh, and though we have done these things and the potential to do them is still present in our flesh (as evidenced by Abraham, David, Lot, and Peter), yet this is not our pattern of life This is not the practice of the believer! Our tenor of life and the bent of our wills is holiness, righteousness and peace. Those who would still live by these principles and practices of the flesh are not redeemed and shall not inherit the kingdom of God.

The flesh is the proud root of depravity and God hating rebellion in every human heart. It always exalts itself, either with great subtlety in proud self-righteousness or in blatant, God defying immorality. It is written, 'If ye live after the flesh, ye shall die' (Romans 8:13).

But the fruit of the Spirit is love, joy, peace, longsuffering, gentleness, goodness, faith, Meekness, temperance: against such there is no law.

(Galatians 5:22-23)

Chapter 32

Read: Galatians 5:22-23

'The Fruit Of The Spirit Is ... '
Here is a blessed contrast to what we saw in verses 19-21. There the Apostle set before us seventeen works of the flesh, products of the carnal mind that hates God, works produced by the efforts of hearts at enmity against the holy Lord God. All who continue in such works must be forever damned. Here he shows us that which is the fruit of the Holy Spirit, that which is produced in (not wrought by, but produced in) the heaven born soul by the almighty grace of God the Holy Spirit.

Paul does not deal with the fruit of the Spirit as many things, but as one. He is describing the fruit (singular) not the fruits (plural) of the Spirit. The fruit of the Spirit is a cluster of fruit, like a cluster of grapes, brought forth in all who are born of God in the new creation of grace. This fruit of the Spirit is not spoken of as that which ought to be in the believer, but as that which is produced in the believer. Paul is not setting before us that which is given to some as an extra-ordinary gift of God, but the common, constant fruit of God the Holy Spirit in all who are born again.

In this cluster Paul specifically names nine things as the fruit of the Spirit: 'Love, joy, peace, longsuffering, gentleness, goodness, faith, meekness, temperance'. With reference to God, all believers have created in them love, joy, and peace. With reference to one another, all are given long-suffering, gentleness, and goodness. With reference to themselves, all who know God are people of faith, meekness, and temperance.

'The Fruit Of The Spirit Is Love'

Man by nature loves himself and really only himself. He 'loves' all other things (family, friends, possessions, etc.) only for what they add to himself. Though many who do not even profess faith in Christ claim to love God, they only love their own concept of what God ought to be. All men by nature vainly imagine that God exists only to benefit men. This is a condition that never changes. 'That which is born of the flesh is flesh; that which is born of the Spirit is spirit' (John 3:6). Love is the fruit of the Spirit, not the fruit of the flesh. Indeed, along with faith, it is the gift of God. When a person is born again, he gains the capacity to love God, to love God as he is revealed in the scriptures, as he is revealed in Christ; to love God as he really is in his true character. He not only gains the capacity to love God, he truly does love God (1 Corinthians 16:22; 1 John 4:19).

All who are born of God love and seek his glory. This is part of the miracle of the new creation in Christ (2 Corinthians 5:17). Because the believer truly loves God, all other loves are never the same. He no longer loves only that which gratifies and exalts the flesh. He always has an eye to that which honours God his Saviour. All other loves are made subservient to this love. And when our love for family and friends, yes, even for men in common, is subservient to love for God, then we truly love others and seek to serve their best interests in all things.

Now, this love is far from perfect. It is nothing about which we have reason to boast. Yet, this is the true testimony of every heaven born soul: 'We love him because he first loved us.' We do not love him as we desire. We do not love him as we know we should. We do not love him as we soon shall. But we do really love him. It is not possible for a man to experience the grace of God in salvation and not love the God of all grace. It is not possible for a man to know the efficacy of Christ's blood in his own soul and not love his gracious Redeemer. It is not possible for a man to have his heart renewed by the power of the Holy Spirit and not love the Spirit of life. In spite of our many weaknesses, sins and failures, we do honestly and sincerely confess, 'Lord, thou knowest all things; thou knowest that I love thee.'

We know also that we would never have loved him if he had not loved us first. The love of God for us precedes our love for him. 'He first loved us'. He loved us before we had any desire to be loved by him. He loved us before we sought his grace. He loved us before we had any repentance or faith. He loved us before we had any being. He loved us eternally. Does he not say, 'I have loved thee with an everlasting love: therefore with lovingkindness have I called thee' (Jeremiah 31:3). He chose us, redeemed us, and called us because he loved us.

Our hearts are so hard and our wills so stubborn that we would never have loved the Lord, if he had not intervened to conquer us with his love. In the midst of our sin and corruption, he passed by, and behold it was 'the time of love'. He revealed his great love for us in Christ. As we beheld the crucified Christ, dying in the place of sinners, the love of God conquered our rebel hearts. Trusting Christ as our only Saviour, we are compelled to love him, 'because he first loved us'.

'The Fruit Of The Spirit Is Joy'
Believers possess and enjoy a gladness of heart, a joy, of which the world knows nothing. Unregenerate men enjoy the pleasures of sin for brief seasons; but theirs is misspent and transient happiness that comes and goes with the empty bubbles they chase. The believer's joy is based on something more substantial. We rejoice in the Lord (Philippians 4:4). With Habakkuk, we sing, 'Although the fig tree shall not blossom, neither shall fruit be in the vines; the labour of the olive shall fail, and the fields shall yield no meat; the flock shall be cut off from the fold, and there shall be no herd in the stalls: Yet I will rejoice in the LORD, I will joy in the God of my salvation' (Habakkuk 3: 17, 18). Having no confidence in the flesh, we 'rejoice in Christ Jesus' (Philippians 3:3).

When Job lost everything, he yet blessed the name of the Lord because the object of his love and joy was God his Saviour, not what God had given him, but God himself. It was only when he feared that the Lord had turned his back that horror and despair cast their ominous shadow over his soul. This is not natural to man, but is the gift and fruit of the Spirit.

Believers do not fake joy. They possess it. We do not walk like giddy air-heads, oblivious to real sorrow and grief, or in denial of it, as so many do. We do, however, possess real and enduring joy, rejoicing in him by whom and in whom we are so monumentally and eternally blessed, being assured of his unfailing goodness and grace (Romans 8:28). Chris Cunningham wrote, 'Our joy is irrepressible because the object of our delight is infinitely and invariably delightful.'

When others despise us, as Michal despised David, we rejoice in God's electing love as David did. When men and Satan hurl accusations against us, as Shemei did against David, we rejoice in the knowledge that our God sends them for our good, to drive us to Christ our Redemption and Righteousness. When our weakness is manifest, we rejoice in Christ, whose strength is made perfect in weakness. When we see our utter insufficiency, we rejoice to know that 'our sufficiency is of God'. When it is obvious that things are out of control, as far as we are concerned and as far as all other creatures are concerned, we rejoice to see God our

Saviour, the Lamb upon his throne. When our bodies are dying, we rejoice in Christ who is our Life.

'The Fruit Of The Spirit Is Peace'

We have peace with God being reconciled to him by the death of his Son, and peace from God being ruled in our hearts by the Prince of peace, and the peace of God because the Spirit of God has spoken peace to our hearts giving us faith in Christ. Though we are, by nature, 'like the troubled sea, when it cannot rest, whose waters cast up mire and dirt' (Isaiah 57:20), by the gift and grace of God the Spirit, we are as lambs under the ever-watchful eye and omnipotent care of the Good Shepherd. Though our sin is ever before us, we have peace in our consciences, knowing that all our sin and guilt is forever put away by the sin-atoning sacrifice of our Lord Jesus Christ. Though, at times, the weight of the world and its care crushes our souls, we have peace of mind, casting all our care upon him who cares for us. And God gives us peace in our hearts, causing us to be fully satisfied and delighted with him, knowing that he is fully and forever satisfied and delighted with us in his Son, who has washed away our sins in his blood and robed us with his perfect righteousness. And when our time on earth is finished, we shall, like Simeon of old, depart this body of flesh in peace, having our eyes fixed upon our Salvation. In that day, we will lay down in peace and sleep, 'for thou, Lord, only makest us to dwell in safety' (Psalms 4:8).

Longsuffering, Gentleness, Goodness

With reference to God, all believers have created in them love, joy and peace. With reference to one another, all are given longsuffering, gentleness and goodness.

'The Fruit Of The Spirit Is Longsuffering'

God the Holy Spirit, when he creates life and faith in our souls, gives us longsuffering, and teaches us to be longsuffering. He gives us patience to endure trials from our heavenly Father and troublesome, irksome things in and done by others. Grace experienced in the soul makes saved sinners slow to anger and ready to forgive. Grace causes people who are by nature easily offended, and quick to retaliate, patiently to bear affronts and be forbearing with those who offend.

Our Lord Jesus is more than an example for us to follow. Everything he did in life, he did in obedience to the Father as our Mediator and Representative, working out perfect righteousness for us. And everything he endured in death, he endured as our Substitute to satisfy the justice of

God for us. But we must never forget that in all his life and death, our blessed Saviour is also our example (1 Peter 2:21-25). Should any ask, 'What is longsuffering?' I say, 'Look to Christ. He is the very embodiment of longsuffering.'

When his disciples displayed an utter ignorance of the things he taught, he patiently taught the same truths again and again. When they were filled with unbelief and fear, he showed them their folly, not by belittling them, but by removing the cause of their fear. Even when they forsook him (and they all did), he did not abandon them. Rather, like the Good Shepherd he is, as soon as he was risen from the dead, he began seeking his scattered sheep. When Peter was ashamed to come to him, he sent his messengers to Peter to tell him that he would meet him in Galilee.

How great is his longsuffering toward us! Throughout the days of our rebellion, with every breath and deed, we spewed out our hatred against him; but his longsuffering was our salvation. We scoffed at him; but he was longsuffering to us. We blasphemed him; but he was longsuffering to us. We despised his blood and righteousness; but he was longsuffering to us. And in all the days of our lives, since he snatched us as brands from the burning out of the very jaws of hell by his omnipotent mercy, how we have sinned and continue to sin against him. Yet, he knows our frame and remembers that we are dust, and refuses to deal with us after our sins and reward us according to our iniquities.

That is what Paul means by this term, 'longsuffering'. God the Holy Spirit makes chosen, redeemed, called sinners longsuffering. Yet, as with our love, joy, and peace toward God, our longsuffering with one another in this world is such horrid short-temperedness that it must be bathed in the blood of Christ, robed in his righteousness, and forgiven by his grace. Yet, God's saints are a people patient and longsuffering with one another. John Newton wrote:

Fear thou not, distressed believer; venture on his mighty name;
He is able to deliver, and his love is still the same.
Can his pity or his power suffer thee to pray in vain?
Wait but his appointed hour, and thy suit thou shalt obtain.

'The Fruit Of The Spirit Is Gentleness'
Longsuffering is accompanied with gentleness, kindness, and courtesy. This gentleness is seen in our attitudes toward others, our speech to and about others, and our treatment of others. This, too, is exemplified in 'the gentleness of Christ'. Gentleness is a mild, peaceful, moderate spirit,

bestowed upon those who are 'made partakers of the divine nature'. It is the spirit of Christ our Saviour (2 Corinthians 10:1) and the spirit he gives by his grace, by which fallen men are made to be great men and wise (2 Samuel 22:36; Psalms 18:35). 'The wisdom that is from above is gentle' (James 3:17). This gentleness is not a passive spirit of compromise and cowardice that destroys manhood and usefulness. That is a vice rather than a virtue, a display of depravity rather than of grace. Our Lord Jesus was the most gentle man who ever lived, and the boldest and most courageous. Charles Buck very accurately says of gentleness, 'It renounces no just right from fear; it gives up no important truth from flattery: it is, indeed, not only consistent with a firm mind, but it necessarily requires a manly spirit and a fixed principle, in order to give it any real value.'

Yet, gentleness is the very opposite of harshness and severity, of pride and arrogance, and of violence and oppression. It is the charitable spirit of brotherly love and kindness that causes God's saints in this world to take great care neither to offend nor hurt another. It causes the believer to seek to relieve the needs and burdens of others, be patient and forbearing with the offences of others, and prevents severe judgment and retaliation. Gentleness is that spirit of meekness and humility that causes believers to restore one another when fallen (Galatians 6:1-2), weep with those who weep, and rejoice with those who rejoice (Romans 12:15). Believers are not bitter but benevolent, not harsh but helpful, not mean but merciful. Truly, gentleness is both greatness and wisdom!

'The Fruit Of The Spirit Is Goodness'

Goodness is a readiness to do good, particularly a readiness to do good to and for one another. Yet, the Apostle Paul, writing as a believer, said 'I know that in me (that is, in my flesh,) dwelleth no good thing' (Romans 7:18). Goodness is not in us by nature. Our Master declares, 'There is none good, but one, that is God'. God alone is good, infinitely good, immutably good, and perfectly good. Fallen man is not good, but bad; and there is no possibility of any man doing that which is good. 'There is none that doeth good, no, not one.' Still, when God the Holy Spirit performs his mighty operations of grace in chosen, redeemed sinners, he makes them to be a people whose lives are marked by goodness. Any goodness found in us or performed by us is God's work in us, the fruit of the Spirit (Romans 3:12; Ephesians 2:10).

What is this goodness that is the fruit of the Spirit? How is it manifest? Is there ever an act performed by, or even a thought in the heart of a believer that is truly and absolutely good and pure, perfect and righteous, worthy of God's acceptance? The answer, of course, is, 'No'. Both the scriptures and an honest consideration of our own life experience compel us to acknowledge these things (1 John 1:8, 10). The Spirit that is in us is good, perfectly good. That which is born of God cannot sin (1 John 3:9); but our old nature is nothing but sin. How, then, can the fruit of the Spirit in us be called 'goodness'?

'Goodness' is that indwelling grace of God the Holy Spirit, that attribute of the divine nature of which we are made partakers in the new birth, which disposes believers to acts of goodness to others. There is much talk in the religious world about 'good works'. As defined by men, good works are measured by the observance of various rules of conduct relating to dress codes, diet, and outward appearance. But in the Word of God good works are always connected with acts of brotherly love, kindness, self-denial, and sacrifice: visiting the sick, feeding the hungry, helping the needy, etc. (Matthew 25:31-46; James 1:26-27).

Good works, works acceptable and well pleasing to God, are works of faith, works by which faith is shown (James 2:14-26). Good works are never spoken of in Scripture except as manifestations of faith. If faith without works is dead, then what are works without faith? A good work is a work of faith, arising from and connected with faith in Christ, without which it is impossible to please God (Hebrews 11:6). Our good works are acceptable and well-pleasing to God only in Christ, only because we are one with Christ, who alone is our Righteousness (Ephesians 4:32-5:2; 1 Peter 2:5).

Faith, Meekness, Temperance

With reference to God, all believers have created in them love, joy, and peace. With reference to one another, all are given longsuffering, gentleness and goodness. And with reference to themselves, all who know God are people of faith, meekness and temperance.

'The Fruit Of The Spirit Is Faith'

As Paul uses the word 'faith' here, it refers not so much to our faith in Christ (though that is included) as it does to our faithfulness as believers in all things. In other words, Paul is saying, 'The fruit of the Spirit is faithfulness'. The one thing God requires of all who serve him as stewards in his house and kingdom is faithfulness. And when God the Holy Spirit makes sinners the willing servants of Christ, he makes them faithful.

There is nothing more admirable in our God and Saviour than the fact that 'he abideth faithful'. And there is nothing more admirable in his

children than faithfulness. Believers are people who are faithful: faithful
to God, faithful to his Word, faithful to his glory, faithful to one another,
and faithful in their lives. This faithfulness certainly includes
dependability; but many are dependable in their responsibilities who have
no knowledge of the eternal God at all. This faithfulness is more than that.
This is an inward principle of grace, an inward, heart fidelity to Christ, by
which the lives of God's saints are regulated in this world.

'The Fruit Of The Spirit Is Meekness'

With regard to meekness (as with all other spiritual matters), it must be
stated and clearly understood that the opinions of unregenerate men are
exactly opposite to the teachings of holy scripture. Meekness is not a
weakness of character that makes men useless wimps. We read in the
Book of God that, 'The man Moses was very meek, above all the men
which were upon the face of the earth' (Numbers 12:3). But I am pretty
confident that had anyone who asked Pharaoh for an example of meekness,
Moses would have been the very last man to come to his mind.

Meekness is a spirit that is not easily provoked, a tamed spirit (James
3:7-10). It is that attitude of heart, created in God's elect by the Holy Spirit
in the gift of faith, that causes believing souls to be at ease in the world.
Where the Prince of Peace reigns meekness reigns. Meekness is that
frame of mind, that disposition of soul in believing men and women, arising
from a recognition of the fact that we are sinners forgiven and accepted of
God in Christ, and that we belong to God our Saviour. We are his property,
his children, and his servants.

This meekness makes believers humble before God and men. We know
that we are nothing but sinners saved by grace. That knowledge causes
us to walk humbly with our God and to be gracious to one another. At the
same time, meekness (true meekness) gives people backbone. It causes
men and women as the children and servants of God to be bold,
courageous, and faithful, knowing that he who is God indeed is our God
and Father. 'The Lord is my light and my salvation; whom shall I fear? The
LORD is the strength of my life; of whom shall I be afraid?' (Psalms 27:1).

Most everyone thinks of the man Christ Jesus as a man of weakness,
which they call 'meekness'. But our Lord Jesus was truly meek. In meekness
he voluntarily bowed to his Father's will and became 'obedient unto death,
even the death of the cross'. In meekness he drove the money-changers
out of the temple. In meekness he set his face like a flint to go up to
Jerusalem. In meekness he denounced as pretentious hypocrites the most
highly respected religious leaders of the day. In meekness he called
idolaters idolaters, adulterers adulterers, and self-serving politicians foxes.

In meekness he cast out the prince of this world and triumphantly conquered death, hell, and the grave in his sin-atoning death.

'The Fruit Of The Spirit Is Temperance'

Temperance is self-control, continence, or control from within. Without question, it is seen in the control of our appetites, in moderation in eating and drinking; but there is much more to temperance than self-discipline. When God the Holy Spirit comes in saving power, Christ sets up his throne in the hearts of saved sinners and makes them kings (1 Peter 2:5, 9; Revelation 1:6; 5:10; 20:6). Kings are men who reign. The Lord Jesus reigns within the hearts of his people, giving them dominion over their passions, over the world around them, and even over death, so that all who are born of God live in this world in temperance, being controlled not by the things around them but by Christ who reigns within them.

This fruit of the Spirit is altogether contrary to nature. It is not something produced by us, but something produced in us by God the Holy Spirit. It is the result of the new birth, the gift of faith in Christ, and the indwelling Spirit of God. If it is ours, it is ours only by grace (1 Corinthians 4:7). It is fruit found in every believer. In some it is but newly planted seed in the heart. In others it is mature fruit. In none is it perfect. But in all it is present. Of this fruit, John Gill wrote,

> It may be observed, that these fruits of the Spirit are opposed to the works of the flesh. So love is opposed to hatred; joy to emulations and envying; peace to variance, strife, and seditions; longsuffering, gentleness, goodness, and meekness, to wrath and murders; faith to idolatry, witchcraft, and heresies; and temperance to adultery, fornication, uncleanness, lasciviousness, drunkenness, and revellings.

'Against Such There Is No Law'

Obviously, these things are in full agreement with God's holy law. To practice such things is to 'by love serve one another'. But Paul's declaration here refers not to the fruit of the Spirit, but to those in whom this fruit is found, to those who walk in the Spirit, to those who are born of God, to those who live by faith in Christ. He is saying, 'There is therefore now no condemnation to them which are in Christ Jesus, who walk not after the flesh, but after the Spirit.' The works of the flesh and those who live after the flesh are under the curse and condemnation of the law. 'But if ye be led of the Spirit, ye are not under the law.'

And they that are Christ's have crucified the flesh
with the affections and lusts. If we live in the Spirit, let
us also walk in the Spirit. Let us not be desirous of vain
glory, provoking one another, envying one another.

(Galatians 5:24-26)

Chapter 33

Read: Galatians 5:24-26

Walk In The Spirit

Paul is continuing with his exhortation to us to 'walk in the Spirit' (v. 16). We recognize that the believer's life of faith in Christ is a life lived by grace, sustained by grace, and worked in us by grace. The fruit of the Spirit within us, and manifest in our outward behaviour is altogether the work of God's unceasing grace and goodness. However, the life of faith in Christ is not a life of spiritual passivity. Rather, it is a life of relentless, determined resolve for the glory of God. While we are made willing by God our Saviour to be his servants, all true believers are willing servants.

A Deliberate Crucifixion

Those who are Christ's are those who are united to him by faith; and they have nailed their flesh to his cross. Believers are people who have deliberately, purposefully, and willingly crucified the flesh. They are a people who belong to Christ (v. 24).

We were his secretly from eternity, given to him in the covenant of grace from eternity by the Father who chose us in him before the foundations of the earth were laid (John 6:39). We were given to him as his sheep and his people, made to be one with him and accepted in him as our Mediator before the world began (Ephesians 1:3-6). And we are his by purchase. The Lord Jesus Christ bought us with his precious blood. We are not our own; we have been bought with the price of Christ's life's blood poured out for us at Calvary. And we are Christ's by the effectual, irresistible call of his Spirit in omnipotent grace. He has saved us by his grace. But there is more.

We belong to Christ by wilful, deliberate faith. In our baptism, the believer's public profession of faith in Christ, we were symbolically buried with Christ in the watery grave. By this we were declaring to Christ, his church, and the world that we were crucified with Christ, that we have been raised from death to life by his grace; that we are his forever to walk with him in newness of life; that we have deliberately given ourselves up to him (Romans 6:3-10). Faith in Christ is the voluntary, wilful surrender of ourselves to him. It is the deliberate denial of self, the surrender of our lives to Christ as Lord (Matthew 16:24-25; Mark 8:34-35; Luke 14:26-33). This is what Paul refers to when he speaks of us having crucified the flesh with its affections and lusts. Confessing Christ as our Saviour and Lord, we have declared (and continually declare) that our old man has no right to live, mortifying therefore 'the deeds of the body' (Romans 8:13; Colossians 3:5-6).

> Chosen in eternal love
> By my God, Who reigns above,
> All I am and own I bring
> Under rule to Christ my King:
> I submit to Christ my God'.
>
> Chosen and redeemed and called,
> Let no fear my heart intrude:
> Christ will feed and clothe His own,
> And protect me by His throne:
> I will trust Him, Christ my God.
>
> Saviour, let me live on earth
> To proclaim Your matchless worth:
> In body and spirit, Lord,
> I would glorify my God:
> I will live for Christ my God.
>
> Though my sinful flesh rebel,
> Force me, Lord, to do Your will:
> When my work on earth is done,
> Bring me safely to Your throne:
> I will see my Christ, my God!

A Determined Consecration

The interpretation I have given of verse 24 is confirmed by verse 25, 'If we live in the Spirit, let us also walk in the Spirit.' Those who are Christ's 'live in the Spirit'. God the Holy Spirit has given us eternal life, and that life is life we have by the Spirit of Christ dwelling in us. 'I am crucified with Christ: nevertheless I live; yet not I, but Christ liveth in me: and the life which I now live in the flesh I live by the faith of the Son of God, who loved me, and gave himself for me' (Galatians 2:20).

Still, this is not a life of spiritual passiveness, but a life of determined consecration to Christ our Saviour. To walk in the Spirit is to live by the rule of his Word, under his influence and direction, constantly surrendering our will to our Saviour's will, ever seeking his glory. Yes, this is something we must continually do. It involves the continual, deliberate renunciation of self, the continual, deliberate surrender of self to Christ; 'Whether therefore ye eat, or drink, or whatsoever ye do, do all to the glory of God' (1 Corinthians 10:31). Some might ask, 'Is such total, constant surrender to Christ reasonable?' Indeed, it is. It is the most reasonable thing in the world, 'I beseech you therefore, brethren, by the mercies of God, that ye present your bodies a living sacrifice, holy, acceptable unto God, which is your reasonable service' (Romans 12:1).

'How much owest thou unto my Lord?' (Luke 16:5). Were this question, which the unjust steward put to his lord's debtors, put to me concerning that immense debt which has made me forever insolvent, how could it be answered? It is an indescribable debt I cannot calculate, much less pay. I am a debtor to God's infinite, free, and sovereign grace.

When I think of my being, I realise that no human ledger is sufficient to calculate even the gifts of creation and providence with which I have been boundlessly blessed all the days of my life. Looking back over all my days, I am compelled to declare to the praise of my God, 'Surely goodness and mercy have followed me all the days of my life.'

But when I think of my well-being in Christ, of the boundless riches of God's free grace bestowed upon my soul in Christ, I am humbled with gratitude and overawed with wonder and praise. The calculation of my debt is infinite. Before God's holy law, I was utterly bankrupt, condemned by the righteous justice of God and under the dreadful penalty of everlasting death in hell. The terrors and alarms of a guilty, screaming conscience held me in fear of death. The accusations of Satan tormented me day and night. What an oppressive load of guilt and sin I carried in my dark soul! My heart sank within me. 'But God, who is rich in mercy, for his great love wherewith he loved us,' (Ephesians 2:4) stepped in, gave me life and faith in Christ, spoke peace to my soul by the blood and righteousness of his darling Son, revealing Christ in me as my all-glorious, almighty Saviour, and my burden fell from my soul! 'How much owest thou', O my soul?

When I think of my Saviour, the Lord Jesus, and remember that he has restored all that I owed, fed my hungry soul, and clothed my nakedness with his own righteous garments, I bow before him in amazement. He has made me to be a man who has done that which is lawful and right before God, as one who has walked in his statutes and kept his judgments. All the bounty of his grace he has given to this sinful man freely, not 'upon usury', but freely, taking no increase from me. Yes, he has ransomed me from the power of death by his death in my stead. He is for me the plague of death and the destruction of the grave (Ezekiel 18:5-13; Hosea 13:14). My ever-blessed Saviour has cancelled all my debts. He has fulfilled all the demands of God's holy law for me. He has silenced Satan, my accuser. He has redeemed me out of the hands of everlasting bondage, misery, and eternal death. He has brought me into his everlasting kingdom of freedom, joy, and glory. He has made me an heir of God and joint-heir with himself! 'How much owest thou', O my soul?

When I consider the love of God my Father in giving his dear Son to be my Saviour, when I meditate upon my great Redeemer's love in coming to save me, when I think about the love of God the Holy Spirit made known to my soul in effectual grace, my heart cries out, 'How much owest thou', O my soul! Oh precious debt! It is ever increasing. Yet, owing it makes me blessed forever!

> Here, Lord, I give myself away, 'tis all that I can do.

A Denied Exaltation

In verse 26 Paul again shows us that this matter of walking in the Spirit, this matter of living in this world for the glory of God, is directly connected with brotherly love. If we would walk in the Spirit, 'Let us not be desirous of vain glory, provoking one another, envying one another.' We must make it a matter of constant determination not to desire and seek honour, esteem, and applause from men. What we are in Christ, we are by the grace of God. He and he alone has made us to differ from others. We must ever abase ourselves and prefer one another. We who know ourselves to be the chief of sinners must take care not to despise and provoke one another by a show of pretentious superiority. And we must not envy the gifts and abilities God has bestowed upon others, but rejoice in them.

'As' And 'So'

The Apostle Paul makes a statement in Colossians 2:6 that goes to the very heart of this matter of walking in the Spirit. There he says, 'As ye have therefore received Christ Jesus the Lord, so walk ye in him'. How did you receive Christ? We did not receive Christ by the works of the flesh, or by the hearing of the law, but by faith (Galatians 3:1-3). That is how we must live, if we would honour God. We honour God, fulfil the law, and magnify our Saviour, only by faith in him (Romans 3:31; Hebrews 11:4-6).

How did you receive Christ? If you have received him, you received him by faith. You came to him as a sinner, trusting him as your Saviour (1 Corinthians 1:30-31). You bowed to him as a servant, receiving him as your Lord. You became the willing servant of Jesus Christ (Exodus 21:1-6). You came to him as a bride, like Gomer, conquered by his love, embracing him as your husband.

As you received Christ Jesus the Lord, so walk in him, trusting Christ's goodness, grace, love, and providence in all things (Psalms 23:1; Proverbs 3:5-6). Walk in faith, following Christ. Worship Him. In everything give thanks to him. Sing praise to him. Ever follow his example (John 13:15; 1 Peter 2:20-24; Ephesians 4:32-5:2).

If we would live in this world for the glory of God our Saviour, if we would walk in the Spirit, we must seek the will and glory of God in all things and above all things. I do not mean that we should endeavour to show people that we love the Lord (Matthew 6:1-17). But I do mean that we ought to be consumed, utterly consumed, with love for Christ: 'Seek ye first the kingdom of God and his righteousness' (Matthew 6:33), 'Set your affection on things above, not on things on the earth' (Colossians 3:2). The secret to satisfaction in this world is serving God; doing his will (John 4:31-34). Daily surrender all things to Christ. Call everything but dung in comparison to him (Philippians 3:7-10). Take up your cross daily, and follow him. Lose your life to Christ, and you will save it. 'Whatsoever he saith unto you, do it' (John 2:5).

I cannot think of a better way of summarising Paul's message in Galatians 5 than by quoting a statement I heard a preacher make when I was a very young man, 'Don't ever lose your sweetheart love for Christ.'

Brethren, if a man be overtaken in a fault, ye which are spiritual, restore such an one in the spirit of meekness; considering thyself, lest thou also be tempted. Bear ye one another's burdens, and so fulfil the law of Christ. For if a man think himself to be something, when he is nothing, he deceiveth himself. But let every man prove his own work, and then shall he have rejoicing in himself alone, and not in another. For every man shall bear his own burden.

(Galatians 6:1-5)

Chapter 34

Read: Galatians 6:1-5

Serving One Another

The Galatians had foolishly been trying to bear the heavy burden of the Mosaic law. They had entangled themselves again with the yoke of bondage. They endeavoured to establish righteousness for themselves by the works of the law. None of them said, 'We are saved by our own works.' Satan does not work in such an open manner. These lawmongers at Galatia were saying, 'We are saved by grace, but only if we keep the law.' Others of them said, 'We are saved by grace alone, in so far as our justification is concerned; but in order to be sanctified we must keep the law as a rule of life.' In reality their doctrine was the same. They were attempting to mix law and grace. They had forsaken the gospel way of salvation by grace alone.

Now Paul says to them, 'Do you want a law to live by? Then live by the rule of the law of Christ – love.' Here is a law that is a living principle. It touches the heart, influences the life, honours God, and is sympathetic towards and helpful to men. The whole law is fulfilled in this one thing – love. Without it, all the pretentious, self-righteous piety men claim to possess is hypocrisy.

It seems quite remarkable to me that those self-righteous people, who apparently want all men to know that they make the law of Moses their rule of life, usually forget that which is the essence and spirit of the law – love. They are (in their own minds) so righteous that they become stern, hard, severe, critical, and judgmental, which is being unrighteous. Even the righteousness of the Mosaic law is a righteousness of love. But I have never found one of those self-righteous legalists who was tender-hearted, kind, and gentle. He looks at the killing letter of the law and becomes as hard and stern as death.

Let this be the law by which we live: 'Love one another' (John 13:34). Reject that which is hard, stern, and severe. 'Be ye kind one to another, tender-hearted, forgiving one another, even as God for Christ's sake hath forgiven you' (Ephesians 4:32). In Galatians 5:13-14 the Apostle urged us to serve one another by love, telling us that it is love that fulfils the law, not religious ceremony and a pretentious show of piety. Here, in chapter 6 he tells us how to serve one another in love.

Restore the Fallen

Paul begins this chapter by telling us that when a brother or sister in Christ is fallen, those who are spiritual (that is to say, believers, those who walk in the Spirit) are to restore the fallen 'Brethren, if a man be overtaken in a fault, ye which are spiritual, restore such an one'. He tells us how to restore them 'in the spirit of meekness'. He explains what the spirit of meekness is 'considering thyself'. Then, he presses his admonition home 'lest thou also be tempted' (v. 1).

The church of God is a family. Believers are brothers and sisters in the household of faith. The love that knits a family together and makes it strong is manifest in the tender care each member of the family has for the rest. In a strong, loving family the whole family rallies to the needs of one. The greater the need is, the more the family's love is poured out to meet the need. And the need is never greater than when one in the family is, by his own folly, fallen.

That is the need to which Paul addresses himself here. Believers never have greater opportunity to show their love to one another, or greater opportunity to exemplify that which James calls 'pure religion and undefiled', than in seeking the restoration of a fallen brother or sister in Christ.

Those who walk in the Spirit must take great care, when they look upon one who is fallen, not to indulge the lust of the flesh; that pride and self-righteousness that is quick to take the judgment-seat, looking down upon the fallen in a pretence of pity that says, 'Stand by thyself, come not near to me; for I am holier than thou.' Let us ever hear our Saviour's words, 'Judge not, that ye be not judged.' Anytime we start to look upon a fallen saint with such self-righteous contempt, we ought to ask ourselves, 'Why dost thou judge thy brother? or why dost thou set at nought thy brother? for we shall all stand before the judgment-seat of Christ.'

It is the lust of the flesh that jumps at the chance to distance ourselves from the fallen, put them out of the church, and show the world that we are a 'holy' people who do not countenance sin. The instruction Paul gives us here is not in any way a detriment to proper church discipline. Rather, it is proper church discipline. The purpose of discipline in the family is not to exclude the fallen member, but to restore him.

There are many who move from church to church, looking for that perfect church. They attend a church only long enough to see a problem, and then they are off to another in their endless search of a congregation that is worthy of such fine people as they think themselves to be. A story is commonly told that illustrates my point.

Frederick the Great of Prussia once toured a prison, interviewing many of the inmates. One prisoner after another insisted that he was innocent of the crime for which he was imprisoned, asserting that he had been falsely accused and convicted. Finally, he spoke to a prisoner who frankly admitted his guilt and acknowledged that his imprisonment was just. Frederick called for the prison guards – 'Quickly! Release this man, lest he corrupt all these innocent men!'

In all things, our Lord Jesus teaches us to be compassionate and tender, not harsh and severe. We are to restore the fallen 'in the spirit of meekness'. Paul's own explanation of this 'spirit of meekness' is given in his next words: 'Considering thyself, lest thou also be tempted.' When we remind ourselves that we are nothing but sinners saved by grace, that our only righteousness is Christ, and that we are kept from doing the very same thing our fallen brother or sister has done, only by the grace of God, we are compelled to be gentle in dealing with the fallen.

The absolute truth of the matter is that we are all sinners (Romans 6:23). If we say we have no sin, or that in anything we have not sinned, we deceive ourselves (1 John 1:8, 10). 'In many things, we offend all'(James 3:2). Sin is not necessarily a matter of wilful rebellion against God. It is often, as stated here, being 'overtaken in a fault'. Stumbles and falls do not imply wilfulness, but weakness. That is not an attempt to excuse sin; but it is an indication of how we are to look upon the sins of our brothers and sisters in Christ, not as crimes to be punished, but as weaknesses requiring help.

When a child falls, you do not beat him, or even scold him. You pick him up, help him, and do whatever needs to be done for him. Regardless of the nature of the fall, when a brother or sister is 'overtaken in a fault', those who trust Christ, those who walk in the Spirit, those who know they are sinners saved by grace alone, are to restore the fallen.

Burden Bearing

Here is another way we are to serve one another in love. 'Bear ye one another's burdens, and so fulfil the law of Christ' (v. 2). Pastor Scott Richardson once said, 'Life in this world begins with a slap on the bottom and ends with a shovel full of dirt in your face; and everything between the two are but bumps and bruises and heartache.' That is exactly the way Solomon describes it. 'For all his days are sorrows, and his travail grief; yea, his heart taketh not rest in the night. This is also vanity. There is nothing better for a man, than that he should eat and drink, and that he should make his soul enjoy good in his labour. This also I saw, that it was from the hand of God' (Ecclesiastes 2:23-24).

Life can be difficult. For some people one heartache seems to follow another, often in rapid succession. Faith in Christ does not change that fact. Believers suffer the same heartaches and sorrows that other people suffer. Many who walk with God in faith, trusting Christ, like David, have spouses who despise them and children who crush their hearts. Many who are made perfect in Christ, like Job, endure bereavement, bodily sickness, emotional anguish, being misunderstood and misrepresented by friends, and at times feel utterly forsaken by God. The fact is we all need help along the way as we make our pilgrimage through this world.

Life in this world is full of trouble and care. If a brother or sister is weighed down by some burden, we are to be alert to their needs and do what we can to help. We must not allow them to carry the crushing load alone. And we must take care not to add to their burden, like the Pharisees (Matthew 23:4), indicating that their burden is somehow connected with their own lack of faith and righteousness, or some secret sin.

We must not divorce verse 2 from verse 1. The two are connected. Paul is specifically telling us that we are to bear our fallen bother or sister's burden of sin, and to bear it as our own, in love ministering to the needs of the fallen, forgiving the fault, and helping them to recover. Someone once said, 'Christians are the only ones who shoot their wounded.' That is not true. Religious people may shoot their wounded, but Christians mend the wounds.

The way we treat those who have fallen is a very real indication of our own relationship with Christ. By thus bearing one another's burdens, Paul says, we 'fulfil the law of Christ' (John 13:34-35). The Judaisers at Galatia were attempting to bring the Galatian believers back under the law of Moses. Here Paul makes a clear contrast, telling us that we are to live and be motivated not by the law of Moses written on tables of stone, but by the law of Christ written in our hearts.

Self-deception

All pride is self-deception. 'For if a man think himself to be something, when he is nothing, he deceiveth himself' (v. 3). If anyone imagines that he is better than his fallen brother or sister, or that he would not do the things the fallen has done because he is stronger, more spiritual, more righteous, or more holy than the one who has fallen, he is simply deceiving himself (1 John 1:7-10). 'Man at his best state is altogether vanity' (Psalms 39:5). 'For I know that in me (that is in my flesh) dwelleth no good thing' (Romans 7:18). We owe our being, our knowledge, our mercies, our preservation, and our gifts to God alone (1 Corinthians 4:7). In ourselves, and left to ourselves, we are nothing and know nothing. All such pride and self-righteousness is an abomination to God (Proverbs 6:16-18). Such an attitude in anyone, John Gill correctly observed, is an indication that, 'He is destitute of the grace of God, he deceives himself and the truth is not in him.'

Self-examination

Now Paul calls for self-examination. We are not to sit in judgment over others; but over ourselves. It is so easy to compare ourselves with others, whom we look upon as weaker or less gifted believers because they have fallen, and to think we are something special, that we are strong, or that we are better than them. What arrogant folly! Let us each prove the sincerity of our faith in and love for Christ by the Word of God. If we are honest, we will find plenty to judge and condemn in ourselves, without having to compare ourselves with others and condemning them.

When Paul says, 'then shall he have rejoicing in himself alone', he is speaking ironically. His meaning is just the opposite of that. We know that is the case because he declares in Philippians 3:3 that all who are born of God 'rejoice in Christ Jesus and have no confidence in the flesh'. He is not here telling us that we are to look within ourselves for personal righteousness, that we may have assurance of salvation. We are to look outside ourselves to Christ alone for assurance (Hebrews 11:1; 1 Corinthians 1:30-31). 'For if a man think himself to be something, when he is nothing, he deceiveth himself' (v. 3).

If we will heed Paul's admonition, we will have every reason to be ashamed of ourselves. We will own and acknowledge our sinfulness and shame, while at the same time rejoicing in a conscience void of guilt before God; because Christ has redeemed us and given us perfect righteousness, complete forgiveness, and absolute acceptance with the holy Lord God (Hebrews 9:12-14; 10:22; 2 Corinthians 1:12). It is in this sense that we are to understand Paul's words. A believer may rejoice 'in himself', in the vindication of his own character before men, though not before God, as Job and David did. The fruit of the Spirit in us is the result, not the cause, of our justification and righteousness before God.

Believers do not point to the sins and faults of others, rejoicing in those things to their own praise, using them to convince themselves or others that they are not like the fallen. That is the attitude of the self-righteous Pharisee and hypocrite.

Judgment Day

Believers understand and live in the awareness that every person will be judged for his own works, not for another's, 'For every man shall bear his own burden' (v. 5). In the Day of Judgment we will answer for ourselves, not for others. Yes, there is a day coming when we shall be judged according to our works (2 Corinthians 5:10; Revelation 20:11-15). 'It is appointed unto men once to die, but after this the judgment' (Hebrews 9:27). The Judge, before whom we must stand, is the God-man, whom we have crucified (John 5:21-23; Acts 17:31; 2 Corinthians 5:10). We will be judged out of the books, according to the record of God's strict justice.

When the books are opened, what shocks of terror will seize the hearts and souls of those who have no righteousness and no atonement before the Lord God! With the opening of the books, every crime, every offence, every sin they have ever committed in mind, in heart, and in deed shall be exposed! 'Judgment was set; and the books were opened' (Daniel 7:10).

I realise that this is figurative language. God does not need books to remember man's sins. However, as John Gill wrote, 'This judgment out of the books, and according to works, is designed to show with what accuracy and exactness, with what justice and equity, it will be executed, in allusion to statute-books in courts of judicature'. In the scriptures God is often represented as writing and keeping books. According to these books we all shall be judged.

What are the books? The Book of Divine Omniscience (Malachi 3:5); The Book of Divine Remembrance (Malachi 3:16); The Book of Creation (Romans 1:18-20); The Book of God's Providence (Romans 2:4-5); The Book of Conscience (Romans 2:15); The Book of God's Holy Law[1] (Romans 2:12); and the Book of the Gospel (Romans 2:16).

---

[1] This book of the law has two tables. The first table contains all the sins of men against God (Exodus 20:3-11). The second table contains all the sins of men against one another (Exodus 20:12-17).

But there are some against whom no crimes, no sins, no offences can be found, not even by the omniscient eye of God himself! 'In those days, and in that time, saith the LORD, the iniquity of Israel shall be sought for, and there shall be none; and the sins of Judah, and they shall not be found: for I will pardon them whom I reserve' (Jeremiah 50:20). Their names are found in another book, a book which God himself wrote and sealed before the worlds were made. It is called, 'The Book of Life' (Luke 10:20; Revelation 20:12). In this book there is a record of divine election, the name of Christ our divine Surety, a record of perfect righteousness (Jeremiah 23:6, cf. 33:16), a record of complete satisfaction, and the promise of eternal life.

The question is often raised, 'Will God judge his elect for their sins and failures, committed after they were saved, and expose them in the Day of Judgment?' The only reason that question is ever raised is because many retain a remnant of the Roman doctrine of purgatory, by which they hope to hold over God's saints the whip and terror of the law. There is absolutely no sense in which those who trust Christ shall ever be made to pay for their sins! Our sins were imputed to Christ and shall never be imputed to us again (Romans 4:8). Christ paid our debt to God's law and justice; and God will never require us to pay. God who has blotted out our transgressions will never write them again. He who covered our sins will never uncover them!

The perfect righteousness of Christ has been imputed to us. On the Day of Judgment, God's elect are never represented as having done any evil, but only good (Matthew 25:31-40). The Day of Judgment will be a day of glory and bliss for Christ and his people, not a day of mourning and sorrow. It will be a marriage supper. Christ will glory in his Church. God will display the glory of his grace in us. And we will glory in our God.

Those who are found perfectly righteous, righteous according to the records of God himself, shall enter into eternal life and inherit everlasting glory with Christ. They that have done good, nothing but good, perfect good, without any spot of sin, wrinkle of iniquity, or trace of transgression, shall enter into everlasting life. (Revelation 22:11).

Who are these perfectly righteous ones? They are all who are saved by God's free and sovereign grace in Christ (1 Corinthians 6:9-11; Romans 8:1, 32-34). Heaven was earned and purchased for all God's elect by Christ. We were predestined to obtain our inheritance from eternity (Ephesians 1:11). Christ has taken possession of heaven's glory as our forerunner (Hebrews 6:20). We are heirs of God and joint-heirs with Jesus Christ (Romans 8:17). Our Saviour gave all the glory he earned as our Mediator to all his elect (John 17:5, 22). And in Christ every believer is worthy of heaven's glory (Colossians 1:12). Glorification is but the consummation of salvation; and salvation is by grace alone! That means no part of heaven's bliss and glory is the reward of our works, but all the reward of God's free grace in Christ! All spiritual blessings are ours from eternity in Christ (Ephesians 1:3).

All who are found guilty of sin in that great and terrible Day of Judgment shall be cast into the lake of fire and there be made to suffer the unmitigated wrath of almighty God forever! One by one, God will call the wicked before his throne and judge them. As he says, 'Depart ye cursed', he will say to his holy angels, 'Take him! Bind him! Cast him into outer darkness' (Matthew 22:1-14).

In that day there will be no mercy, no pity, no sorrow, no hope, and no end for the wicked! To hell they deserve to go! To hell they must go! To hell they shall go! Let all who read these lines beware. Unless you flee to Christ and take refuge in him, in that great day the wrath of God shall seize you and destroy you forever! I beseech you now, by the mercies of God, be reconciled to God by trusting his darling Son! In that great and terrible day let us be found in Christ, not having our own righteousness, but the righteousness of God in Christ.

In that great day, 'every man shall bear his own burden'.

Let him that is taught in the word communicate unto him that teacheth in all good things. Be not deceived; God is not mocked: for whatsoever a man soweth, that shall he also reap. For he that soweth to his flesh shall of the flesh reap corruption; but he that soweth to the Spirit shall of the Spirit reap life everlasting. And let us not be weary in well doing: for in due season we shall reap, if we faint not. As we have therefore opportunity, let us do good unto all men, especially unto them who are of the household of faith.

(Galatians 6:6-10)

Chapter 35

Read: Galatians 6:6-10

Sowing In The Spirit

Paul continues to give us instructions about what it is to 'walk in the Spirit'. Just as the Lord Jesus 'went about doing good' (Acts 10:38), those who walk in the Spirit, that is to say, all who follow him, all who are his disciples, go through this world doing good (Ephesians 2:10). Those who sow to the flesh (who live after the flesh) shall reap eternal woe. And those who sow to the Spirit (who live after the Spirit) shall reap life eternal in Christ (Romans 8:5-6; Galatians 6:8). Of course, Paul is not telling us that we are justified, sanctified, or even that we gain or lose reward in heaven upon the basis of our works. He is simply telling us that believers are people whose faith in Christ is manifest by their works. Let us ever trace our mercies to their Source: 'It is God which worketh in you both to will and to do of his good pleasure' (Philippians 2:13).

Pastoral Support

In verse 6 Paul tells us that those who teach the Word of God (pastors of local churches, missionaries, and evangelists) are to be supported financially by those who profit from their labours. The doctor who ministers to your bodily health, the policeman who protects you, the carpenter who builds an addition on your house, the mechanic who changes the oil in your car, and the neighbourhood boy who mows your lawn for you are all compensated according to their service. Even so, the man who studies the Word, seeks a message for your soul from God, prays for you and teaches you the Word of God (the most important service of all) is to share in your material substance. Gospel preachers are to be supported and maintained in their livelihood by the voluntary generosity of those for whom they labour. This is one of the clearest statements in the Bible about the support of gospel preachers. All who profit from the preaching of the gospel are expected to give of their means for the support of those who preach the gospel, 'Let him that is taught in the word communicate unto him that teacheth in all good things.'

The fact is every local church needs money to operate. Buildings must be erected. Bills must be paid. Office supplies must be purchased. Equipment must be maintained and salaries must be paid. We are to preach the gospel freely to all men, seeking nothing in return; but in order for us to preach the gospel freely, someone has to pay for it. How is the work of the ministry to be maintained? How should local churches raise the money needed to support pastors, missionaries, and various works for the furtherance of the gospel? These questions need to be answered plainly and frankly from the Word of God.

There is no scarcity of material in the holy scriptures regarding the financial support of the gospel ministry. It is a subject that appears again and again throughout the Bible. Under the Mosaic economy of the Old Testament those who ministered about the holy things of divine service lived upon the things of the temple. Those who served the altar were partakers of the altar (1 Corinthians 9:13). God prescribed by law that the priesthood, the children of Levi, should receive a tenth of all the possessions of the children of Israel, a tenth of their money, property, crops, and herds, for their service in the tabernacle of the congregation. The Jews were required to pay a tithe to be used exclusively for the financial support of the ministry of the Levitical priesthood (Numbers 18:21). Failure to do so, for any reason, was regarded as robbing God himself (Malachi 3:8-9).

However, we are not under the law today. God's people are no more required to pay a tithe in this gospel age than we are required to keep the sabbath day, or observe the Passover (Colossians 2:16-23). We are free from the law. A. D. Muse, the late pastor of Hearts Harbor Tabernacle in Louisville, Kentucky, used to say, 'If you tithe, you're under the law. And if you don't tithe, you're an outlaw.' In other words, the person who just pays his tithe is a mere legalist, and anyone who does not do that much is an antinomian. Anyone who uses his freedom from the law as an excuse for being a niggardly miser and selfishly refuses to give of his means for the support of the gospel of Christ is, I fear, without grace. God's people give. They give generously, and they give cheerfully.

The instructions given in the New Testament regarding the financial support of the gospel ministry are unmistakably clear. Those men and women who believe the gospel of the grace of God are expected to support generously those who preach it. Not only is this expected, among God's saints it is practiced. God's children are not miserly, self-centred worldlings. They are stewards who use what God has put in their hands for the cause of Christ. They need only to be instructed from the Word of God, and they gladly submit to it.

Our Lord Jesus Christ tells us plainly and repeatedly that those who preach the gospel are to live by the gospel (Matthew 10:9-10; Luke 10:4-7; 1 Corinthians 9:14; 1 Timothy 5:17-18). Those men who faithfully preach the gospel of God's free and sovereign grace in Christ are to be supported and maintained by the people to whom they minister. Faithful missionaries should be as fully and generously supported by the churches that send them out as the pastors of those local churches.

There were times when Paul and his companions were required to make tents to support themselves in the work of the gospel. It was an honourable thing for them to do so. Paul tells us that his goal was not to enrich himself, but to avoid being a burden to young churches (1 Thessalonians 2:9) and to avoid causing an offence to young, weak believers (1 Corinthians 9:15-19). But the fact that God's messenger had to spend his time and efforts making tents was a shameful reproach upon the churches. Those churches that were established in the gospel should have assumed the responsibility of supplying Paul's needs and the needs of his companions, as they travelled from place to place preaching the gospel. The New Testament clearly makes it the responsibility of every local church to provide for the financial, material support of those who preach the gospel of Christ.

A Reasonable Precept
The word 'communicate' (v. 6) means 'to share with or distribute to'. It comes from the word 'communion' and basically means the same thing as 'fellowship'. Paul is saying, 'Let everyone to whom the gospel is preached have fellowship with and participate in the preaching of the gospel by supplying the earthly, material needs of those who preach it.' Edgar Andrews explains it thus,

Paul's formula is very simple: those who are 'taught the word' should share their material wealth with 'him who teaches'. In other words, the congregation should support its minister(s) financially, and do so (as the word 'share' implies) at the same standard of living as they themselves enjoy. This was the principle that God laid down for the support of the Levites by the remaining tribes of Israel in Old Testament times (though the New Testament transmutes obligation into willingness). Where pioneer missions are involved, and until there is a congregation to support the preacher, the sending church or churches will bear this responsibility. But let us also notice that when Paul and Barnabas were sent out by the church at Antioch (Acts 13:3), they did not spend the first six months securing pledges for their support! On the contrary, they departed immediately for Cyprus, to preach the Word of God. They knew they had been sent out, not only by the church, but by the Holy Spirit, who was well able to care for their needs as they arose (Acts 13:4-5).

To whom is this communication to be made? Paul did not lay down a blanket rule that we should give financial support to every preacher, evangelist, or missionary who comes along claiming to speak for God. Those who deny the gospel of Christ, preachers of free-will, works religion, are not to be supported by God's saints (2 John 9-11).

Supporting The Ministry
Paul's doctrine is this: those preachers who faithfully teach the Word of God are to be supported by the church; particularly, they are to be supported by the churches they pastor. We must not let ourselves be deceived by personality, charm, or flowery speech. God's prophets are not always personable, but they are always profitable. Their delivery is not always impressive, but their message is always instructive. Their preaching is not always stirring, but it is always sound. Every preacher must be judged by one thing: what does he preach? What is his doctrine? God's servants faithfully instruct men and women in the Word by preaching the gospel of Christ. They teach their hearers the Word of truth; and those who hear them are taught in the Word of truth. If a man is sent of God to preach the gospel, he will preach with such unmistakable clarity that all who hear him regularly will be taught the doctrine of Christ.

If you want to know what a man preaches, ask the people who hear him. If he consciously and consistently preaches the gospel, they will know it (see John 18:19-21). It is impossible for a person to hear a man preach the gospel regularly and not know, at least in his head, the doctrine of the gospel. He will know his lost condition of depravity and condemnation by nature (Romans 5:12; Ephesians 2:1-3). He will have some understanding of the doctrine of Christ: our Lord's divine person, his incarnation and virgin birth, his representative obedience to God for his people, his effectual, sin-atoning, substitutionary death. Those who are privileged to hear a man faithfully preach the gospel will know that salvation is by grace alone through faith in Christ alone. All who hear the gospel faithfully preached are taught what happened in the garden, what happened on the cross, and how God saves sinners. And the man who faithfully preaches those things is worthy of the financial support of God's people.

It is the responsibility of God's church to generously supply the needs of every man who faithfully preaches the gospel of God's free and sovereign grace in Christ. This is only reasonable. Are you taught the good things of the gospel? Then it is your reasonable and equitable responsibility to supply the material needs of the man who teaches you. You should supply him with good things materially who supplies you with good things spiritually (1 Corinthians 9:11). It is the ordinance of Christ that, 'They which preach the gospel should live of the gospel' (1 Corinthians 9:14). No man who preaches the gospel of the grace of God should be required to provide for himself or his family (Acts 6:2-4; 2 Timothy 2:4). This support of the ministry must begin with each local church supporting its own pastor. Once that is taken care of, every local church should assume responsibility for the support of faithful missionaries. Those churches that are well established should also assist in the support of smaller churches and their pastors.

God's servants are not ambitious, greedy men. Faithful men will not abuse, or take advantage of, the generosity of God's people (1 Corinthians 9:17-18). But God's preachers should never be expected to live as paupers. Those men who labour in the Word and doctrine of Christ, faithfully giving themselves to the work of the ministry, are to be supported generously in a comfortable life-style.

I am often asked, 'How much should the church pay its pastor?' I often reply', How much does it take for you to live?' The pastor has a wife and children to clothe, feed, house, and educate, just like you. He will incur many necessary expenses that you do not. His home is a virtual free hotel for God's people, and he wants it to be. His table almost always has a few extra mouths to feed, and he wants them there. He has miles to travel and books to buy, necessary for his work. All these things require cold, hard cash every week. When the church contemplates the pastor's salary, a good rule of thumb is this: pay the pastor at least as much as the average income of the working men in the congregation; and then add enough to cover his additional expenses. If the church is not able to do what is needed, it is expected and responsible to do the best it can, and this is only reasonable.

Cheerful Giving

How is this financial support to be secured? This may seem strange to some; but the way to secure financial support for the gospel of Christ and those who preach it is in fact not to secure it. God will supply the needs of his church and his servants by the free, voluntary, generous gifts of his people. The moment a preacher, a missionary, or a church begins to secure its financial stability on its own, it leans upon the arm of the flesh and dishonours God.

There are some things, dishonouring to God and contrary to the gospel of his grace, which must not be done. God's church must never be brought back under the law by having the law of the tithe imposed upon them. We must never solicit pledges from people, hold bake sales or rummage sales, or set up investment schemes to raise money for God's work. God's servants and his churches must never beg and grovel for help from men, as though the work of God depended upon man's assistance. Nor must we ever solicit the aid of unbelievers. I know these things are commonly practiced in our day; but they are contrary to every principle of grace and faith. God's church operates by faith, and faith looks to God, not man! Any work that is of God will have its needs supplied by God through the free, voluntary gifts of God's saints (2 Corinthians 9:7).

If a pastor wants the people to whom he preaches to be generous, he must be generous. In all things, like a shepherd, the pastor must lead God's sheep and show them the way by personal example. The moment men and women detect selfishness, greed, and unfaithfulness in their pastor, these things will be reflected in them.

The Word of God supplies us with an abundance of instruction about the matter of giving. All of 1 Corinthians 9 and 2 Corinthians chapters 8-9 are taken up with this subject. But there are no commands given to the people of God anywhere in the New Testament about how much we are to give, when we are to give, or where we are to give. Tithing and all systems like it are totally foreign to the New Testament. Giving, like all other acts of worship, is an act of faith and grace. It must be free and voluntary, or it is unacceptable. However, there are some plain, simple guidelines laid down in the scriptures for us to follow. Here are ten things revealed in the New Testament about giving.

1. Our giving should be planned (2 Corinthians 9:7).
2. Our giving must be free, voluntary, unconstrained (2 Corinthians 9:7).
3. Our giving must be motivated by love and gratitude towards Christ (2 Corinthians 8:7-9).
4. Our giving must arise from a willing heart (2 Corinthians 8:12).
5. Every believer should give to the work of the gospel according to his personal ability (1 Corinthians 16:2).
6. Every believer should give a portion of his goods for the cause of Christ (1 Corinthians 16:2).
7. Our gifts for the gospel should be liberal and sacrificial (2 Corinthians 9:5-6; Mark 12:41-44).
8. We are to give as unto the Lord (Matthew 6:1-4).
9. This kind of giving is well-pleasing to God (2 Corinthians 9:7; Philippians 4:18; Hebrews 13:16).
10. If we are willing to give, God will supply us with the ability to give (2 Corinthians 9:10: Luke 6:38; Philippians 4:19).

Someone once said, "There are three kinds of giving: grudge-giving, duty-giving and thanksgiving. Grudge-giving says, 'I have to.' Duty-giving says, 'I ought to.' Thanksgiving says, 'I want to.'"

A Recognised Principle
The Judaisers and false teachers at Galatia were persuading these men and women not to support the men who faithfully preached the gospel of Christ to them, and devised many excuses for them not to do so, which the Galatians readily seized. Paul warns them not to be fooled; 'Be not deceived; God is not mocked: for whatsoever a man soweth, that shall he also reap (v. 7).

People are easily led astray from what they know to be right by personal greed and covetousness. They often excuse their miserliness by their own earthly cares and responsibilities, or by finding some petty fault with the preacher. Neither excuse is valid. If we work hard and live within our means, we will not be too financially strapped to give. Nor do our personal likes or dislikes of something about God's messenger in any way lessen our responsibility to support him in the work of the gospel. Men with money often try to exert control over a pastor by how much they give, or refuse to give. It should not need saying that God's people do not have this attitude. It is also true that God's servants cannot be controlled by money!

Men and women who find excuses not to give to the cause of Christ and work of the gospel mock God. Paul is saying, 'You cannot insult God and get away with it!' Remember, in the context Paul is talking about the support of the gospel ministry. If a man comes to you in the name of God, preaching the gospel of Christ, and you refuse to give of your means to support him, you insult God! And you will not get away with it!

It is a universal law, applying to every realm of life that 'whatsoever a man soweth, that shall he also reap' (v. 7). Generally speaking, whatever we sow, as to kind, quality, and quantity, we will reap. If a farmer sows wheat, he reaps wheat. If he sows sparingly, he will reap sparingly. If he sows bountifully, he will reap bountifully. If he sows good seed, he will reap a good harvest. If he sows nothing, he will reap nothing. Everyone understands that in the natural world; but here Paul applies it to the things of God.

'He that soweth to his flesh shall of the flesh reap corruption'. In other words, if we use what God puts in our hands to pamper our flesh and gratify our personal greed and covetousness, if we spend our substance upon luxuries for ourselves and our families, or hoard it up to increase our riches, we shall of the flesh reap corruption. Paul is telling us that the way we use, or abuse, our money reveals the true state and condition of our hearts (see Matthew 6:19-24).

'But he that soweth to the Spirit shall of the Spirit reap life everlasting.' This does not mean that men and women can earn salvation, or even a greater degree of heavenly reward and glory by what they give to the cause of Christ. The text simply means that, if we lay out our worldly substance for the cause of Christ, the preaching of the gospel, and the good of his kingdom, we will reap that for which we have sown it 'life everlasting'! Our use of what God puts in our hands does not secure anything for us, but it does reveal the true state and condition of our hearts (Matthew 25:24-30).

A Required Perseverance

Satan uses many things to discourage us, and God uses many things to try us. We do not see immediate results. Our circumstances, the economy of the nation and the needs of our families all change. We sometimes begin to think, 'Maybe I ought to stop, or at least curtail my giving. Nothing much appears to be accomplished by it. The kingdom of God will get along all right without my few dollars in the offering plate'.

To such thoughts, Paul says, 'Don't give up now!' 'In due season', at God's appointed time, 'we shall reap, if we faint not' (vv. 9-10). The seed sown will spring up again, and the bread cast upon the waters will be found after many days. But there must be a time of waiting between the sowing of the seed and the reaping of the harvest. This time of waiting is to try our faith, to prove whether we really believe God. It is our responsibility to use what God has given us for the cause of Christ, to sow to the Spirit and to wait for God to give the increase. He will give it in his way, at his time, for his glory. Robert Hawker's comments on this verse are excellent ...

> The Apostle's train of argument is, that the Lord's people should never be weary, nor faint in their minds, at any exercises they meet with, in the present time-state of their existence. Christ is their portion. And in due season, on his account, and for his sake alone, they will reap the blessed fruits of that inheritance, to which, as his people, they are begotten, by his soul-travail, blood-shedding, and righteousness. The expression is not unsimilar to what is said in Hebrews 6:12, 'Be ye not slothful, but followers of them who, through faith and patience, inherit the promises'.

The Household Of Faith

By doing good 'especially unto them who are of the household of faith', Paul means communicating to the needs of men and women, particularly to the needs of God's children, and, in this context, to the needs of his servants. While the time of life lasts, let us use what God gives us for the good of his people and the furtherance of the gospel. If we do so, then we partake of and have fellowship with God's servants in their work (Matthew 10:40-42; 3 John 8).

Paul is calling for commitment to Christ. If I am committed to something, I throw my life into it; and if I am committed to the cause of Christ in this world, I throw my life into his cause. That means that I do whatever has to be done and give whatever has to be given to get the job done. The very least that I can do is give! Let us give ourselves in unreserved commitment to Christ and the cause of the gospel of his grace for the glory of our God.

Ye see how large a letter I have written unto you with mine own hand. As many as desire to make a fair show in the flesh, they constrain you to be circumcised; only lest they should suffer persecution for the cross of Christ. For neither they themselves who are circumcised keep the law; but desire to have you circumcised, that they may glory in your flesh. But God forbid that I should glory, save in the cross of our Lord Jesus Christ, by whom the world is crucified unto me, and I unto the world. For in Christ Jesus neither circumcision availeth any thing, nor uncircumcision, but a new creature. And as many as walk according to this rule, peace be on them, and mercy, and upon the Israel of God. From henceforth let no man trouble me: for I bear in my body the marks of the Lord Jesus. Brethren, the grace of our Lord Jesus Christ be with your spirit. Amen.

(Galatians 6:11-18)

Chapter 36

Read: Galatians 6:11-18

Glorying In The Cross

In these final verses of this tremendous Epistle the Apostle Paul seems determined to leave his readers with their hearts and minds fixed resolutely upon 'the cross of our Lord Jesus Christ'. Throughout these chapters, he has been showing us that it is in the cross of Christ that the law of God finds its fulfilment and end, that it is Mount Calvary and not Mount Sinai that saves, and that all the blessings of grace, righteousness, salvation, and eternal life flow to sinners only by the merits of the cross. His message throughout this Epistle (throughout all his Epistles) is set before us in this one dogmatic assertion, 'God forbid that I should glory, save in the cross of our Lord Jesus Christ'.

Paul's Concern

Paul wrote much longer epistles than this (Romans, First and Second Corinthians, and Hebrews), but some of those epistles to the various churches were dictated by him to others (Romans 16:22). This epistle was written with his own hand (v. 11). He calls attention to this fact as an expression of great affection for the saints at Galatia. He cared deeply for them and was very concerned for their well-being. The errors to which they had been exposed, and the fact that many had fallen by Satanic deception into the errors of the legalists, caused him great grief. Oh, for a heart that cares for others and that is broken when their peace is threatened by error or sin!

False Teachers

In verses 12 and 13, Paul identifies the false teachers he has been exposing throughout this epistle and states plainly what the motives of such men are. They are hypocrites, motivated by their own personal interests, and not the glory of God and the good of men's souls. They do what they do to be seen of men. Their religion is nothing but an outward show by which they seek the approval and applause of men (Matthew 6:1-5). By force of influence, doctrine, church creeds, and the opinions of others like themselves, they try to constrain believers to be regulated by the rule of law and observe religious ceremonies, holy days, and customs, rather than living as those who have been made free in Christ (Galatians 5:1-4).

They sway men and women to adopt their legalists rules, 'lest they suffer persecution' from the religious people who are offended by 'the simplicity that is in Christ' and the preaching of the total sufficiency and efficacy of Christ as our Saviour. Christ crucified is our atonement. Christ's obedience is our righteousness. Our works contribute nothing to our acceptance with God. We are complete in him.

These religious teachers, who preach the law, teach the law, and boast of their regard for the law are nothing but hypocrites. They do not keep the law themselves; and they know it (Galatians 3:10). Yet, they require others to do what they cannot do, so that they can boast before men about the number of people who follow them, and how 'holy' they are. Henry Mahan observes that, 'Every religious person glories or rejoices in something. These false teachers glory in the flesh, in the outward form, in the noise they make, in the work they do and in the souls they have won.'

Glorying In The Cross

True faith brings needy sinners to Christ, puts on Christ, and walks in Christ. Faith brings sinners to the cross and glories only in the cross of our Lord Jesus Christ, by whom the world is crucified unto us and we unto the world. Though faith is not righteousness, it is the believer's connection to righteousness. Faith finds in Christ and enjoys in Christ the assurance of perfect, indestructible righteousness before God through the merits of God's own Son. Joseph Irons saw this when he wrote:

> What sacred Fountain yonder springs
> Up from the throne of God,
> And all new covenant blessings brings?
> 'Tis Jesus precious blood.

Faith in Christ assures the believing sinner of eternal life and everlasting righteousness in the ages to come, depending upon the perpetuity of that righteousness which can never change. We shall never put off that Christ whom we put on when we believed (Romans 13:14; Galatians 3:27). The garments of salvation shall never wear thin. The robe of righteousness in which the Lord God has clothed us shall never wax old. The beauty our Saviour has put upon us (his own beauty) is a beauty that fadeth not away.

Faith abides ever at the cross. It never takes us away from the cross of our Lord Jesus Christ, to which at first it led us. Many seem to think that believers quickly get beyond the cross and leave it behind. Like the legalists at Galatia, they never openly do so, but their subtle doctrine is that the cross has done all it can for us once we believe the gospel, and teaches that once we believe we are to abandon the cross and go forward; that to remain always at the cross is to be babes, not men of faith. Nonsense!

What is the cross? Paul is not talking about the historic fact that Christ died upon the cross. The knowledge of that fact, though it is necessary to salvation, is not salvation. Neither is Paul referring to the literal, wooden cross upon which Christ died. He was not an idolater, a worshipper of religious relics. He knew that there is no superstitious, spiritual value in that piece of wood. And he certainly is not suggesting that we glory in some sign, symbol, representation, or form of the cross.

When Paul speaks of the cross, he is talking about the glorious, soul saving doctrine of the cross, the gospel of our Lord Jesus Christ. He is talking about blood atonement (Romans 5:6-11), legal propitiation (Romans 3:24-26), substitutionary redemption (2 Corinthians 5:18-21), and free justification (Romans 5:19).

As used here in Galatians 6:14, and commonly used in the Epistles of the New Testament, the word 'cross' refers to the gospel of Christ. Pagans glory in religious relics. Idolaters glory in religious images, signs, and symbols. Ignorant people glory in religious feelings, emotions, and experiences. God's people glory in the gospel of Christ, not in the 'old rugged cross' sentimentalists sing about, but the old, old story of redeeming blood. We glory in the revelation of the glory of God. We can no more part with that than we can part with life eternal. In this sense, to turn our back upon the cross would be turning our back upon Christ crucified. It would be giving up our connection with the Lamb of God slain upon the cursed tree! This we cannot, must not, and shall not do!

All that Christ did and suffered from the manger to his resurrection glory forms one glorious whole. No part of our Redeemer's work shall ever become needless or obsolete. To forsake any part of his work is to forsake him. I rejoice in the incarnation of Christ. Yet, I know that the incarnation cannot save. I delight to follow my Master into Gethsemane. Yet, I know that his agony there was not the finished work. I glory in the cross. My face is always toward it. My eye is ever on the crucified One. I am convinced that the sacrifice there was completed once for all. I never cease to look into the empty tomb with delight. I rejoice to know that it is the risen, ascended, exalted, reigning Christ who gives eternal life to this needy sinner.

Leaving nothing behind, I trust the whole Christ and the whole of his work for all my righteousness, justification, forgiveness, acceptance, and everlasting salvation.

Glory In The Cross

The word 'glory' means to exalt, to boast of, and to rejoice in. Paul exalted, boasted of, and rejoiced in the sin atoning death of the Lord Jesus Christ upon the cursed tree. He exalted the doctrine of the cross as the only theme of holy scripture and the singular subject of his preaching (1 Corinthians 2:2; 9:16). He saw 'Christ crucified' as the whole counsel of God, the message of all the types, promises, and prophecies of the Old Testament, the basis of hope for sinners, the motive of all godliness, and the message he was sent to proclaim.

He rejoiced in the cross, the gospel of Christ, as the only grounds of his confident hope before God. He trusted Christ alone as his Saviour (Philippians 3:3; 1 Corinthians 1:30). He counted all his religious works, knowledge, and experiences to be nothing but dung that he might be found in Christ, robed in his righteousness and washed in his blood.

And he preached the cross, boasting of Christ's death as the only means of reconciliation to and acceptance with God, the only means of salvation for guilty sinners (Galatians 2:21). If righteousness cannot be gained by man's obedience to the law of God (and it cannot!), then no man can be saved by anything else he might do. Nothing can save a man's soul, nothing can bring a sinner to God, nothing can make a sinner acceptable in the sight of God, but the cross of our Lord Jesus Christ.

It is 'the cross of our Lord Jesus Christ' that makes it possible for the holy Lord God to be both 'a just God and a Saviour'. It is the cross of Christ that makes it possible for God to be both 'just and Justifier'. Sinners have hope before God only because of 'the cross of our Lord Jesus Christ'. Therefore, saved sinners rejoice to say with the Apostle, 'God forbid that I should glory, save in the cross of our Lord Jesus Christ, by whom the world is crucified unto me, and I unto the world.'

Crucified

Faith in Christ, the assurance of redemption by Christ, caused the Apostle Paul to look upon the world as a thing crucified to him (v. 14). He knew that he had no more reason to fear his most implacable enemies in this world than a man would to fear someone crucified and dead. Happy is that person who learns this! Because our Lord Jesus Christ, by his death upon the cross as our Substitute and Redeemer, has overcome the world, conquered Satan (the prince of this world) and cast him out, and vanquished death, hell and the grave, since he has put away our sins by the sacrifice of himself, we are more than conquerors in him (Romans 8:32-39). We have nothing to fear in this world or from this world. As the children of Israel looked upon Pharaoh and the Egyptian army slain by God in the Red Sea and sang praise to him, so we ought to look upon all that opposes us in this world as dead and sing praise to God our Saviour who has 'triumphed gloriously'. Let us neither love the world, nor the things that are in the world, but look upon them as dead things. The gospel of the grace of God experienced in the soul teaches us to despise the riches, honours, and applause of the world.

The profits, pleasures, and praises of dead men are as worthless as dung. That is exactly how they are to be looked upon and counted by all who seek Christ (Philippians 3:7-15). But, as Paul uses the term 'world' here in the book of Galatians, he is specifically referring to 'the weak and beggarly elements of the world' (Galatians 4:3-9), the carnal ordinances and ceremonies of the law. He is declaring that since 'Christ is the end of the law' (Romans 10:4), the law's sabbath days, sacrifices, and services are to be looked upon by us as dead things. As it is written, 'Wherefore, my brethren, ye also are become dead to the law by the body of Christ; that ye should be married to another, even to him who is raised from the dead, that we should bring forth fruit unto God'. And again, 'For I through the law am dead to the law, that I might live unto God. I am crucified with Christ: nevertheless I live; yet not I, but Christ liveth in me: and the life which I now live in the flesh I live by the faith of the Son of God, who loved me, and gave himself for me' (Romans 7:4; Galatians 2:19-20). Our all-glorious Redeemer took 'the handwriting of ordinances that was against us, which was contrary to us, and took it out of the way, nailing it to his cross' (Colossians 2:14).

The world had no more attraction for Paul than a corpse, and he had none for the world, but was despised by it for Christ's sake. So it shall ever be with those who follow Christ. As the law was dead to him and had no power over him, so he was dead to the law by the sacrifice of Christ. He had nothing to do with those weak and beggarly elements of bondage.

A New Creature

Here is the reason why we must have nothing to do with legal, works religion, why we must look to, trust, and glory only 'in the cross of our Lord Jesus Christ' – 'For in Christ Jesus neither circumcision availeth any thing, nor uncircumcision, but a new creature' (v. 15). Circumcision and the carnal ordinances of the law are utterly meaningless, being totally abolished by Christ. Being uncircumcised is no barrier to the blessings of the gospel and all the privileges of the children of God.

It must be stated that Paul is not here suggesting that baptism, or the refusal to confess Christ in believer's baptism are meaningless things. Those who give such a perverse interpretation of Paul's words here ignore the teaching of Scripture regarding gospel ordinances. John Gill wrote,

> Though baptism is of no avail in the business of salvation, yet it cannot be said of it, as of circumcision, that it avails not anything as a command; for it is a standing ordinance of Christ; or as an emblem and sign, for it is significative of the death and burial, and resurrection of Christ; or as a privilege, for it is of use to lead the faith of God's people to his blood and righteousness for pardon and justification; for he that believes, and is baptised, shall be saved; and it is necessary to church communion. And, on the other hand, it cannot be said that non-baptism avails not; it is a bar to church fellowship; and a neglect of baptism in those who are the proper subjects of it, is resented by Christ, and is a rejecting of the counsel of God against themselves; which was the case of the Pharisees, in the time of John the Baptist.

That which is significant and meaningful, the only thing that is, is 'a new creature', or a new creation (2 Corinthians 5:17). This new creation is 'Christ in you, the hope of glory' (Colossians 1:27), 'the hidden man of the heart' which is not corruptible (1 Peter 3:4). This new creation is that work of God performed for us at Calvary when Christ made all things new, putting away our sins and giving us his perfect righteousness, reconciling us to God in justification. It is also that which God performs in us, causing us to be reconciled to God in regeneration, faith, and conversion (2 Peter 1:4; 1 John 3:9). Again, John Gill's explanation is excellent.

> This is a 'new' creature, in opposition to the old man; and because it is a principle in man, which never was there before. It consists of a new heart and spirit, of new eyes, ears, hands, and

feet, expressive of new principles and actions, of new light, life, love, desires, joys, comforts, and duties. Now this is of avail. It is a branch of the new covenant of grace, which God has therein promised to bestow on his people. It is an evidence of interest in Christ, the new and living way to the Father, and eternal life. Such are newborn babes, regenerated persons, and have a right to and meetness for the kingdom of God. They shall possess the new Jerusalem, shall dwell in the new heavens and new earth. They are called by the Lord's new name, the adopted children of God; and have a new song put into their mouths, which none but redeemed and newborn souls can sing; and shall drink the new wine of endless joys and everlasting pleasures with Christ, in his Father's kingdom.

By virtue of our union with Christ in his death and resurrection and by the power and grace of God the Holy Spirit, all who are born of God are new creatures in Christ. We are no longer under the sentence of condemnation, but entirely free from the law, free in Christ, having past from spiritual death to spiritual life; in Christ we possess eternal life. We now live in the Spirit, are led by the Spirit, and shall never come into condemnation (Romans 8:1-17). All merely outward religion is utterly meaningless. True Christianity is the work of God in us, transforming us into the sons of God (John 4:24; Philippians 3:3). It is the life of God in you, Christ in you, being made 'partakers of the divine nature'. That cannot be accomplished by outward ceremonies, or by the will and choice of a man, but by the creative power of God alone. In this work of the new creation 'all things are of God' (2 Corinthians 5:18).

The Israel Of God
In verse 16 Paul pronounces a blessing of peace and mercy upon all the Israel of God: 'And as many as walk according to this rule, peace be on them, and mercy, and upon the Israel of God.' No blessing of grace is conveyed to anyone because of his physical descent (John 1:12-13). The Israel of God does not refer to the physical nation of Israel (Abraham's physical seed), but to the church of God's elect (Abraham's spiritual seed), made up of all believers. All the Israel of God shall be saved by Christ (Romans 11:25-27). Peace and mercy shall be theirs forever.

Who are these people, this 'holy nation', these chosen heirs of eternal life? Who can rightfully claim this promise of peace and mercy in Christ? Only those who 'walk by this rule': the rule of faith. This is the rule of every believer's life: not law but love (2 Corinthians 5:14-15), not works but faith (1 John 3:23). Those who are God's elect are those who renounce all confidence in, dependence upon, and trust in themselves, and any thing done or experienced by them (Philippians 3:3), believing on the Lord Jesus Christ as their only and all-sufficient Saviour (1 Corinthians 1:30-31), glorying only in the cross of our Redeemer.

Those who make merchandise of the souls of men boast of their works and the works they get others to do, just as the Judaisers at Galatia gloried in circumcision, sabbath keeping, and carnal ceremonies. Paul cared for none of those things. He was determined not to be troubled by those who trouble God's churches with their false doctrine (v. 17). He counted their enemies his enemies, and washed his hands of them (2 Corinthians 11:13-15).

He bore in his body the scars of Christ. Paul was stigmatised in reputation as a preacher of Christ, his cross, and God's free grace to sinners without works. He bore the stigma gladly. He bore it not only in his constantly maligned reputation, but in his very body, in the scars he bore in his body as the result of the things he had suffered for the preaching of the gospel (2 Corinthians 6:4-10; 11:16-33). He holds them before us as a soldier might hold up the stub of an arm lost in battle as the only argument needed to prove his bravery and devotion. All the claims of those false prophets of success and authority in the preaching of legal works and will worship, Paul hereby mocks as hypocrisy and deceit. His obedience to his Master was made obvious by the things he suffered in his Master's cause. With that, he closes the epistle, expressing his love for God's people as his brothers and sisters in Christ, desiring for them the boundless blessing of God's manifest grace in Christ. 'Brethren, the grace of our Lord Jesus Christ be with your spirit. Amen.'

END

Bible Verses Index

Old Testament

New Testament

Other Titles by Don Fortner
available from
Go Publications

BASIC BIBLE DOCTRINE

Don Fortner

An easy to read summary of Bible teaching, contains 77 subject chapters from creation to the end times. An excellent reference for new believers and those who seek an overview of scriptural teaching with a strong free grace emphasis.

Basic Bible Doctrine

Donald S. Fortner

Published by:

Go *publications*
THE CAIRN, HILL TOP,
EGGLESTON,
CO. DURHAM,
DL12 0AU
TEL/FAX : 01833 650797

Clothbound Hardback,
660 pages

ISBN   978-0-9527074-9-3

www.ingramcontent.com/pod-product-compliance
Lightning Source LLC
Chambersburg PA
CBHW020456100426
42812CB00024B/2677